Doomsday Cult

The time we live in will not last long. While it lasts, married men should be as if they had no wives; mourners should be as if they had nothing to grieve them, the joyful as if they did not rejoice; buyers must not count on keeping what they buy, nor those who use the world's wealth on using it to the full. For the whole frame of this world is passing away.

*   *   *

It seems to me God has made us apostles the most abject of mankind. We are like men condemned to death in the arena, a spectacle to the whole universe—angels as well as men. We are fools for Christ's sake . . .

*"The First Letter of Paul
to the Corinthians"*
(7:29-31; 4:9-10, NEB)

Doomsday Cult

*a study of conversion,
proselytization,
and maintenance of faith*

JOHN LOFLAND
University of Michigan

Prentice-Hall, Inc.
Englewood Cliffs, New Jersey

If the names of persons or companies in this book bear any similarity to those of actual persons or companies, the similarity is purely fortuitous.

Current Printing (Last Digit):
10   9   8   7   6   5   4   3   2   1

Prentice-Hall International, Inc., London
Prentice-Hall of Australia, Pty. Ltd., Sydney
Prentice-Hall of Canada, Ltd., Toronto
Prentice-Hall of India (Private) Ltd., New Delhi
Prentice-Hall of Japan, Inc., Tokyo

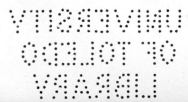

Acknowledgments

During the course of this study I received invaluable aid and support from Berkeley sociologists Erving Goffman, Herbert Blumer, Neil Smelser, and Philip Selznick. Only a small part of my debt to them is discharged through this public confession. As friend, colleague, and devil's advocate, Rodney Stark's unflagging interest in the project stimulated me to continual re-examination of my methods of data collection and analysis. Discussions with and observation by Travis Hirschi, Fred Templeton, Shelia Mc-Laughlin, Paul Forman, and Richard Santee were helpful in developing a more adequate empirical and conceptual portrait of the DP cult. In a variety of ways known to her, my wife, Lyn, made this work possible. As is necessary and proper, I alone am responsible for the numerous defects that reflective readers will naturally discern.

This investigation was supported in part by a Public Health Fellowship from the National Institute of Mental Health.

v

68 03791

Contents

List of Central Characters ix

1. Introduction 1
2. The Cult World View 14

part one
Conversion 29

3. Dispositions 31
4. Situations 50

part two
Proselytization 63

5. Disembodied Access 65
6. Embodied Access 90
7. Promotion Vehicles 120
8. Prospect Alignments 143
9. Promotion Tactics 175

part three
Faith and Hope   191

10.   Faith and the Encompassing Culture   193
11.   Faith and Cult Events   212
12.   Mechanics of Hope   244

Postscript   257

appendix
How the Data Were Collected   269

List of

Central Characters

Alfred	Bright teenager and moral cynic who became a DP
Alice	Wife of Merwin, part of housewife trio of Bertha and Minnie Mae
Bertha	Hallucinating and sanctified housewife who, along with Minnie Mae, deserted her family for the DP
Soon Sun Chang	The DP Korean Christ and Messiah
Dagna	Freshman seeker who giggled convulsively in the presence of young males
Earl	Resident of DP Center who promoted the proselytization tactic of peddling cosmetics door to door
Elmer	Halting introvert and college flunk-out who still longed for intellectual achievement before becoming a DP through Merwin
Elsa	Ludwig's maiden sister
Greta	German immigrant who lived in the Evangeline Residence for Young Women and fostered the flow of female freshman seekers to the DPs

Han	Karate champion who operated DP Judo School with Colonel Kim
Colonel Kim	Diplomatic aide in Korean Embassy who ran a Judo school as a front for DP proselytization
Yoon Sook Lee	Former college professor and leader of DP cult in America
Leo	Sometime convert and ex-GI who alternated residence between DPs' and a mental hospital
Lester	Former seminarian, graduate student in linguistics, and ambivalent homosexual who became a DP
Lucy	Freshman seeker and friend of Dagna
Ludwig	German immigrant and despondent college student who became a DP
Merwin	Beatnik recluse with dreams of financial empires before becoming a DP; Alice's husband
Minnie Mae	Arkansas-bred housewife who, accompanied by Bertha, deserted her family for the DP
Pierre	French immigrant and DP resident who was "patently disorganized"
Rev. Salvador Santini	Spiritualist minister who exploited DPs for membership in his church; partner of Stein
Stein	Pompous partner of Santini in exploiting DPs
Trouver	Social welfare investigator who became erotically entangled with Minnie Mae
Walter	Exploitive resident and metaphysician who conceived reality in terms of "vibratory levels"

Doomsday Cult

chapter 1

Introduction

Most of us most of the time have a fair agreement with one another about the nature of the "real world." We share a world view, an order of things taken for granted about the attributes of objects, events, and human nature.[1] This is a peculiar and intriguing feature of social life; but even more interesting is the fact that despite such massive agreement, little groups continually break off from this conventional consensus and espouse very different views of the real, the possible, and the moral.

Such splintering is of special interest because espousers of "deviant" world views must engage in the painful and frightening venture of going against established conceptions. Having taken their stand, they must live in the midst of the conventional majority's overt disdain or even active suppression of them. To be an ideological minority is to be largely bereft of the supports that accrue by mere virtue of conformity—supports consisting in large measure of the simple fact that a multitude of others agree with us.

In view of the powerful forces supporting ideological conformity, one must ask how it is possible for little groups continually to break off and set up counterideologies and, having done this, how it is possible for them to maintain their positions. Are there not pressures that lead to the breakdown of these positions and a return to the dominant perspective?

Among the many types of ideological splinter groups in our society, religious cults are of particular relevance in attempting

---

[1] Tamotsu Shibutani, "Reference Groups as Perspectives," *American Journal of Sociology*, Vol. LX (May, 1955), 564.

to answer these questions. Their world views are, by definition, quite different from the dominant American perspective, making them prima facie incredible; their ideological systems are highly complex and articulate, making them susceptible to criticism; and their adherents typically attempt to win others to the faith, exposing them to criticism. We should expect, therefore, that their problems as an ideological minority are particularly acute.

This book examines one such religious cult. It seeks to exploit this special relevance to the study of ideological splintering by tracing certain general social processes as they operate in this more sharply focused setting. From such a study we can perhaps gain insight into the operation of the same but less sharply defined processes, operating in a variety of contexts.

The cult in question, here called "The Divine Precepts" (DP for short),[2] is headquartered in Bay City on the Pacific Coast of America. It constitutes the American wing of a body of more than 5,000 millenarians in Korea who give allegiance to a Mr. Chang, a "Christ-Messiah," who teaches that the world is going to be transformed and made perfect by 1967. While God and "spirit forces" will affect this upheaval, the believers must also play a role and assemble a foundation of 144,000 converts[3] before that year. Led by a female Korean charged with the mission of saving America, the American branch, studied in 1962-63, was composed of more than twenty predominantly young, white believers. These "future world rulers" typically lived communally and devoted their total resources to the quest for converts.

Following from the problems stated, I shall pose three generic questions and seek to provide answers specific to the DP's, while also attempting to suggest the general relevance of these answers. These questions are: (1) How do deviant groups go about recruiting members? (2) How do persons come to be involved in "far

---

[2] This and other names that might tend to compromise the anonymity of participants have been changed.

[3] Revelation 7:4-5: "And I heard the number of those who had received the seal. From all the tribes of Israel there were a hundred and forty-four thousand."

out" activities? (3) How do adherents of such groups maintain their own involvement in the face of an encompassing and disapproving parent society? These questions may be thought of as an *involvement sequence*, or natural history, moving from group efforts at *proselytization*, through actual *conversion*, to the *maintenance of faith and hope*. These form, respectively, Parts II, I, and III of the study. (Although proselytization is logically prior to conversion, it will be discussed second in order to reduce the expository problems involved in introducing DP personnel.)

These three analytic questions are best understood against the background of (1) a brief descriptive introduction to the cult and (2) a more detailed overview of the analysis to be offered.

DESCRIPTIVE INTRODUCTION
TO THE DP CULT

During the late 1940's and early fifties, a young Korean electrical engineer, Mr. Soon Sun Chang, received a series of what he took to be messages from God, acknowledging him as none other than the returned Christ, the Lord of the Second Advent. Chang was also convinced that through these divine encounters, a new body of knowledge, The Divine Precepts, was being revealed to him. This doctrine unveiled the laws or principles by which God governs man, explained the causes of mankind's problems and God's purposes in human history, and disclosed the manner in which the perfected and eternal kingdom of God would shortly be established on earth.

By the late fifties, Mr. Chang had assembled several hundred followers in and around Seoul. To these believers he announced that the seven years from 1960 to 1967 would be the "Last Days" of the world as we know it, the period of "cosmic tribulation and judgment." By the end of the seventh year, the world would undergo a dramatic, supernaturally caused transformation through which his faithful followers would become rulers of a restored, eternal, and perfect Garden of Eden. Although this imminent transformation would be effected by "descending spirit forces,"

God's Chosen People would be obliged to play a role. Before 1967 they would be required to assemble 144,000 converts to constitute a "remnant" or "foundation of the new world." These would provide an élite to govern the theocracy of the "New Age." Since the restoration of man to God's grace would involve not just Korea but the entire world—although Koreans were God's Chosen People—the foundation had to include persons from twelve nations.

Toward this end, in 1959 Chang sent one of his earliest converts, a forty-four-year-old, English-speaking former university professor, Miss Yoon Sook Lee, to the United States. During the next four years, which she spent on the Pacific Coast, Miss Lee was involved with hundreds of people, but managed to convince only about twenty to accept the faith and help usher in the "Cosmic Era." These converts forsook their unconverted former associates and families, whom they regarded as enmeshed in the "Satanic" and dying world, to take up communal living and devote their finances and energy to the crucial quest for more converts. Like many of the early Christians, these people served as totally committed agents for "God's newly revealed plan."

The present study deals almost exclusively with the development of the American Pacific Coast branch from 1959 through mid-1963.[4]

Inasmuch as this material will be treated in terms of its relevance to one or another of the three questions to which we shall address ourselves (and will frequently violate temporal sequence), it is helpful to outline briefly the events of these four years, the better to understand a rather complicated collection of persons and places.

Northwest Town: January, 1959-May, 1960.   The DP in America began in the Pacific Northwest in a town of some 75,000 persons. Although relatively populous, Northwest Town was still basically a large rural settlement, situated as it was at the end of a farming valley and in the midst of a logging and wood products

---

[4] Field work and data-collection procedures are described in the Appendix.

manufacturing area. Much of the town's size and economic well-being were due to the presence of the state university (Northwest University).

Lee arrived there in January, 1959, in the role of a university student. She attended the university full-time through May, 1960, while working as a domestic. From September, 1959, to May, 1960, she was the caretaker of a local women's civic club. This group owned a mostly unoccupied bungalow that they used periodically for social events. It was here that Lee met with the first persons interested in the Divine Precepts. During this period, she also worked up an English draft of the DP revelation for use as a study text.

By May, 1960, twelve persons were regularly attending her bible study group in the clubhouse. Five of these were to become the core of her future cult enterprise: *Minnie, Bertha,* and *Alice,* young working-class housewives; and *Merwin* (Alice's husband) and *Elmer,* Merwin's co-worker in a plywood plant.

Maple Hill: May, 1960-December, 1960. The first four of these persons lived in a small settlement informally know as Maple Hill, which was seven miles outside Northwest Town. Due to a number of factors, other interested persons fell away from Lee in May, 1960, and at the invitation of Merwin and the others, Lee moved to Maple Hill, where she resided in a ramshackle house next door to Merwin and Alice. Soon Elmer, who lived on a farm with his parents some thirty miles out of town, moved in with Lee. Lee gave this quintet intensive instruction in the DP, and that summer the husbands of Minnie and Bertha became concerned that she was exercising too much influence on their wives. In September, 1960, the wives, convinced of their obligation to help save the world, deserted their families. This caused a good deal of tension in Maple Hill, but Lee and her remaining agents stayed on in order to work with a new set of prospective converts. However, other problems arose, and in December, 1960, the DP's migrated down the Pacific Coast to join Minnie and Bertha, who had settled in Bay City.

Bay City: January, 1961-June, 1962. Situated on the central Pacific Coast, Bay City was the commercial and seaport center of an environing metropolitan complex. The six DP's rented a seven-room flat in a multiracial, working- and lower-class district, began to live together, got unskilled jobs, and set out to convert the city. A variety of efforts in the first nine months produced an average of less than one new person per day calling at the DP Center. But one new enduring convert, *Alfred,* a seventeen-year-old, recent high school graduate, was added to the DP faithful, and at least four other persons were now professing faith.

In the fall of 1961, it was decided to make better preparation for the future by revising and reprinting the DP book and by purchasing a house to use as training headquarters when the movement really began to grow. They completed the printing in February, 1962, and in March the group moved to their new three-flat house, a few blocks from their original location.

After about a month of concentrated renovation of what had been a slum dwelling, a new surge of proselytization activities began. By June, these new efforts appeared to have failed, or were at least clearly in the process of failing. Two more converts, *Ludwig,* a German immigrant and college student, and *Leo,* a fork-lift operator, joined the faithful, but this was small success indeed.

State U. City and State College Town: July, 1962-June, 1963. In July, Lee decided it was time for each convert to go out on his own and be a missionary, as she had been in Northwest Town in 1959. The Bay City Center was to be maintained as headquarters, but each convert was required to establish his own residence and circle of converts in adjacent cities. The most successful and active of these in subsequent months were Minnie's cell in State University City and Bertha's in State College Town. The former city, which derives its name from the university situated there, was half an hour by car from the Bay City Center, and State College Town, the site of a large public college, was about an hour's drive away.

The results of proselytization were nil through the summer, but then in September, 1962, *Lester,* a twenty-five-year-old former naval officer and seminary student, at that time a graduate student at State U., converted to the DP. Minnie and Ludwig took up residence in Lester's flat, thus forming another DP cell. In State College Town, Bertha soon formed a cell with a female senior at State College, and four additional persons began to profess the faith.

Extensive proselytization activities were conducted in the winter of 1962-63, especially in State U. City, but little additional progress was made. By the spring of 1963, DP's felt it necessary to get out to new places. Dispersion of converts to additional state cities (and to Germany) followed.

*   *   *

Thus we have gained some sense of the contrast between the DP and conventional culture, its demand for total commitment, and its proselytization intensity. We may proceed now to a statement of the questions to be posed and an overview of the answers to be suggested.

OVERVIEW OF THE ANALYSIS

Because my discussion of the concrete DP materials will become somewhat detailed at times, it is perhaps useful to provide a reference guide to the more detailed conceptual apparatus that guides the conversion, proselytization, and faith and hope analysis. Chapter references for particular topics appear at the beginning of their respective summary paragraphs.

Part I. The first process to be discussed, *conversion*, concerns the conditions under which one may expect persons to take up a deviant role. This question will be approached in terms of a developmental model consisting of seven accumulating conditions, which, in their total combination, would seem to account for conversion.

Chapters 3-4. For conversion it is necessary that a person:

1. experience enduring, acutely felt tensions;
2. within a religious, problem-solving perspective;

3. which lead to defining himself as a religious seeker;
4. encountering the cult at a turning point in his life;
5. wherein an affective bond to adherents is formed (or pre-exists);
6. where extra-cult attachments are low or neutralized;
7. and where, to become a "deployable agent," exposure to intensive interaction is accomplished.

Conditions 1, 2, and 3 may be thought of as *background* factors, while 4-7 are *situational* or *interactional* elements. The reader will note that the analysis stresses the importance of *situated* conditions. There has been an overly strong tendency in psychodynamic and sociological conversion accounts (and in discussion of recruitment generally) to focus on explanatory variables that are somehow lodged in the person or precede his contact with a group. The thrust of the present formulation is that factors operating at the time of contact also play a crucial role in the consummation of perspective displacement.

Part II. The second process, *proselytization* or *recruitment,* is viewed as two temporally sequential phases:

1. *Strategies of access:* In what ways and under what conditions can missionaries gain access to and the attention of nonbelievers for the purpose of conversion?

2. *Promotion of conversion:* After gaining access, what are the ways in which missionaries can attempt to promote prospects into accepting a world view?

The DP's central operating goal of making converts has generated some rich case materials for the analysis of proselytization. Insofar as possible within the DP data, an attempt is made to delineate generic types of strategies-of-access and conversion-promotion tactics. The strategies-of-access data also provide materials for the analysis of the generalized circumstances in which persons have interactional access to one another.

Chapter 5. The first phase of proselytization is classified in terms of *embodied* (face-to-face) and *disembodied* (mediated) *communications, overt* or *covert presentations,* and their applications in religious or secular and conventional or deviant social gatherings.

There were two primary flurries of disembodied appeals in the period under study. The first (January-June, 1961) was composed of handbills, newspaper advertisements, news stories, mailed lecture announcements, and a radio program. The second (May-December, 1962) used news stories, a sound truck, personal letters to university foreign students, and mailed invitations to "get together" parties. Both flurries were perceived by the group as massive failures—and in fact they were.

Chapter 6. Although the DP's experimented with various kinds of embodied access strategies, their basic strategy—the one to which they always returned—was the more or less systematic application of covert presentations in religious gatherings. Religious, as opposed to secular, places were favored because the DP's felt that there were more predisposed persons there, because there were more religious gatherings available for infiltration, and because religious gatherings assume the sincerity of their participants and have universal mutual access rules that make interactional access quite easy. Covert presentations were favored because DP's were likely to be ejected if they announced what they were up to, because they appreciated the necessity of building affective bonds before telling prospects their doctrines, and because covert presentations were the only ways in which they could be polite and display regard for the occasion. DP's assumed the religious place roles of seeker-onlooker, spiritualist, and member. The less frequent overt presentations in religious places consisted of literature distribution and proselytizing professional religionists in their places of business. Access strategies in the less favored secular places involved manipulation of the roles of employee, patron, and salesman.

None of these strategies was very successful. Persistent failure to be effective was a source of chronic despair that had to be managed.

Chapter 7. Access was typically accomplished in some location outside a DP headquarters, where the aim was to generate some sort of initial interest that would induce the prospective convert to undertake the *second phase,* that of appearing in a DP residence, where the actual full-scale promotion of conversion could begin. The tactics employed in this phase also varied over time, were objects of hesitancy and vacillation and were subject to a number of peculiar vicissitudes.

The DP's had two primary promotion vehicles. One was the *briefing session,* which was intended to give the prospect an overall view of the DP perspective. In Bay City in March, 1961, this session was formalized into a four and a half hour tape recording. The reluctance of prospects to sit through this led to its progressive shortening. It was all but abolished by June, 1963. The other vehicle, the *study group,* was organized around serialized oral readings from Miss Lee's English translation of the Divine Precepts. This format also appeared to produce little interest, and it too was under consideration for abolition in June, 1963.

Chapter 8. Prospects were not a homogeneous category of persons, but rather displayed a number of different alignments to the cult, most of which presented vexing problems. The six primary postures were: (1) the *patently disorganized,* persons who had difficulty formulating and controlling their action in terms of situational proprieties; (2) *countermissionaries,* religious persons who determined to convert the DP's to some other "true religion"; (3) *exploiters,* persons who attempted to extract some nonreligious and unapproved benefit from the DP's, primarily cheap bed and board, power, and sex; (4) *conventionals,* the "squares" who happened into association with the DP's; (5) *veteran seekers,* primarily middle-aged women who as a matter of course merely studied each new religious doctrine that happened through the area; and (6) *freshman seekers,* primarily deprived young women who were tentatively beginning a career of occult seekership.

Chapter 9. DP promotion tactics clustered around efforts to promote friendship bonds through affectation of warmth and permissiveness; to assume consciously a moral front; to open the DP believers to extensive interaction with prospects; and to foster congruence with the DP perspective through introducing prospects to spiritualistic literature, doctrines, and organizations. Tactics for promoting prospects in the first few weeks of association were well-developed. There was hesitation, however, on how to manage those prospects who continued their association for longer periods without converting. This difficulty arose because the DP's expected spontaneous participation and freely granted compliance. Although they lacked well-worked-out tactics for managing this contingency, threats of immediate misfortune and future damnation caused by spirits were sometimes employed as the final ploys of these aborted promotions.

· *Part III.* The third process, the *maintenance of faith and hope*, concerns the question of how it is possible for persons to maintain their faith in the truth of a highly deviant, obscure, and stigmatized world view, and, in the millenarian case, keep up a sense that the millennium is imminent.

Chapter 10. Some students have suggested that deviant or radical constructions of reality are particularly vulnerable to information from the encompassing culture and require special mechanisms and arrangements that function to protect the faith of the adherents. I suggest, however, that at least the DP perspective provided elegant and abundant faith supporting cognitions and escaped cognitive contradiction. This derived from a radical revision of causal sources wherein all natural events were ascribed to good or evil supernatural causes or forces that were locked in a life and death struggle. These forces' continuing hostile encounters were constantly manifest in everyday life. The thoroughgoing elaboration and application of such a revision produced a qualitatively different and viable "system of truth."

The primary sources of the cult's experience are analyzed for the ways in which the espousers' operating code constructed and managed everyday "raw" reality. The believers' decoding of the public media productions of 1962 are reviewed to indicate how it was not only possible, but easy for them to read international,

national, and local events as pointing to the end of the world. Their perimeter experience with conventional religious rhetoric, direct spirit manifestations, work happenings, and prospect reluctance will all further suggest that events in the external world were supportive of their faith.

Chapter 11. Experience arising from the association of converts with each other that might be thought to be threats to faith are shown to have been supportive because of the nature of the system in which such experience was conceived. Among the negative experiences with supportive significance discussed are Miss Lee's erratic and authoritarian leadership style, peer convert irritations and conflicts, doubts and defection, and physical denial. More obvious supports of faith—such as direct spiritual experiences, interunit success stories and visits, tales of Korean charisma and suffering, and cult symbols and ceremonials—are also discussed.

These concrete types of raw reality suggest that the DP world view had few, if any, problems of cognitive contradiction. The DP's did not have to barricade themselves from the external world in order to sustain their faith. Quite the contrary, with their transcendent ideology, they happily operated in the midst of ongoing, ordinary life.

Chapter 12. Because the DP's frequently perceived themselves as massive failures in accomplishing their conversion goals, their central problem was that of keeping up a sense of hope, a sense that success in making thousands of converts was imminent. An analysis of their three-year organizational history (1960-63) and their repeated failures to attain their conversion goals reveal four mechanisms that appeared to regenerate hope of success.

*   *   *

These are, in brief, the main lines of the analysis set forth in the following chapters. Before turning to the question of conversion, however, it is necessary to present one last preliminary topic:

the substance of the DP world view. Some grasp of its content will establish the kind of credulity that belief in it required and also introduce the "dilemma of disclosure," a basic theme of the proselytization analysis.

chapter 2

The Cult
World View

DP's wanted the entire world to know and accept their ideology, but only certain parts were felt to be appropriate for disclosure to outsiders. Other parts should be held in secret until prospects were sufficiently instructed to understand them properly. The secret portions were controversial and, moreover, they made no sense apart from an acceptance and understanding of the less esoteric sections of the system.

Because of this and other concerns, the DP was divided into a more or less *public* portion, for outsider consumption, and a *sympathetic prospect* portion for insider consumption. This informational line was, by and large, upheld, although DP's sometimes "spilled" insider doctrines to what turned out to be unsympathetic outsiders.

Outsider Portions: "The Completed Testament." The portion felt to be appropriate for outsider's consumption was contained in the 200-page "Completed Testament" entitled *The Divine Precepts.* This book, the holy scripture of the cult also functioned as a text for outsiders. (Although the complete and final word of God, it had Lee's name on the title page.)

The Divine Precepts opens with a preface by Lee alleging the chaotic state of current religion and the need for a new revelation to "bring mankind back to the true religion." She states that a "full revelation and the ultimate solution to the questions of life and the universe [has] been revealed." Because of this revelation "we are living in a period of great transition" which began in 1960. The "crossing junction" between "good and evil" began when evil went from an "aggressive" to a "defensive" position and "good" took over the offensive. "Evil is doomed to decline rapidly. The principality of this world, the Satanic sovereignty, is to be destroyed completely."

The Biblical Book of Revelation has been fulfilled through God's new revelation, her preface continues, and "the new history of God's sovereignty has begun." This "new revelation" is said to have been "divinely revealed" to Mr. Chang, "a dedicated religious leader and philosopher in Korea." Chang is mentioned only in the preface and only in these terms. He is not declared to be "the Lord of the Second Advent," although he is said to have discovered "the hidden meaning of human history" and to be the leader of a group in Korea, whose "spiritual gifts" (e.g., healing, spirit guidance) are then described.

The preface closes with a plea to read the book in sequence and to pray to God concerning doubts.

The divine text itself is divided into twelve chapters. The first six chapters give a detailed and repetitious exposition of the precepts that constitute most of the premises upon which the world view is built.

The First Precept asserts the universality of "three stages of creation": formation, growth, and perfection. It is divinely ordained that all things must pass through these stages (e.g., "plants pass through the stages of seed, tree, and fruit").

Second, all things exist in "complementary associations"; i.e., in pairs (e.g., male and female, positive and negative, right and left). Everything is created "in the image of God," who, therefore also has a dual nature; namely, "the dual characteristics of male and female."

Third, there is an "action of give and take" between all complementary associations. All existence is maintained only through the action of give and take.[1] Between men and women this is manifest in love, in "stimulating joy and happiness."

---

[1] The second and third precepts are, in part, the Yin and Yang notion. Lee claimed that Chang discovered them (from God) and that they were

Fourth, God created man so that He, too, could exist in complementary association and experience the action of give and take and "feel the energy of life, the joy of love."

Fifth, there is a spirit world and a material world. The spirit world is "the world of cause and purpose." "Whatever happens in this physical world has its cause in the [spirit] world and leaves the result there." Man has both a spirit body and a material body.

Sixth, God originally intended that man's spirit should grow through the three stages of development and attain perfection. First, he would be a "form spirit," whose body would "appear white like white linen"; then a "life spirit" and "shine with light," but . . . only reflective light . . ."; and finally a "divine spirit," or "luminous being," and "shine with a bright luminescence within [himself]." In the original plan, man's spirit would grow to perfection and communicate with God and the spirit world and live in perfect harmony and love.

Chapter Two explains how this spiritual paradise was intended but never gained. As in the classic Christian myth, God created an Adam and Eve who lived in a Garden of Eden, where they were to develop spiritually. When they were fully developed— i.e., had reached spiritual perfection—God planned to bless them in marriage, and they and their offspring would live happily ever-after; before that time they were to refrain from sexual contact.

They had approached the top of the spiritual growth stage when the Archangel, Lucifer, became jealous of this pair, took a strong erotic interest in Eve, and "ventured to join together with [her]." Lucifer thereby violated God's precept. Eve tried to rectify this by sexual congress with Adam, but that only compounded the sin. By copulating without God's permission, Adam and Eve "stained their blood" and "the world came under Satanic rule." They committed the Original Sin and "fell far below the forma-tion stage."

---

his greatest precepts. Upon reading a newspaper account of the 1962 Nobel Prize awards, Lee commented that one day soon Chang would get a Nobel Prize for, among other things, his discovery of these precepts.

As in some versions of Christianity, all evil in the world, all problems of man, are due to this primordial violation of God's will. Indeed, history is little more than a footnote to this central happening. Because of the Fall, man experiences an "inner struggle" between good and evil. His spirit wants to act for good, but his body is dominated by Satan. Moreover, before the Fall man could communicate with the "spirit world," but since then this ability has been "damaged" and only a few people can now receive spirit messages.

The Fall, and Satan's domination of man were, and are, possible because God does not directly rule man before he attains perfection; if He ruled man directly, He could abolish Satan in an instant. Rather, God governs His relations with man by the Divine Precepts. Under these precepts, man must discover for himself the "secret crime of Satan." "Satan could dominate the world because no one had discovered his crime and accused him before God by pointing out the original nature of it."

Chapters Three, Four, and Five repeat and amplify the above points, preview later assertions and set down DP prophecies. Relative to the latter, it is said that there will be a "new heaven" above "Paradise" and that "Jesus will no longer be the central sun." "The new Lord will be the new sun of the heaven." The "end of the world" does not mean annihilation, but rather that a "complete change in world order will come about, even within a decade." This change will, however, be accompanied by unprecedented "economic collapse" and "moral corruption" which will produce "darkening clouds of fear and anxiety." Persons in the spirit world can only attain perfection by cooperating with people on earth. They will, therefore, aid the forces of good by intervention in "human affairs at the individual, national and international levels."

During these last days and before the final victory, Christians will oppose the new dispensation but after a "sufficiently large number" of people realize the Divine nature of these happenings, the New Dispensation will be swept into power.

The "Cosmic Judgment" will culminate in a final, nonnuclear conflict between democracy and communism. Democracy will win, but will then give way to "a new ideology . . . revealed by God." Democracy is the preferred form of government in a "Satanic world," where no one has "Divine wisdom," but "In the Golden Age the ruler will govern the world with Divine wisdom, Fatherly Love, and absolute Divine power. This ruler will not be elected by the people, but will be appointed by God."

Chapter Six defines "resurrection" as the process of restoring man's original nature. "The goal of resurrection is the attainment of perfection." Since man fell below the formation stage, it is God's intent that in the course of history he should collectively work himself back up again and attain perfection.

Chapters Seven, Eight, and Nine explain the divine "providence of restoration" from Adam and Eve to the failure of Jesus. Restoration proceeds by the "precept of restitution," according to which man is a "depraved sinner" and "a debtor to God." To be forgiven by God man must indicate his intention to reform by thoroughly rejecting Satan. He does this by undergoing hardship and diligently working his way back into God's favor. Satan, however, seeks to continue his control of man, and thus makes restoration an extremely difficult task.

The course of restoration to God is likened to the action of a "delicate beam-balance." When man desires God's favor, God exerts force on His side of the beam-balance. Satan, however, then exerts a counter force on His own side. Sometimes Satan even exerts His force first and God has to counter with His "Divine influence." In order to return to God's favor, then, man must constantly reject "Satan's unrelenting attacks." Moreover, if man fails to reject an attack of Satan, he must make *restitution* to God for the failure.

Human history is the long and sad tale of man's efforts to achieve restoration, his failure to do so and his acts of restitution. The "providence of restitution" in history began with God's attempt to establish a "foundation of faith" through Cain, who was to make restitution for the Fall by subjugating himself to Abel and showing love to him. However, he felt "jealousy and hatred toward Abel" and killed him. Because of Cain's failure a foundation of faith could not be laid in Adam's family and sixteen hundred years elapsed before another family could be chosen.

DP numerology is introduced at this point to explain the significance of 1,600 years. The numbers 3 and 4, their addition and multiplication (by each other and 10) are of particular significance. All manner of things are said to happen in threes (e.g., three stages of creation). Four is important, for it is the number of the "heavenly Unit of the Four Positions," which is the "Divine ideal of creation," meaning "God, Adam, Eve, and their children." "Hence the number four and its multiples have been directly related to the time intervals associated with progress toward the fulfillment of the providence of restoration."

Therefore, 1,600 years (or 10 generations, for ten is the "number of completion") elapsed because it was a "complete spiritual cycle" and ". . . had to be spent for a complete separation from Satan." [2]

God then chose Noah and his family for a foundation of faith and sought to begin a new creation after the flood. To accomplish restitution, Ham, "the God-favored . . . second son" had to be confronted by a "state of nakedness" to see if he had the original sense of innocence or was still afflicted with the shame of fallen man. He felt shame upon seeing his naked, and drunken father and thereby "failed God's test." The flood was rendered useless and it was necessary to wait for another spiritual cycle of ten generations in order to arrive at Abraham.

After some preparatory restitutive acts, Abraham was finally to separate good and evil by cutting some birds in two and offering them to God. He did not cut them in two, thus voiding the recently completed 400 years of restitution. In order to make restitution for Abraham's failure, the people of Israel had to "struggle in the Satanic world for an equal length of time."

---

[2] Such numbers and calculations have of course been quite popular among millenarians. See Hans Kohn, "Messianism," *Encyclopedia of the Social Sciences*, Vol. X, pp. 356-363, and the survey by A. H. Silver, *A History of Messianic Speculation in Israel* (Boston: Beacon Press, 1959), esp. Chap. 10, "The Five Methods."

Therefore "Abraham's descendants were doomed to be enslaved 400 years in Egypt."

After this, God sent Moses to lead the Israelites out of Egypt. They wandered in the desert 40 additional years for another misdeed. Then Moses made the mistake of striking a rock twice in order to obtain water, rather than once, as instructed by God. Moses would have "restored Adam" by striking it once, but the second blow "symbolically struck the restored Adam, Jesus." Jesus was thus given back to Satan, nullifying the 400 years of restitution through slavery in Egypt. The subsequent 400 years of Judges made "restitution for the 400 years of slavery in Egypt."

The Israelites then built the Temple of Solomon in order to put man in a new dispensation. This effort failed because of "Solomon's love for many foreign women" and attention to "other gods."

Because of King Solomon's corruption, the fulfillment of the ideal of the Temple was delayed 610 years: 400 years of Divided Kingdoms, 70 years of exile in Babylon, and 140 years of returning periods from exile.

In spite of all these errors, or perhaps because of them, "the Jews had come to the final stage of trial preceding the coming of the Messiah." In order to have this great day, they finally accomplished "total restitution for their entire history by separating themselves from Satan for the next 400 years." Jesus arrived and began to teach, but the prestigious John the Baptist failed to recognize Jesus as the Messiah and to testify to him. As a result, the Jews failed to follow Jesus and the "providence of universal restoration" was not accomplished. Although Jesus failed in his main mission, all was not lost. By belief in Jesus, one could at least attain "spiritual salvation" to the "growth stage." Thus, man's first 4,000 years end in a failure to attain the earthly paradise.

One can now see the emerging outlines of the DP images of man and God. Man is a faithless and sinful creature who lives in darkness, cut off from God because of his repeated errors. Although God's heart is broken as He cries for the return of man, He is also a stern judge who has punished generations of humans for small and unknowing transgressions of His rather obscure precepts.

Chapter Ten interrupts the historical narrative to argue that Jesus himself will not appear at the Second Advent. The Old Testament is said to show that "God never uses, a second time, the same person who once failed to fulfill His dispensation." A different man must play the Christ role, a man who will "subjugate Satan completely" and restore "the entire universe." Like Jesus, he will suffer rejection and the faithful will be difficult to find. Many anti-Christs will appear, because "before truth appears, falsehood stalks ahead."

Chapter Eleven interprets the nearly 2,000 years since Jesus. This period has accomplished restitution for the 2,000 years from Jacob to Jesus that were "lost" because of Jesus' crucifixion. Moreover, the last 2,000 years were "not merely a prolongation" but also a development. "The 2,000-year period from Jacob to Jesus was the Formation Stage, or the Old Testament Age; the 2,000 years after Jesus comprised the Growth Stage, or the New Testament Age." Further, God's dispensation in the present, the New Testament Age, has followed the pattern of the Old Testament Age. There are "seven comparable periods of major religious developments":

1. 400 Years of Slavery of the Israelites in Egypt.
   400 Years of Persecution under the Roman Empire.
2. 400 Years under the Judges.
   400 Years under the Church Patriarchs.
3. 120 Years of the United Kingdom.
   120 Years of the United Christian Empire.
4. 400 Years of Divided Kingdom of North and South.
   400 Years of Divided Empires between East and West.
5. 70 Years of Exile of the Israelites in Babylon.
   70 Years of Exile of the Papacy.
6. 140 Years of Return from Exile of the Israelites.
   140 Years of Papal Reinstatement and Renaissance.
7. 400 Years of Preparation for the Messiah.
   400 Years of Preparation for the Second Advent.

The major events of the New Testament Age are chronicled under these categories, showing how events are converging upon the Second Advent.

The final chapter describes the forty years before 1960 which was "an historical encapsulation of the 400 years since the Protestant Reformation . . . and serves as restitution to God for the entire 6,000-year history of His providence." In "three universal events," Satan was, or is being defeated. First, his German protégés were defeated in World War I in order to make "restitution . . . to God and [invoke] retaliation against Satan for Adam's failure." Second, in World War II, "the ambition of Hitler to rule the world under Satan represented, symbolically, the opposite of the one world under God which Jesus was to have established." Hitler's defeat was retaliation against Satan for the unfulfilled mission of Jesus. Third, communism is Satan's attempt to "thwart the fulfillment of God's providence. . . . It must . . . and will be banished. . . . God has already started the final stage of His Divine plan. . . ."

The final pages of the book ask: "What nation will be chosen for the fulfillment of God's Will?" God always undertakes a new dispensation with a different people; therefore He will now choose a different nation. Only a formula for determining the identity of this nation is provided. The Lord of the Second Advent must be "from the East," for Revelation says: "Then I saw another angel ascend from the East." This nation must have been "tried for a long period in its history through unmerited sufferings and persecution. . . . In the last days, the sufferings of this nation will become more intense and much of their blood will be shed." Also, "this chosen nation must be free of any sin of aggression . . . as were the Jews." Finally, in order to be a "symbolic representation of the whole world, which is now divided between Cain and Abel, . . . this chosen nation must itself be divided into two sections, . . . symbolizing Cain and Abel." "The establishment of the kingdom of heaven and the destruction of Satanic rule will be effected in this country first, and from there it will spread universally."

The Lord of the Second Advent will be recognized by his

discovery of "the secret crime of Satan" and his ability to subjugate Him. He will also be able to "disclose and put into operation the schedule for the establishment of the New World."
The book closes:

The New Age has now begun. The Lord of the Second Advent will
rule the heaven and the earth with Divine wisdom and power and
Fatherly love, and his kingdom will last forever.

This, in brief, is the DP Bible and the publicly espoused portions of the DP world view. The book is long because of elaborate
biblical quotations and narrative, a considerable amount of repe-
tition, and a marked propensity for clarifying interpretations by
giving analogies and parallels. These practices make it rather
difficult to decipher the volume's thrust and argument.

Insider Portions. If one studied the book and appeared sympathetic and accepting, he could learn the insider portions. However, many of the sensitive doctrines could be inferred from the
book, and DP's lacked formal procedures for disclosing insider
portions. One picked them up piecemeal as he "grew" in the DP.

The primary questions concerning the insider's understanding
are raised by the book itself. What was the nature of the "crossing junction" of 1960? Who and where is the Lord of the Second
Advent? How exactly did he get to be Christ? Who is this new
chosen people? When and in what manner will this new kingdom
come about? What is man's part in effecting this transformation?
What should one do to prepare for it?

Mr. Chang was often named and discussed but was rarely
declared to be the Lord of the Second Advent. His status was
simply assumed in interaction. He earned his Christhood through
being born in the "second Israel" (Korea) at the right juncture
of the long spiritual cycle and through being concerned with
man's depraved and evil state. Chang had to *earn* his role by
diligently deciphering God's partial revelations that spanned seven
years and by passing a series of God's tests. One of the most
important of these necessitated a journey into the spirit world
and an appearance before God on His throne. On this occasion,

Jesus and his hosts assembled on one side of God's throne and Satan and His supporters on the other. In front of the throne stood a display board containing seventy possible causes of Man's Fall from Eden. Chang could pass a crucial test for Messiahship by picking the correct answer and thereby revealing the "secret sin of Satan." He ran his hand over the possible answers while astutely watching the hosts of Jesus and Satan out of the corner of his eye. He saw that Jesus' hosts rejoiced and Satan's people cringed when he came close to the right answer. By using this clue, Chang picked copulation. He walked up to God and announced his choice. God said he was wrong. Chang repeated that copulation was the original sin. Again God said he was wrong. A third time Chang asserted copulation as the correct answer. With that, God embraced him and announced: "You are My son."

This "discovery" [3] only secured his nomination. To be the Christ he had to "restore" himself (i.e., rid himself of original sin) and assemble a group of other restored people as the foundation of a new, perfect world. The accomplishment of this restoration was the mysterious and seldom revealed "crossing junction between good and evil" in 1960. Concretely, the forty-year-old Chang married one of his seventeen-year-old female converts. The original sin was sexual, so Chang had to marry at the numerologically significant age of forty and become the "Second Adam" with his "Second Eve." [4] His marriage symbolically

---

[3] Curiously, Lee and the DP's actually seemed to believe that copulation as the original sin had been discovered only by Chang. The notion is of course an enshrined part of popular folklore, and as early as the fourth century was a leading theory of the Fall among Christian theologians. See N. P. Powell, *The Ideas of the Fall and of Original Sin* (London: Longmans, Green & Company, Ltd., 1927), esp. pp. xii, 45, 58, 77, 86, 204, 226, 227, 271-273, 304, 340, 411. See also C. Nordhoff, *The Communistic Societies of the United States* (New York: Hillary House Publishers, Ltd., 1961), pp. 120-125, 132-134; and T. Schwartz, *The Paliau Movement in the Admiralty Islands, 1946-54* (New York: American Museum of Natural History, 1962), esp. pp. 252-253, 258.

[4] It was the original mission of Jesus to marry at age forty, but he of course lived only to age thirty-three.

restored man at the individual level and fulfilled Revelation 19:7-8:

Alleluia! The Lord our God, sovereign over all, has entered on His reign! Exalt and shout for joy and do Him homage, for the wedding day of the Lamb has come! His bride has made herself ready.

The New Age began with individual restoration, and in subsequent years Chang was to restore man symbolically at the tribal, national, and international levels. Thirty-six Korean couples were matched and married in 1961 in order to effect the symbolic tribal restoration. Seventy-two simultaneous marriages in 1962 accomplished national restoration. International restoration would require 144 couples drawn from twelve nations and was to occur sometime before 1967. To be a true part of the New Age, one was required to marry, not just anyone, but a mate of Chang's choice. Such mating was known as "the blessing."

Sexual activity was the original corruption that "stained man's blood." Therefore one should abstain from sex until given in blessed marriage. A period of separation also served to purify one and allow taint-free congress with a similarly purified consort.

The foregoing matters were secret, but still more so was the belief in a fully restored world within seven years of 1960. Revelation 7:4 had to be fulfilled within that period: "And I heard the number of those who had received the seal. From all the tribes of Israel there were a hundred and forty-four thousand." Upon attaining this number the "spirit world" would become visible to everyone and cause mass DP conversions. The current order would collapse in the process, and DP's would assume the reins of the new theocracy.

DP's were circumspect in speaking of Korea's "true role," lest outsiders doubt these Americans' loyalty. In safe company, Korea was venerated as "the motherland" and "God's chosen nation." Korean was to be the official and universal language of the New Age. Shortly before 1967, Korea was to "serve as the priest nation for the rest of the world." According to Lee:

People from all over the world will go to Korea to study the new philosophy, the Divine Precepts. Korea will be the center from which the spiritual truth and blessings of the New Age will reach out to every corner of the earth.

In return for spiritual blessings, richer nations would send Korea their material wealth. Revelations 21:24-27 describes this New Age arrangement:

I saw no temple in the city; for its temple was the sovereign Lord God and the Lamb [Mr. Chang]. And the city had no need for sun or moon to shine upon it; for the glory of God gave it light, and its lamp was the Lamb. By its light shall the nations walk, and the kings of the earth shall bring into it all their splendour. The gates of the city shall never be shut by day—and there will be no night. The wealth and splendour of the nations shall be brought into it.

As is apparent, strong beliefs in Korean national deliverance and Koreans as a superpeople are found in the DP.

The public portions of the DP were remarkably bereft of instructions on what one should do with his life in light of the DP. Insiders of course believed in total dedication to the cause. Indeed, the New Age was to be stratified on the principle of how much work an individual performed in bringing it about. In fact, the principle of "work rendered" was the cult's paramount moral law. The moral demands and dilemmas of the current social order were irrelevant because a new order was just around the corner. It was on this basis that Lee counseled converts to give up their spouses and friends, quit or change jobs, and stop schooling. There was no need to confront traditional moral problems, such as whether or not to meet violence with violence. They were irrelevent, because in a few years moral dilemmas would no longer arise.

Outsiders were inclined to view DP's as retreating from the world, but DP's conceived of themselves in a radically different manner. They alone were *really in* the world and *really knew* what was happening. Moreover, they saw themselves as eternity's cadre, as having imminent access to incredible power. They would have more power than any historical ruler and more spiritual status than all previous religious adepts, including Jesus. Although aware of their current and manifest incompetence to rule the world, come the New Age and their blessing, each would undergo profound change in personality, personal knowledge, and leadership competence. "I'm just an ordinary guy now," one convert said, "but after I'm blessed I'll be above the pettiness of everyday life and I'll be able to see things as they really are."

Chang would not have time to judge everyone's blessing, so élite converts would help in deciding on the rewards appropriate for the world's population. Latecomers to the kingdom would find it much more difficult to achieve spiritual and material advance and would do so only by this élite's permission.[5]

Beyond a conception of the New Age as a severely graded hierarchy of eternal perfection and bliss for the élite, little else was promulgated as inviolate doctrine on what to expect. Chang was still receiving revelations on the character of life in the New Age, so detailed depiction was not yet possible. Nevertheless, DP's engaged in considerable speculation on its character. Many speculations followed an "as you like it" line, although Lee reported Chang to have said that the social order would be built upon units of New Age (i.e., rematched) monogamous marriages. The elementary unit was to be three families living together, three such units under the authority of another three-family unit. The society would pyramid in this manner up to Chang and his family. A planning committee of sorts in the Korean movement was said to have already drawn up a master chart and filled some top posts. Such a structure was necessary because persons at the bottom would still have evil thoughts. Other proximate families would be able to "spiritually detect" deviationist tendencies and bring quick corrective action.

During informal descriptions of this kind, DP's sometimes openly admired some aspects of communist *social organization* (especially the Chinese version). Communistic systems displayed *forms* of the New Age that failed to make people happy because they were dominated by Satan. They were Satan's "imitation" of

---

[5] Cf. "It is God's people who are to judge the world. . . . The world is to come before you for judgment. . . . Are you not aware that we are to judge angels?" The First Letter of Paul to the Corinthians 6:1-3.

God's plan, but would work under God. Thus all the "instruments of production" would be owned by God. Children would be rotated from home to home or raised in communal nurseries.

The spirit and material worlds would again merge in the New Age and allow for all manner of marvels. According to Lee, Chang said, for example, that fertilization of crops would be unnecessary —"you simply plant prayfully and things will grow." One DP—a science fiction fan—was fond of predicting travel from one place to another through simply "willing" the trip. Further, one would be able to create material objects by simply thinking about them. Such developed "mind power" would make learning very easy. One willed mastery of materials and it would be done. In general, all the problems of man—poverty, ignorance, disease (spiritual and physical)—would disappear.

The DP was, then, a relatively complex and articulated *millenarian* world view. It was a ". . . phantasy of salvation which is to be

1. collective, in the sense that it is to be enjoyed by the faithful as a group;
2. terrestrial, in the sense that it is to be realized on this earth and not in some otherworldly heaven;
3. imminent, in the sense that it is to come both soon and suddenly;
4. total, in the sense that it is utterly to transform life on earth, so that the new dispensation will be no mere improvement on the present but perfection itself;
5. accomplished by agencies which are consciously regarded as supernatural." [6]

This is what they believed. In the next two chapters, I shall try to explain how they came to believe it.

---

[6] N. Cohen, "Medieval Millenarism: Its Bearing on The Comparative Study of Millenarian Movements" in S. Thrupp, ed., *Millennial Dreams in Action* (The Hague: Mouton & Co., 1962, Supplement II of *Comparative Studies in Society and History*), p. 31.

part one

Conversion

My brothers, think what sort of people you are, whom God has called. Few of you are men of wisdom, by any human standard; few are powerful or highly born. Yet to shame the wise, God has chosen what the world counts folly; and to shame what is strong, God has chosen what the world counts weakness. He has chosen things low and contemptible, mere nothings, to overthrow the existing order.

"The First Letter of Paul
to the Corinthians"
(1:25-28 NEB)

chapter 3

Dispositions

In this part, I shall present a model of the conversion process through which persons came to see the world in terms set by the perspective of the Divine Precepts.

The logical and methodological structure of the analysis is based on a developmental conception.[1] That is, I will offer a series of more or less successively accumulating factors, which in their total combination would seem to account for conversion to the DP's. Seven such factors will be presented, all of which together seem both necessary and sufficient cause for conversion to occur.

The sequential arrangement of the conditions may be conceived as a funnel; that is, as a structure which systematically reduces the number of persons who can be considered available for recruitment and at the same time increasingly specifies who is available. At least theoretically, since the mission of this band of world savers was to convert America, all persons in this country could be considered as targets. Each condition thus serves both to narrow the range of people available and to show why only a handful of them ultimately responded to the DP call.

Furthermore, the temporal order in which conditions are met may vary. Typically, and perhaps ideally, the conditions develop

---

[1] Cf. Ralph Turner, "The Quest for Universals in Sociological Research," *American Sociological Review*, Vol. XVIII (December, 1953), 604-611; Howard S. Becker, *Outsiders* (New York: The Free Press of Glencoe, Inc., 1963), esp. pp. 22-25; and, Neil J. Smelser, *Theory of Collective Behavior* (New York: The Free Press of Glencoe, Inc., 1963), pp. 12-21.

Portions of Chaps. 3 and 4 were previously published in the *American Sociological Review*, Vol. XXX (December, 1965), 862-875, in collaboration with Rodney Stark.

as presented. However, the ordering principle has been one of *activation* rather than of temporal occurrence alone. That is to say, some conditions may pre-exist for a considerable time prior to their becoming relevant to DP conversion, or they may develop only in time to accomplish conversion. The time of activation is the same in either case.

It was not possible to obtain complete data pertinent to all seven steps of the conversion model on all twenty-one persons who were classified as converts as of mid-1963. However, full information on all seven factors was available for fifteen cases. All known data on all cases conformed to the model, and speculative inferences about unknown items, based on what information did exist, strongly suggested that these too met each condition. In presenting biographical data in the following sections to explain and document the model I shall focus on the most central of the early converts, although material from less central and later converts will also be drawn upon for illustration. As an overview, it may be helpful to know that they were primarily white, Protestant, young (typically below age thirty-five), some had college training, most were Americans from lower-middle-class and small town backgrounds, and the rest were immigrants.

How can one determine when a person has *really* in some deep sense taken up a different perspective? The most obvious evidence is of course his own declaration that he has done so. This frequently takes the form of a tale of regeneration, about how terrible life was before and how wonderful it is now.[2] But verbal claims alone are insufficient, because they are easily made and just as easily falsified. Indeed, several persons who professed belief in the DP's were regarded as insincere by all core members.[3] However, a display of loyalty and commitment, such as giving time, energy, and money to the DP enterprise invariably brought ratification of the conversion from all core members. But to require such a display as a necessary indication of true conversion

---

[2] Peter Berger has provided us with a delightful characterization of the reconstructive functions of such tales. See his *Invitation to Sociology* (New York: Doubleday & Company, Inc., 1963), Chap. 3.

[3] See, for example, Chap. 8, the cases of Stein and Santini.

raises problems too. A few persons who made only verbal professions were universally regarded as converts by core members. To avoid this difficulty, I shall distinguish between two classes, or degrees, of conversion: *verbal converts*, those fellow travelers and followers who professed belief and were accepted by core members as sincere, but who took no active role in the DP enterprise; and *total converts*, who exhibited their commitment through deeds as well as words.

The data indicate that, up to a point, the same factors account for both types of conversion. In my initial discussion the two groups will be treated together. Later I shall attempt to show how failure to transform verbal into total conversion is a consequence of the failure of the last stage in the conversion sequence to develop.

A Model of Conversion

To account for the process by which persons come to be world savers for the DP, I shall be concerned with two types of conditions or factors. The first type, which may be called *predisposing conditions*, comprises attributes of persons *prior* to their contact with the cult. In current sociological language, these may be thought of as background factors operating to produce a pool of appropriate persons from which the DP converts may be drawn. However, it is unfortunate that a convention has grown up in sociology of treating various kinds of demographic characteristics, structural and/or personal frustrations, and so forth, as reasonably complete accounts of factors that "push" people into groups that are dedicated to protest against the prevailing social order. Not that these factors are unimportant, or that such models are inaccurate, but they are woefully incomplete. One might put the character of their incompleteness in a Meadian paraphrase of T. S. Eliot: Between the impulse and the act falls the shadow.

The second type of conditions concerns this shadowy area, the contingencies of social situations. By *situational contingencies* I refer to those conditions that develop through direct confrontation and interaction between the potential convert and DP members, conditions that can lead to the successful recruitment of

persons already well disposed toward the enterprise. Many of those who qualified for conversion on the basis of predispositional factors entered into interpersonal relationships with the DP's, but because the proper situational conditions were not met, they did not convert.

Let us now turn to a discussion of each of the factors operating within these two classes.

I. TENSION

It would seem that no model of human conduct entirely escapes some concept of tension, strain, frustration, deprivation, or the like, as a factor in accounting for action. And not surprisingly, even the most cursory examination of the life situations of converts over the years before they embraced the DP reveals that they labored under what they at least *perceived* to be considerable tension.

This tension is best characterized as a felt discrepancy between some imaginary, ideal state of affairs and the circumstances in which they actually saw themselves. It is suggested that such acutely felt tension is a necessary, but far from sufficient condition for conversion. It provides some disposition to act. But tension may be resolved in a number of ways (or remain unresolved). Hence to know that these people were in a tension situation says little about *what* action they might take.

Just as there can be myriad consequences of tension, so too can the sources be disparate. Some discovered, concrete varieties were: unrealized longing for wealth, knowledge, fame, or prestige; hallucinatory activity for which the person lacked any successful definition; frustrated sexual and marital relations; homosexual guilt; acute fear of face-to-face interaction; disabling and disfiguring physical conditions; and, perhaps of a slightly different order, a frustrated desire for a significant, even heroic, religious status—to "know the mind of God intimately"—and to be a famous agent for His divine purposes.[4]

---

[4] It is currently fashionable to reduce this last to more mundane, "real" causes. This may be possible. However, it is not necessary here to prejudge the phenomenology.

Some of these tensions may be sketched in the form of brief life histories of a few central believers. The case of Miss Lee, the Messiah's emissary in America, illustrates the theme of aspiring to be an important religious figure.

Miss Lee was born and raised in Korea and converted to Chang's cult in 1954, when she was thirty-nine. During her early teens she was subject to fits of depression and used to sit on a secluded hilltop and seek spirit contacts. She began receiving visions, hearing voices, and generally hallucinating, a pattern she was to maintain thereafter. Her teenage mystical experiences convinced her that she had a special mission to perform for God. Hence, at the age of nineteen, she entered a Methodist seminary in Japan. She was immediately disenchanted by the "worldly concern" of the seminarians and the training she received, although she stuck out the five-year course. Prior to entering the seminary, she had become engrossed in the spiritualistic writings of Emmanual Swedenborg, who soon began to appear to her in visions. Her estrangement from conventional religious roles was so great that upon graduation from the seminary she, alone among her classmates, refused ordination. She returned to Korea at the start of World War II, and by 1945 was a professor of social welfare at a denominational university in Seoul. In 1949 the Methodist Board of Missions sent her to a Canadian university for further theological training. There she wrote her thesis on Swedenborg, who continued to visit her in spirit form. In Canada, as in Japan, she was bitterly disappointed by the "neglect of things of the spirit," raised concern among the faculty by constantly hiding to pray and seek visions (often in the dorm basement), and occasionally stole away to Swedenborgian services. Her spirits continued to tell her that she was a religious figure of great importance. Returning to her academic life in Korea, she fell ill with chronic diarrhea and eventually nephritis, both of which resisted all medical treatment. After two years of this, her health was broken and she was completely bedridden. At this time her servant took her to see Chang.

Thus is summarized the portrait of a desperately estranged spinster, with secret convictions of grandeur, frequent heterodox hallucinations, and failing health, who felt herself inextricably immersed in the mundane affairs of modern religious bureaucracy.

Although embedded in a different cultural context, the cases of *Bertha* and *Lester* follow lines rather similar to Miss Lee's, but include an important sexual theme.

Bertha (age twenty-nine at conversion), the daughter of German immigrants, was raised in a suburban town. After high school she attended one of those modeling schools operated in large cities for naïve, fame-hungry girls, regardless of suitability. She returned shortly to marry a local boy employed as a stereotyper in a printing plant. On her wedding night she spent two hours locked in their hotel bathroom, and subsequently did not alter her evaluation of sexual intercourse. Several years later the couple separated briefly, reunited, and after five years of marriage (1955) had their first child. The second came in 1957, and they moved to the West Coast. There Bertha began having private religious hallucinations, including sanctification—being made holy and free of all sin. She went to various ministers to tell of her marvelous experiences, but was not warmly received; indeed, most advised psychiatric help. She began, then, to tell her husband that one day she would be very important in the service of the Lord. Following a homosexual episode with a neighbor woman, Bertha demanded to be taken elsewhere, and the family moved to Northwest Town, in April, 1959. There they settled in rural Maple Hill, a collection of half a dozen houses about seven miles from town. This was soon to be the scene of the initial formation of the cult group, and here she came to know two neighbors, Minnie Mae and Alice. These young housewives drew the attention of other neighbors by spending many hours a day in the nearby general store, sometimes drinking beer and often complaining a good deal about their husbands. During this period, Bertha attended churches of various denominations and continued to have frequent ecstatic religious experiences, mostly while sitting alone in a clump of bushes near her house, where she was also reported to have spent a good deal of time crying and moaning.

An N.R.O.T.C. cadet, *Lester* (age twenty-five at conversion) was commissioned an officer in the United States Navy upon college graduation. While at sea he underwent a series of religious and hallucinatory experiences and was given an early discharge in order to enter a Lutheran Seminary in State U. City. His continuing mystical perceptions, such as "fiery red balls," aroused a good deal of curiosity and opposition among his fellows and the faculty. After an abortive part-time year, he left the seminary to take up full-time graduate study in linguistics at nearby State U. (As an undergraduate major in this field, Lester had mastered at least the rudiments of eleven languages.) He remained convinced that he was destined to be a one-man revitalization movement in the church and took an extremely active role in campus student religious programs, meanwhile increasing his preoccupation with spiritualism and his own psychic experiences. For his first full-time year of graduate school he was awarded a Woodrow

Wilson fellowship. But he was much more concerned about his religious life—and a new interest. He went to live with a young ex-Hungarian aristocrat, well-known in the area as a practicing homosexual. The young Hungarian led Lester to organized spiritualism, where his religious preoccupations and hallucinations were greatly reinforced and increased. But Lester found these groups wanting. They contented themselves with mundane affairs and seemed uninterested in speculations on larger theological matters. In addition, Lester was highly ambivalent about his homosexuality, unable to explain it, unable to accept it, and unable to quit it. Then he met Miss Lee.

As in the previous cases, *Ludwig* was subject to hallucinatory episodes that for a time lacked satisfactory definition. Other of his tensions focused upon failure to achieve his educational aspirations.

Ludwig (age thirty-four at conversion) grew up under Hitler's Third Reich. At age sixteen he was taken into the Nazi army in Hitler's 1944 "total mobilization," and reported having for a time been a front line combat soldier. He immigrated to the United States at age twenty-nine and worked as a stock broker's clerk in New York for two years before moving to Bay City, where he enrolled in a junior college. Subsequently he transferred to State U. as a junior in industrial engineering. While he had done well in junior college, his grades fell at the university and he began to fear the possibility of flunking out. Despondent, he contemplated suicide. Although Ludwig was antireligious, feeling that talk about God and such was nonsense, he frequently experienced what he perceived as "super-real" dreams. These often involved scenes of bombing, fire storms, and combat from his youth. When alone (which was most of the time), it would sometimes seem as if someone were standing behind him; but that someone—or thing—would be gone when he turned around. After entering the university, these events became more frequent and began to concern him intensely. He started reading about spiritualism and attending spiritualist churches, where he became a firm believer in occult phenomena. However, he was dissatisfied that spiritualism did not give him a larger view of things or provide an encompassing meaning and direction to his life. At best, it only interpreted his dreams and feelings of spirit presence.

The case of *Elmer* illustrates another kind of frustrated ambition, that of attaining status as a man of knowledge and invention.

Elmer (age twenty-six at conversion) was born on a farm in North Dakota, whence his parents fled the drought and depression for the West Coast during the late thirties and settled on a farm near Northwest Town. Elmer was slightly built, with something of a vacant stare. After high school he flunked out of the university after one semester and spent the next two years in the army, where he flunked medical technician school. After the army he enrolled in a nearby state college and again lasted only one semester. He then returned to his parents' farm and took a job in the plywood factory. Elmer conceived of himself as an intellectual and aspired to be a learned man. He undertook to educate himself and collected a large library toward this end. Unfortunately he was virtually illiterate. In addition to more conventional books, he subscribed widely to occult periodicals, such as *Fate, Flying Saucers, Search,* and so on. He also viewed himself as a practical man of invention, a young Thomas Edison, and dreamed of constructing revolutionary gadgets. He actually began assembling materials for a tiny helicopter for use in herding the cows and a huge television antenna to bring in stations hundreds of miles away. Elmer also had severe interaction problems. He was unable to speak to others above a whisper and looked constantly at his feet while talking. He had great difficulty sustaining a conversation, often appearing to forget what he was talking about. But despite his "objective" failures at intellectual accomplishment, Elmer revealed a picture of a person still clinging to a belief in his own potential. The consequences of failure were largely to make him withdraw in order to preserve this self-image from his inability to demonstrate it.

Although not as intensely concerned with spirit matters or hallucinations as some others, *Alfred* displayed a moral concern over what he felt to be a low rate of compliance with religious ethics. This had produced in him an angry, cynical view of the world. In turn, this moral concern was very likely provoked by the restrictions imposed during and after a rather exotic illness.

Alfred (age seventeen at conversion) grew up on a farm near Northwest Town, a neighbor of Elmer's parents. He was reared in the standard, active way of life of rural America, but in the tenth grade became very fat, prone to bruises, and hyperactive. He developed a round, moon face and reddish complexion, which made him appear mentally retarded. Specialists diagnosed his affliction as overactive adrenal glands and failure of the body to discharge liquids, which were building up in body tissue and causing obesity. These conditions were corrected, but thereafter he was required to live a relatively sedentary life. Prior to his illness, Alfred had been an outdoor type and had aspired to prominence on high school athletic teams. Although mediocre in this area, he had trained for various sports by putting himself through a daily regimen of five to seven miles of road work. Medical directives closed off this career. He now shunned the "frivolity" of high school youth culture, spent a good deal of time alone, and read widely, developing a fascination for the apocalyptic books of the Bible and far right wing political writings. He grew increasingly preoccupied with strict moral codes and what he saw as a widespread and deplorable evasion of them. He felt that his church was filled with hypocrites, viewed local businessmen as crooks, and thought that most people were "lazy, spend-thrift, materialistic slobs." As editor of the school paper, he continually attacked the administration for not running a "tight ship" (e.g., failing to apprehend boys who smoked in the lavatories). Even though he was a top student (salutatorian, 98th percentile on a national senior achievement examination) and his teachers fondly regarded him as one of the few intellectually alive students they had known, Alfred felt that his teachers disliked him for his attacks on the school. Knowing Elmer, and learning that he was in Bay City with a "religious group," Alfred decided to visit him the summer after graduation and to work in Bay City before entering Northwest University.

Bertha's friend *Minnie Mae* did not aspire to significant status, religious or otherwise. She pined rather for the more modest goal of marital satisfaction.

Minnie Mae (age twenty-seven at conversion) was born in Possum Trot, Arkansas, of hillbilly farmers. She was one of eleven children, began dating at twelve, and married at fifteen, having completed only rural elementary school. She and her young husband left Arkansas for lack of jobs and settled in Northwest Town. Her husband took a job in a plywood factory. Although the young couple did not join a church, they came from a religious background (Minnie Mae's mother was a Pentacostal lay preacher), and they began attending tent meetings near Northwest Town. During one of these Minnie Mae began speaking in tongues and fell into a several-hour trance. After this her husband discouraged church activities. The couple had three children at roughly two-year intervals, and until 1960 Minnie Mae seems to have spent most of her time caring for these children and watching television. She reported tuning in a local channel when she got up in the morning and keeping it on until sign-off at night. In 1958 the couple built a small house in Maple Hill. Here her behavior and conversations with neighbors began to reveal severe dissatisfactions with her marriage. She repeatedly complained that her husband had intercourse with her only about once a month, but she also reported being very afraid of getting pregnant again. Furthermore, she wanted to get out and have some fun, go dancing, etc., but her husband wanted only to watch TV and to fish. She sadly wondered often if she had missed her fling and let life pass her by through marrying too young. And often she complained about her husband's opposition to fundamentalist religious activities.

Merwin and *Alice* are of quite a different pattern. Theirs was not an intensely religious concern; indeed, their grandiose ambitions lay in fortune.

Merwin (age twenty-nine at conversion) was raised in a Kansas hamlet where his father was the railroad agent. After high school he tried a small Kansas junior college for a year, did poorly, and joined the marines, where he was in the band. Discharged in 1952, he spent one year at the University of Kansas, majoring in architecture, and did well, so he transferred to what he felt was a better school in Northwest Town. Here he was less successful and fell into a pattern of frequently dropping out, then going back. Estranged and alone, he bought a few acres in Maple Hill and a small ramshackle cottage, and took up a recluse existence—he rarely shaved or washed, brewed his own beer, and dabbled in health foods, left-wing political writings, and occult publications, while supporting himself by working in a plywood plant. Next door, about twenty yards away, lived Alice, her two children, and her husband, also a plywood plant worker. Alice's husband, however, worked a swing shift, while Merwin worked days. This arrangement resulted in Alice filing for divorce and moving over to Merwin's. The husband departed without undue resistance. Following their marriage, Merwin began to put his plans for financial empire into action. He considered a housing development, a junkyard, and finally bought a large frame house in Northwest Town to convert into a boarding house for students. After he had bought furniture and made other investments in the property, the city condemned it. Merwin filed bankruptcy and returned to Maple Hill to lick his wounds and contemplate his next business venture. Merwin had long been disaffected with the established religions and considered himself an agnostic for awhile. But he was also interested in the occult. These interests were developed by his co-worker Elmer.

Alice, also a small town girl, had traded for what she felt was a better man, one who was "going places," but after the bankruptcy these hopes seemed to be fading. She still bragged a great deal to Minnie

Mae and Bertha that Merwin would be a big man someday, but there was little evidence to support her.

These case histories provide some concrete notion of the kinds of things that bothered pre-converts. It would appear that problems we find among them are not *qualitatively* different or distinct from those presumably experienced by a significant, albeit unknown, proportion of the general population. Their peculiarity, if any, appears to be *quantitative*; that is, pre-converts felt their problems to be acute and experienced high levels of tension concerning them over rather long periods of time.

It might in fact be said that from the point of view of an outside observer, their circumstances were in general not massively oppressive. One can probably find among the general population large numbers of people laboring under tensions that would seem to be considerably more acute and prolonged.

Perhaps the strongest qualitative characterization of tension supportable by the data is that pre-converts felt themselves frustrated in their various aspirations and *experienced* the tension rather more acutely and over longer periods than most do.

Obviously, explanation cannot rest here, for such tensions could have resulted in any number of other resolutions, and in fact they usually do. Thus these unresolved problems in living are only part of the necessary scenery, but the props, the stage itself, and the drama of conversion remain to be constructed.

II. TYPES OF PROBLEM-SOLVING PERSPECTIVES

On the basis of the first factor alone, only those without enduring, acute tensions are ruled out as potential DP converts. Since conversion is hardly the only response to problems, it is important to ask what else these people could have done, and why they didn't.

It seems likely that there were very few converts to the DP's for the simple reason that people have a number of conventional and readily available alternative ways of defining and coping with their problems. By this I mean that they have alternative perspectives, or rhetorics, that specify the nature and sources of problems and offer some program for their resolution. There are many such alternatives in modern society, but I shall briefly describe three particular types: the *psychiatric*, the *political*, and the *religious*. In the first, the origin of problems is typically traced to the psyche, and manipulation of the self is advocated as a resolution to problems. Political solutions, mainly radical, locate the sources of problems in the social structure and advocate its reorganization as a solution. The religious perspective tends to see both sources and solutions to difficulties as emanating from an unseen, and in principle unseeable, realm.

The first two rhetorics are both secular and are the most often used in contemporary society. It is no longer appropriate to regard recalcitrant and aberrant actors as possessed of devils. Indeed, modern religious institutions, in significant measure, offer secular, frequently psychiatric rhetorics concerning problems in living. The predominance of secular definitions of tension is a major source of loss of potential converts to the DP. Most people with acute tensions "get the psychiatric word" especially, either by defining themselves as grist for its mill or by being forced into it. Several persons met other conditions of the model but had adopted a psychiatric definition of their tensions and failed to convert. The following case is striking in this regard.

Thirty-year-old *Freda*, a divorcee with a history of mental hospitalization and profuse hallucinations, met Minnie in a chance encounter on a local bus. A college graduate, she was living in a women's residence hall in State U. City and working as a secretary, all the while longing to get married again. She was unsuccessfully participating in local, organized matchmaking groups or lonely hearts clubs and taking numerous university extension courses. She said that she had no close friends and was, in fact, observed to be a very unhappy young woman, noticeably "at loose ends." Minnie and she began to associate extensively. Holding back the more bizarre DP assertions, Minnie gradually worked Freda into the DP view of history and the modern world. Freda became very fond of Minnie. To anticipate the model somewhat, Freda met the conditions of tension, cult-affective bonds, and low extra-cult bonds. She had recently been unemployed and was still at a turning point. However, she did not have a religious perspective. After nine years of psychotherapy she was a veritable fount of psychiatric self-conception. Otherwise she was an excellent candidate for conversion.

In a few cases, persons were ambivalent about psychiatric self-images, and the DP came into direct competition with the mental hospital. Thus in one exaggerated instance, Leo, an ex-GI, literally alternated residence between the DP headquarters and the psychiatric ward of the veterans hospital, never seeming able to decide once and for all which rhetoric to adopt for his circumstances.

All pre-converts seemed surprisingly uninformed about conventional psychiatric and political perspectives for defining their problems. Perhaps largely because of their backgrounds (many were from small towns and rural communities), they had long been accustomed to defining the world in religious terms. Although conventional religious outlooks had been discarded by all pre-converts as inadequate, "spiritless," "dead," etc., prior to contact with the DP's, *the general propensity to impose religious meaning on events had been retained.*

Even within these constrictions in the available solutions for acutely felt problems, a number of alternative responses still remain. First, it must be recognized that people can persist in stressful situations and do little or nothing to reduce their discomfort. This is something that students of social life too often tend to underestimate. The case of Minnie, for example, gives an idea of the way in which tension can be sustained for years with no remedial activity. Except for the emergence of certain situational factors, this tension would doubtless never have erupted.

Second, people often take specifically problem-directed action to change those portions of their lives that are troublesome, without at the same time adopting a different world view to interpret them. Thus, for example, Bertha and Minnie Mae might have simply divorced their husbands, and presumably Lester could have embraced homosexuality. Clearly many pre-converts attempted such action (Merwin *did* start a boarding house, Elmer *did* attend college, etc.) but none found a successful direct solution to his difficulties.

Third, there exists a range of maneuvers that "put the problem out of mind." In general these constitute compensations for, or distractions from, problems in living. Such maneuvers include addiction to the mass media, preoccupation with childrearing, or immersion in work. More spectacular bypass routes are alcoholism, suicide, promiscuity, and the like. A number of such tentative strategies have been mentioned above in the case histories of pre-converts. Recall, for example, the summer of 1959, when Minnie Mae, Alice, and Bertha hung around the general store during the day getting high on beer. One is forced to wonder whether if this activity had occurred in a more urban setting, with bars and strange men available, their subsequent lives might not have been very different.

In any event, it may be assumed not only that many people with tensions explore these strategies, but also that some succeed and hence become unavailable as potential DP recruits.[5]

III. RELIGIOUS SEEKERSHIP

Whatever the reasons, pre-converts failed in their attempts to find a successful way out of their difficulties through any of the strategies outlined above. Thus their need for solutions persisted, and their problem-solving perspective was restricted to a religious outlook. However, all pre-converts found that conventional religious institutions failed to provide adequate solutions. Subsequently, each came to see himself as a seeker, a person searching for some satisfactory system for interpreting and resolving his discontent. Given their generally religious view of the world, all pre-converts had, to a greater or lesser extent, defined themselves as looking for an adequate religious perspective and had taken some action to achieve this end.

-----

[5] It perhaps needs to be noted that this discussion is confined to isolating the elements of the conversion sequence. Extended analysis would have to give attention to the factors that *in turn* bring each conversion condition into existence—that is, to develop a theory for each of the seven elements, specifying the conditions under which they develop. On the form that this would likely take see Ralph Turner's discussion of "the intrusive factor," *op. cit.*, 609-611.

Some went from church to church and prayer group to prayer group, routing their religious seeking through relatively conventional institutions. A male convert in his early twenties recounted:

My religious training consisted of various denominations, such as Baptist, Methodist, Congregationalist, Jehovah's Witnesses, and Catholicism. Through all my experiences, I refused to accept . . . religious dogma . . . because it was Truth I was seeking, and not a limited belief or concept.

Likewise, over the years Lee surreptitiously participated in a variety of little Korean tongues-speaking and prophetic groups, attended Swedenborgian churches while in Canada, and was an ardent student of all manner of heterodox figures. Bertha also attended a variety of church services and prayer meetings, giving allegiance to none. And while bedridden for a year as a result of a car accident, Leo had taken up the Bible and read it numerous times searching for "spiritual meaning." Upon recovery he had "church hopped," looking for religious definition.

Others began exploring the occult, reading the voluminous literature of the strange, the mystical, the spiritual, and tentatively trying a series of occult groups, such as Rosicrucians, spiritualists, and the various divine sciences. Ludwig and Lester assiduously attended spiritualist churches and read religious-metaphysical books in search of the higher philosophy in terms of which they could understand spirits and themselves. Elmer laboriously waded through books on spiritualism, flying saucers, various "new" Bibles, treatises on witchcraft and hypnotism, and occult periodicals; visited mediums; attended flying saucer clubs; and perused Hindu and East-West mutant world views. In working next to Merwin eight hours a day, Elmer introduced him to this range of topics, which Merwin soon accepted as viable formulations. He, too, became an avid follower of the occult-metaphysical. Witness too the spiritual travails of the following couple:

In April, 1960, my wife and I . . . [began] to seek a church connection. [We] began an association with Yokefellow, a spiritual growth organization in our local church. My whole religious outlook took on a new meaning and a broader vision. I grew emotionally and spiritually during the next two and a half years.

However, as I grew, many spiritual things remained unanswered and new questions came up demanding answers which Yokefellow and the Church seemed not to even begin to touch upon. . . . My wife and I became interested in the revelation of Edgar Cayce and the idea of reincarnation, which seemed to answer so much. We read searchingly about the Dead Sea Scrolls, we decided to pursue Rosicrucianism, we read books on the secret disclosures to be gained from Yogi-type meditation. The more we searched, the more questions seemed to come up. Through Emmet Fox's writings I thought I had discovered a path through Metaphysics which through study would give me the breakthrough I longed for.

Or the seekership might display some amalgam of conventional and unusual religious conceptions, as illustrated in this sad tale told by a male convert:

I was reared in a Pentacostal church and as a child was a very ardent follower of Christianity. Because of family situations, I began to fall away and search for other meanings in life. This began . . . when I was about twelve years old. From that time on, my life was most of the time an odious existence, with a great deal of mental anguish. These last two years have brought me from church to church trying to find some fusion among them. I ended up going to Religious Science in the morning and fundamentalist in the evening.

Floundering about in the area of the religious was accompanied by two fundamental beliefs that define more specifically the ideological components of the religious-seeker pattern. Although concrete pre-convert beliefs varied a good deal, all of them espoused the following religious-seeker postulates about the nature of ultimate reality.

First, there was believed to be an active supernatural realm from which spirits of some variety could intervene in the material world. Such entities could, at least sometimes, break through from the beyond and impart information, cause "experiences," or take a hand in the course of events.

Second, there was espousal of a teleological conception of the universe, a belief that there exists a purpose for which every object and event is created. This included general notions, such as that the earth is as it is in order to meet the needs of man, and that man manifests the physical structure he does in order that he might do the things he does. More important, man himself as a phenomenon must be on earth because somewhere, sometime, somehow, it was decided that Homo sapiens should exist to *fulfill a purpose* or purposes. And of course this also applies to individuals, each of whom has some purpose and some sort of "job" to perform.

Typically, the positing was little more specific than this, or at least more specific terms of espousal were only tentatively held. The religious seeking itself was in terms of finding some more detailed formulation of and answers to these vague, existential axes.[6]

A few words on the general question of the importance of prior beliefs in effecting conversion are necessary at this point. A number of discussions of conversion have placed relatively great emphasis on the existence of a strong congruence between previous ideology and a given group's appeal.[7] Others seem to treat the degree of congruence as unimportant so long as the ideology is seen as embodied in what appears to be a successful movement.[8] Both views are extreme.[9]

The data suggest that only the two *gross* kinds of congruence

---

[9] Some readers might conclude that the supernatural entities and teleological postulates already constrict the range of possible clientele to a tiny proportion of the American population. Although a majority are probably excluded, it should also be pointed out that a minority of many millions does espouse these postulates. See Charles Y. Glock and Rodney Stark, *Religion and Society in Tension* (Chicago: Rand McNally & Co., 1965), Chaps. 3, 5 and 8.

[7] See, for example, H. G. Brown, "The Appeal of Communist Ideology," *American Journal of Economics and Sociology*, Vol. II (November, 1943), 161-174; Gabriel Almond, *The Appeals of Communism* (Princeton: Princeton University Press, 1954).

[8] See, for example, Eric Hoffer, *The True Believer* (New York: New American Library of World Literature, Inc., 1958), p. 10.

[9] Cf. Herbert Blumer, "Collective Behavior," in Joseph B. Gittler, ed., *Review of Sociology* (New York: John Wiley & Sons, Inc., 1957), pp. 147-148.

that make up the ideology of religious seekership were necessary for conversion to the DP. Presumptively important items, such as a more or less fundamentalist belief in Christianity, millenarian expectations, and hallucinatory experience, were far from universal among pre-converts. Although some believed in a vaguely defined "New Age" that would appear gradually, most *became* apocalyptic pre-millenarian (in the sense of a New Age soon and suddenly) rather than choosing the DP as an outlet for previously held eschatological hopes. The role of these gross points of congruence is suggested in the DP's substantive appeals to pre-converts.

Active spirits were rampant in the DP view of reality. Converts lived with an immediate sense of unseen forces operating upon and intervening in the physical order (e.g., the weather) and human affairs, from the relations among nations, through the latest national disaster, down to their moment-to-moment lives. Nothing occurred that was not related to the intentions of God's or Satan's spirits.

For persons holding a teleological conception of reality, the DP doctrines had the virtue of being grandly teleological and offering a minute and lawful explanation of the whole of human history. They systematically revealed and defined the hidden meaning of individual lives that had lacked coherence and purpose. The ideology of course explained all hallucinatory behavior in terms of spirit manifestations and of how these spirits had been preparing the pre-convert to be able to see the truth of the DP.

Although acute and enduring tensions in the form of frustrated aspirations are not an ideological component, in the sense of being a more abstract postulate about the nature of reality, it should be noted here that the DP also offered a proximate and major payoff. Converts were assured of being virtual demigods for all eternity, beginning with a rule over the restored and reformed earth within the immediate future. By 1967 God would impose the millennium upon the earth, and those who converted early, before the truth of the message became self-evident, and thus helped to bring about the inevitable, would occupy the most favored positions in the divine hegemony. Converts gave particular stress to this advantage of conversion in their proselytization:

"those who get in early," one member often put it, "will be in on the ground floor of something big."

Religious seekership emerges, then, as a further portion of the path through the maze of life contingencies that leads to DP conversion. It is a floundering among religious alternatives, an openness to a variety of frequently esoteric religious views, combined with failure to embrace the specific ideology and fellowship of some set of believers.[10] This seekership functioned to provide the minimal points of ideological congruence that made these people further available for DP conversion.

---

[10] Further suggestive materials on seekers and seeking may be found in H. T. Dohrman, *California Cult* (Boston: Beacon Press, 1958); Leon Festinger, Henry Riecken, and Stanley Schachter, *When Prophecy Fails* (Minneapolis: University of Minnesota Press, 1956); Sanctus De Santis, *Religious Conversion* (London: Routledge & Kegan Paul, Ltd., 1927), esp. pp. 260-261; H. Taylor Buckner, *Deviant-Group Organizations*, unpublished masters thesis, University of California, Berkeley (1964), Chap. 2. For discussion of a generically similar phenomenon in a quite different context, see Edgar H. Schein, *Coercive Persuasion* (New York: W. W. Norton & Company, Inc., 1961), pp. 120-136, 270-277.

chapter 4

Situations

The necessary attributes of pre-converts stated thus far could all have persisted for some time before these people encountered the DP and can be thought of as background factors, or predispositions. Although they appeared to have arisen and been active in the order specified, they are important here as accumulated and simultaneously active factors during the development of succeeding conditions.

IV. THE TURNING POINT

We now turn to situational factors in which timing becomes significant. The first of these is the striking universal circumstance that at the time when they first encountered the DP, all pre-converts had reached or were about to reach what they perceived as a turning point in their lives. That is, each had come to a moment when old lines of action were complete, had failed, or had been or were about to be disrupted, and when they were faced with the opportunity or necessity for doing something different with their lives.[1]

Thus Miss Lee's academic career had been disrupted by long illness from which she recovered upon meeting Chang:

On the third day [of residence with Chang's group] my nephritis was gone and also the swelling on my face. Until this day I could not eat

---

[1] Everett C. Hughes, *Men and Their Work* (New York: The Free Press of Glencoe, Inc., 1958), Chap. 1; Anselm Strauss, "Transformations of Identity," in Arnold Rose, ed., *Human Behavior and Social Processes* (Boston: Houghton Mifflin Company, 1962), pp. 67-71. Cf. the oft-noted "cultural dislocation" and migration pattern found in the background of converts to many groups, especially cults.

normal food because of indigestion and nephritis, but now I could eat and digest rice, highly seasoned pickles, pork, and fish. In this way I was healed from my years-old trouble. I was quite happy and I felt light inside my body.

Bertha was newly arrived in a strange town; Lester was disaffected with graduate studies after having quit the seminary; Ludwig had entered a new school and was failing; Alfred was just graduated from high school; Minnie Mae no longer had a preschool child at home to care for; Merwin had just failed in business after leaving school; and Elmer had returned to his parents' farm after failing in college for the second time.

Turning points in general derived from having recently migrated, lost or quit a job (a business in Merwin's case), or graduated from, failed in, or quit an educational institution. Perhaps because most converts were young adults, turning points involving educational institutions were relatively frequent. This is seen in the cases above and is additionally illustrated by a graduate student who had just failed his Ph.D. qualifying examinations and two second-semester college seniors who had vague and unsatisfying plans for the future. Recovery from or the onset of an illness, marital dissolution, and other changes, extant or imminent, such as Minnie Mae's new freedom, were relatively infrequent.

The significance of these various kinds of turning points lies in their having produced an increased awareness of and desire to take some action on their problems, *combined with a new opportunity to do so.* Turning points were circumstances in which old obligations and lincs of action had diminished, and new involvements had become desirable and possible.

V. CULT-AFFECTIVE BONDS

We come now to the moments of contact between a potential recruit and the DP's. In order for persons who meet all four of the previously activated steps to be further drawn down the road to full conversion, an affective bond must develop or already exist between the potential recruit and one or more of the DP members. The development or presence of some positive, emotive, interpersonal response seems necessary to bridge the gap between first exposure to the message and coming to accept its truth. That is, persons developed affective ties with the group or some of its members while they still regarded the DP perspective as problematic, or even "way out." In a manner of speaking, final conversion was coming to accept the opinions of one's friends.[2]

Miss Lee's recollections of her conversion to the DP's provides a graphic illustration:

In addition to this change [her recovery from illness] I felt very good spiritually. I felt as if I had come to life from a numb state and there was *spiritual liveliness and vitality within me by being among this group.* As one feels when he comes from a closed, stuffy room into the fresh air, or the goodness and warmth after freezing coldness, was how my spirit witnessed its happiness. *Although I could not agree with the message intellectually, I found myself one with it spiritually.* I reserved my conclusions and waited for guidance from God. [Italics added.]

Miss Lee further revealed that she was particularly attracted to Mr. Chang and lived in his home in order to enjoy the pleasure of his company, until finally she decided that his message was true.

Her statement that she "could not agree with the message intellectually" is particularly significant. Other converts reported and were observed to experience similar reservations, while at the same time building strong bonds with members of the group. Thus, for example, Lester, the most highly intellectual of the converts, displayed extremely strong attachments to the middle-aged Miss Lee and manifested the "intellect problem" for some weeks after he had turned his life over to her. At one point late in this period he could still reflectively comment to an observer:

---

[2] Cf. Tamatsu Shibutani, *Society and Personality* (Englewood Cliffs, N.J.: Prentice-Hall, Inc., 1961), pp. 523-532, 588-592. Edgar Schein reports that in prison "the most potent source of influence in coercive persuasion was the identification which arose between a prisoner and his more reformed cellmate" [*Coercive Persuasion* (New York: W. W. Norton & Company, Inc., 1961), p. 277]. See also Alan Kerckhoff, Kurt Back, and Norman Miller, "Sociometric Patterns in Hysterical Contagion," *Sociometry*, Vol. XXVIII (March, 1965), 2-15.

I have not entirely reconciled [the DP world view] with my intellect, but Miss Lee keeps answering more and more questions that are in my mind, so I am beginning to close the holes I have found in it.

It is particularly important to note that conversions frequently moved through *pre-existing* friendship pairs or nets. Thus, in the case of the formation of the original core group, an affective bond had first to develop between Miss Lee and Bertha (the first to meet Miss Lee and begin to espouse her views), but once that took place, the rest of the original conversions were supported by prior friendships. Bertha was part of the housewife trio of Minnie Mae and Alice; Merwin was Alice's husband; Elmer was Merwin's friend and co-worker. Subsequent conversions also followed friendship patterns, or else friendships developed that linked the pre-convert to the converts.

The building of bonds that were unsupported by previous friendships with a new convert often took the form of a sense of instant and powerful rapport with a believer. Consider, for example, this account by a young housewife of first seeing Lester while attending an Edgar Cayce Foundation retreat:

I went to [one of the] Bible class[es] and saw Lester in our class. I had seen him for the first time the night before and had felt such love for him. He was my brother, yet I had not met him. He looked as if he were luminous! After the class I wanted to talk to him. But our project group had a discipline that day—complete silence. I did not want to break it, yet I felt such a need to talk to him. I prayed and asked God what He would have me do. I received such a positive feeling. I took this as an answer and sought out Lester. When I found him, I did not have anything to say. I just mumbled something. But he seemed to understand and took me to the beach, where he told me, "He is on earth!" Oh, what joy I felt! My whole body was filled with electricity.

The less than latent sexual overtones of this encounter were seen in a number of other heterosexual attachments that led to conversion—and in quite a few that did not. Thus Ludwig heard about the DP from Greta at a gathering of local German immigrants. In his initial visits to the DP and in his subsequent cult career, he was observed to display high interest in this reasonably attractive German girl. On one occasion he commented, with a wink and a grin, that when the partners were being passed out in the new age Greta would have her pick of the men. Everyone would want her; but the implication was, he would get her. Even after four years of cult membership, Elmer could hardly hide his feelings in this testimonial:

Early in 1960, after a desperate prayer, which was nothing more than the words, "Father if there is any truth in this world, please reveal it to me," I met Miss Lee. This day I desire to never forget. Although I didn't fully understand yet, I desired to unite with her. . . .

It is suggested, then, that although potential converts might have difficulty in taking up the DP perspective, when the four previous conditions *and* an affective tie were present, they came to consider the DP seriously and to begin to accept it as their personal construction of reality.

VI. EXTRA-CULT-AFFECTIVE BONDS

It may be supposed that non-DP associates of the convert-in-process would not be entirely neutral to the now live possibility of his taking up with the DP's. We must inquire, then, into the conditions under which extra-cult controls in the form of emotional attachments are activated, and how they restrain or fail to restrain persons from DP conversion.

By virtue of recent migration, disaffection with geographically distant families and spouses, and very few proximate, extra-cult acquaintances, a few converts were "social atoms" in the classic sense. For them extra-cult attachments were irrelevant. This appeared to be the situation in Alfred's case, for example.

More typically, converts were effectively without opposition because, although they were acquainted with persons, no one was intimate enough with them to become aware that a conversion was in progress, or, if they knew, did not feel that there was a sufficient mutual attachment to justify intervention. Lee was ill and isolated from university life and associates until some time after her firm conversion. Elmer neglected ever to tell his parents that he was becoming or had become a DP.

Lester's social round was built predominantly around participation in religious groups, and one might on that account suppose that he had numerous affective bonds with other regular participants. However, although he was a well-known figure and appreciated for his task-contributions, he was an outsider to any local circles of intimacy. Many people knew him, but no one was a personal friend. He was in groups, but not of them. Further, Lester's relations with his two sets of parents and step-parents and with his homosexual partner evidenced considerable strain and ambivalence.

Ironically, in many cases positive extra-cult attachments were to other religious seekers, who, even though not yet budding converts themselves, provided impetus to continue investigation or entertainment of the DP rather than exercising a countervailing force. Indeed, such extra-cult persons might only be slightly behind their friend or friends in their own conversion process. Such was the case in the sequence of conversions among the network formed by Bertha, Minnie, Alice, Merwin, and Elmer.

In the relatively few cases where there were positive attachments between conventional extra-cult persons and a convert-in-process, control was minimized or not activated because of geographical distance and intentional avoidance of contact or communication about the topic during the period when the convert was solidifying his faith. Thus, for example, during his pre-convert period Ludwig failed to inform his mother in Germany, to whom he was strongly attached, and only wrote her about the DP months after his firm acceptance. (She disowned him.)

During and after the period of tentative acceptance of course, converts possessed a rhetoric that helped to neutralize their affective conflicts. The following open letter to the "DP family" written by a young soldier far from home conveys the powerful (and classic) content of this facilitating and justifying rhetoric:

I wrote my family a very long, detailed, but yet very plain letter about our movement and exactly what I received in spiritual ways, plus the fact that Jesus had come to me himself. The weeks passed and I heard nothing, but I waited with deep trust in God.

This morning I received a letter from my mother. She . . . surmised that I was working with a group other than those with the "stamp of approval by man." She . . . called me a fanatic, and went on to say: "My fervent constant prayer is that time will show you the fruitlessness of the way you have chosen before it consumes you entirely. A real, true religion is deep in the heart and shines through your countenance for all to see. One need not shout it to the house tops either."

At first it was the deepest hurt I had ever experienced. But I remember what others in our [DP] family have given up and how they too experienced a similar rejection. But so truly, I can now know a little of the rejection that our beloved Master experienced. I can now begin to understand his deep grief for the Father as he sat peering out of a window singing love songs to Him because he knew that the Father would feel such grief. I can now begin to feel the pain that our Father in heaven felt for 6,000 years. I can now begin to see that to come into the Kingdom of heaven is not as easy as formerly thought. I can now see why many are called but few are chosen. I began to understand why men will be separated, yes, even from their families. I begin to see the shallowness of human concern for God as a Father and their true blindness. Oh, my heart cries out to Our Father in grateful praise and love for what He has given.

*   *   *

[In the words of Miss Lee:] "As we get closer to the Father the road shall become more difficult"; "Only by truly suffering can we know the Leader and the heart of the Father"; "You shall be tested." "He will come with a double-edged blade." Only now am I beginning to realize the deep significance of these words. Only now am I beginning to know the heart of the Father and the great suffering of our Lord.

When there were emotional attachments to extra-cult, nonseeking persons, and when these persons were physically present and cognizant of the incipient transformation, conversion became a nip and tuck affair. Pulled upon by competing emotional loyalties and their discordant versions of reality, pre-converts were thrown into intense emotional strain.

A particularly poignant instance of this involved a newlywed senior at State University. He began tentatively to espouse the DP as he developed strong ties with Lester and Miss Lee. His young wife struggled to accept but failed to meet a number of conditions leading to conversion, and in the end seemed nervous, embarrassed, and even ashamed to be at DP gatherings. One night, just before the group began a prayer meeting, he rushed in and tearfully proclaimed that he would have nothing further to do with the DP's, even though he still thought their message was probably true. Torn between affective bonds, he opted for his young bride, and it was only months later that he finally lost all belief in the DP.

When extra-cult bonds withstood the period of affective and ideological flirtation with the DP's, conversion failed to be consummated. However, most converts did not seem to have the kind of external affiliations in which the informal control over belief that is exerted among close friends could be exercised. They were so effectively unintegrated into any network of conventional people that for the most part they could simply fall out of relatively routine society virtually unnoticed and take their co-seeker friends (if any) with them.

VII. INTENSIVE INTERACTION

The combination of the six previous factors seems sufficient to bring a person to *verbal conversion* to the DP, but one more contingency must be met if he is to become a deployable agent,[3] or what I have termed a *total convert.*

As mentioned earlier, most, but not all, verbal converts ultimately put their lives at the disposal of the cult. It is suggested that such commitment took place as a result of intensive interaction with DP's and failed to result when such interaction was absent. By intensive interaction is meant actual daily, and even hourly physical accessibility to DP total converts. Such intensive exposure offers the opportunity to reinforce and elaborate upon the initial, tentative assent that has been granted the DP world

---

[3] On the concept of the "deployable agent" or "deployable personnel" in social movements, see Philip Selznick, *The Organizational Weapon* (New York: The Free Press of Glencoe, Inc., 1959), pp. 18-29.

view. It is in such prolonged association that the perspective comes alive as a device for interpreting the moment-to-moment events in the verbal convert's life.

The DP doctrine has a variety of resources for explaining the most minor everyday events and for relating them to a cosmic battle between good and evil spirits in a way that places the convert at the center of this war. Since all DP interpretations point to the imminence of the end, to participate in these explanations of daily life is more and more to come to see the necessity of one's personal participation as a totally committed agent in this cosmic struggle.[4]

The need to make other converts and to support the cause in all ways was the main theme of verbal exchanges between the tentatively accepting and the total converts—and, indeed, among the total converts themselves. Without this close association with those already totally committed, such an appreciation of the need for one's transformation into a total convert failed to develop. In recognition of this fact, the DP's gave greatest priority to attempting to get verbal converts (and even the merely interested) to move into the cult's communal dwellings. Indeed, during her early efforts in Northwest Town, Miss Lee gained verbal conversions from Bertha, Minnie Mae, Alice, Merwin, and Elmer many months before she was able to turn them into total converts. And this transformation did not in fact occur until Miss Lee moved into Alice and Merwin's home (along with Elmer), placing her within a few dozen yards of the homes of Minnie Mae and Bertha. This resulted in daily exposure of the verbal converts to Miss Lee's total conversion, which produced their increasing engrossment in the DP until they came to give it their entire personal and material resources. Recalling this period, Minnie Mae reported a process that also occurred during other verbal converts' periods of intensive interaction. When she would begin to waver in her faith, unwavering believers were fortunately present to carry her through this "attack of Satan."

It is also instructive to consider that Ludwig remained in a

---

[4] Cf. Schein, *op. cit.*, pp. 136-139, 280-282.

state of verbal conversion from February, 1962, until midsummer of the same year. Even at the beginning of summer he had been most concerned with getting a job to finance his return to college in the fall. (He had not flunked out, after all, but passed with A's, a feat he attributed to spirits whispering answers to him during exams.) He argued that the time was not right, that he would "work himself to death" and still not get converts, and that therefore he would continue with college. However, that summer Minnie moved to State U. City as a missionary. Ludwig now lived only a few minutes away from a DP, and he and Minnie began phoning and seeing one another many times a day. Within a few weeks they "collectively" decided to become a missionary team and found lodging under the same roof. Ludwig had become a full, committed convert, and he never returned to college.

That fall, Lester became a verbal convert and remained so until Minnie and Ludwig were evicted from their dwelling. Lester magnanimously offered them refuge and, following the departure of his homosexual roommate, Ludwig and Minnie moved in. From then on, Lester threw himself with a vengeance into witnessing and reorganizing his life. Within three months he had sold his two violins, postponed a needed throat operation, cashed in his life insurance ($450), and turned all proceeds over to the group. He gave up his Ph.D. aspirations and left school after receiving his M.A.

Most verbal converts were induced out of their tenuous state through contrived or extant intensive interaction within a few weeks or, more typically, a few months. However, in a few instances the interval between assent and total commitment spanned a year or more. Thus when Elsa, Ludwig's maiden sister, associated with the DP's and came to entertain the perspective, some eleven months of subtle and not so subtle pressures were required to move her out of her private apartment and into communal dwelling. Within two months she went from rather lukewarm belief to total dedication, and she subsequently returned to Germany as a DP missionary. The following ecstatic testimonial given during her second month of cult residence stood in stark contrast to her previously reserved and inhibited statements:

In the beginning of May I moved into our center in Bay City. A complete new life started for me. Why had I not cut off my self-centered life earlier! Here under Miss Lee's care and guidance I felt God's power and love tremendously, and very soon it became my only desire to wholeheartedly serve our Father. How fortunate I am being a child and student of our beloved mother and teacher. She reflects in all her gestures, words, and works the love and wisdom of our Lord and Master.

Thus it is that verbal conversion and resolutions to reorganize one's life for the DP's are not automatically translated into total conversion. One must be intensively exposed to the group supporting these new standards of conduct. The DP's did not find proselytizing, the primary task of total converts, a very easy activity to perform. But in the presence of people who supported one another and balmed their collective wounds, such a transformation became possible. Those who accepted the truth of the doctrine but lacked intensive interaction with the core group remained partisan spectators and failed to play an active part in the battle to usher in God's kingdom.

A NOTE ON CULT FORMATION

With this model at hand it is possible to explore briefly the conditions under which a lone proselytizer can assemble a circle of converts, thereby transforming a private world view into a collective perspective.

First, it appears necessary that there be a set of persons who meet the first five conditions and who are *at the same time linked together in a pre-existing friendship net*. In this way conversions do not have to proceed one by one through successive, unacquainted individuals who meet the requisite conditions. When pre-converts are linked together prior to the appearance of the proselytizer, to interest one is to interest all. Not only is the matter of location simplified, but the problem of forming affective bonds is eliminated. In the DP case, one found such a net among Bertha, Minnie, and Alice, with Alice linked to Merwin and Merwin to Elmer.

Second, the stage is then set for the members of this friendship net to meet the last two conditions of the conversion process under a slightly different form of condition VII. Rather than a believing group with which to interact intensively, the preconverts require *intensive exposure to each other and to the world view carrier*. Perhaps the most crucial contingency in the formation of the DP was the existence of Merwin's empty house into which Lee could move when she left Northwest Town. She thereby gained close and continuous access to her budding converts and granted them easy access to her. (They already of course had access to each other.) In the multitude of days and nights that Lee was able to spend with her charges, a feeling of new and special group identity could be built. She could handily mold notions of what the world was about from their daily grievances. Without such physical proximity, the tenets of the DP could not have been kept so constantly before them or made so directly meaningful as a system.

Such a formulation is usefully contrasted with the kind of sociological explanation usually offered to account for the origins of religious groups. Typically, a characterization of macrosocial conditions and the "hard times" they produce are correlated with the appearance of various new religions. When the interest is merely in macrosocial conditions and incidences of various new collectivities, one need not take exception to this kind of analysis. But if the interest is in the factors that *account for* the emergence of new groups, then it seems clear that one must study people in association. Failure to do this has been a regrettable lapse in the social sciences. When social scientists finally come to this type of study, notions like that of "pre-existing friendship nets" will necessarily become relevant as operant explanatory concepts.

Looking forward to a general theory of the origins of religious groups, the DP pattern may be suggested as universal. This appears to be the case, at least, on the basis of the small amount of information now available. Thus we find that persons who came to have faith in the 1954 upheaval forecast by Mrs. Marian Keech were without exception acquainted with one or more co-believers long before Mrs. Keech made her prediction.[5] In a somewhat better known case, it is found that Joseph Smith, Jr.'s first followers were not random, atomized persons assembled out of a mass society, but rather his parents, two brothers, a neighbor, the local school master (who had once boarded at the Smiths), and the school master's parents and brother.[6] Likewise, in a very well-known instance, Muhammad's first converts were his wife, brother-in-law, and a paternal cousin.[7]

Perhaps it must be concluded that so long as a prophet is without honor in his own country he will be no prophet.

CONCLUDING REMARK

In view of the character of the set of conditions outlined, it might be wondered what competitive advantage the DP's had over other unusual religious groups. In terms of background conditions, I am suggesting that they had little, if any, advantage. In terms of situational conditions, their advantage lay merely in the fact that they got there and actually made their pitch, developed affective bonds, and induced people into intensive interaction. As with so much in life one may say that "there but for the grace of God go I"—within the limits of the conditions specified. It is to be hoped that the present effort will contribute to dispelling the tendency to think that there must be some deep, almost mystical connection between world views and their carriers. Like conceptions which hold that criminals and delinquents must be different from others, so our thinking about other types of deviants has too often assumed some extensive characterological conjunction between participant and pattern of participation.

---

[5] Leon Festinger, Henry Riecken, and Stanley Schachter, *When Prophecy Fails* (Minneapolis: University of Minnesota Press, 1956), esp. pp. 75-94 and p. 243.

[6] Fawn Brodie, *No Man Knows My History* (New York: Alfred A. Knopf, Inc., 1945), Chaps. 1-4.

[7] P. K. Hitti, *The Arabs* (Chicago: Henry Regnery Co., 1949), pp. 32 and 63.

part two

Proselytization

I am a free man and own no master; but I have made myself every man's servant to win over as many as possible. To Jews I become like a Jew, to win Jews; as they are subject to the Law of Moses, I put myself under that law to win them although I am not myself subject to it. To Gentiles, who are outside the Law, I made myself like one of them, although I am not in truth outside God's law, being under the law of Christ. To the weak I became weak, to win the weak. Indeed, I have become everything in turn to men of every sort, so that in one way or another I may save some. All this I do for the sake of the Gospel, to bear my part in proclaiming it.

"The First Letter of Paul to the Corinthians" (9:19-23 NEB)

Behave wisely towards those outside your own number; use the present opportunity to the full. Let your conversation be always gracious, and never insipid; study best to talk with each person you meet.

"The Letter of Paul to the Colossians" (4:5-6 NEB)

chapter 5

Disembodied Access

The concept of access refers to circumstances where two or more persons, not formerly in a situation of information flow, come into such a state. It denotes the gap between a prior state, in which a set of persons are not receiving some kind of written or spoken communication, and a subsequent state in which they are.

This is an era of a wide variety of mass communication devices, such that people are highly accessible. Thus the problem of access seems less important and has received less attention than the subsequent problem of winning some sort of consent within that access. I should therefore like to treat the bridging of this access gap as a problem in itself, as a phase of the involvement sequence that is not to be taken for granted.

Approached from the perspective of those who possess what they feel to be an important message to be imparted, the access gap is indeed a major problem. How can one best gain the attention of people not yet aware of this message?

This was without doubt the central and most perpetually perplexing question faced by the DP's. How, then, did they actually go about their task? My analysis will attempt to delineate the varieties of strategies developed and to explain the relative frequency with which these were employed. By strategy I mean a person's or group's main line of action, in much the same way the term is used in military parlance to refer to overall plans for engaging the enemy (e.g., direction, time, place). Strategy is to be distinguished from tactics, which have to do with maneuvering in the face of the enemy. I shall also describe some of the tactics employed directly upon gaining access.

My explication will be organized primarily around two sets of distinctions that formed the DP's main access decisions and had the most far-reaching consequences for them: (1) the decision as to whether access was to be sought by *embodied* or *disembodied* means, and (2) whether the presentation of the message was to be *overt* or *covert*.

The embodied-disembodied distinction refers to the problem of whether to approach individuals face to face or to impart information through such means as radio and newspapers. The overt-covert presentation distinction refers to the problem of whether to make it clear to the transmittee that the access was instituted in order to "sell" a millenarian doctrine (overt) or to withhold the apocalyptic content and stimulate interest on some other presentational basis, such as sex (covert).

These choices were a cause of great vacillation and hesitancy to the DP's. Over time they shifted among the four types, sometimes concentrating upon one, sometimes engaging in all simultaneously. In this and the following chapter, emphasis will be placed upon a description of these strategies. Chapter 12 will discuss factors that appeared to affect long-term persistence and change in access strategy.

Although less central, attention should also be called to some additional decisions that were sources of vacillation. Among these were the problems of whether to concentrate upon instituting access to people in religious or secular places (e.g., churches *vs.* street corners) and religiously deviant or conventional places (e.g., spiritualist *vs.* mainline churches). There was also some concern over whether to focus on what were called "big people" or "little people" (institutional leaders and influentials *vs.* followers and the unaffiliated) and "young people" or "old people" (people under or over the age of forty). As will become clear, these decisions produced dilemmas. Something of value was lost in opting for one or another, and consequently any decision was unstable.

The focus, then, is the outward-extending and pulsating perimeter of the cult as it attempted to locate those cracks in the façade of the establishment through which access could be gained and interest stimulated.

*   *   *

During the four and a half years under analysis, the DP's engaged in at least thirteen separate and concrete episodes of disembodied access attempts.

Tentative Gestures: Northwest Town, 1959-60. Although a few disembodied access attempts were planned, none came to fruition in Northwest Town. When Lee was still alone in the early months of 1959, she rewrote a chapter of her ongoing manuscript as a magazine article. It was entitled "The Cross Was Not Enough" and sent off to some seventy religious magazines of all varieties, including the august *Christian Century.* In it she argued that God did not really want Jesus to be crucified; that that event was only a secondary choice forced upon him by the failure of the Jewish masses to recognize Jesus for what he was—the Messiah come to re-establish the earthly Garden of Eden. Gradually all the manuscripts found their way home accompanied by rejection slips, letters condemning heresy, or polite dismissals.

The urge to inform the masses with disembodied messages did not assert itself again until late in 1960, when Merwin and Elmer began to sponsor the use of a handbill, promotion of the almost completed DP book, and spot radio announcements. All such plans were cut short by Bertha's and Minnie's desertions of their families.

FIRST FLURRY: JANUARY-JUNE, 1961

Newspaper Ad for a Mass Meeting, January, 1961. The actual use of disembodied attempts began in January, 1961, a few days after Lee had assembled her five committed converts in Bay City. The strongest advocate of disembodied access, Merwin, proposed renting a hall and lecturing the DP. It would have to be advertised, and since Bay City had three large-circulation newspapers, they seemed to be the most worthwhile vehicles. Two of these, the *Tribune* and the *Daily News,* leaned to journalistic sensationalism while the *Times* made its appeal to the moderate and the middle class. The *Tribune* and *Times* had about equal circulations, with the *Daily News* trailing far behind. Opting for a moderate channel, a recurrent theme in the DP, the *Times* was chosen. The cheapest advertising means were selected; namely, space in the classified section under the heading "special notices." Beginning Friday, January 6, the following appeared, along with notices about business cards, debt disclaimers, and an adoption service.

A NEW MESSAGE
Never told before. Reason and
purpose of Creation—What God
is going to do in the next 7
years. Lectures Mondays 7:30
p.m., January 9th, 16th, 23rd
and 30th. No charges, Bay City
Lions Club Hall, 772 Clayton
Street.

The ad was planned to run at least twenty-four days. It ran from Friday through Monday and did not appear again. The DP's appeared in the Lions Club Hall on Monday evening expecting to have attracted a crowd. One person was present. They loaned him a copy of the recently bound DP book, and they never saw him or the book again. The ad was cancelled and the Lions Club let them out of their lease. They decided the time was not right for this approach.

First Handbill, January, 1961. Following this, Merwin promoted, and got Lee to accept, the notion of going from door to door with handbills. Merwin did most of the distributing, choosing a tidy working- and lower-middle-class neighborhood. Because of his reluctance to engage in face-to-face proselytization, Merwin placed more in the doors than in people's hands. About 1,000 handbills were distributed in this way in January and February.

The handbill gave a postal box number where one could purchase the DP book, and a phone number to call and find out about study groups. But not a single person availed himself of this opportunity.

Unlike most handbills, this one was long and complex. It was typed single-spaced, filling the entire sheet with almost fifty lines of text. Unlike the usual handbill style of frequent capitalization, not a single word was in all capitals and no part stood out. It was hardly designed to catch even a fleeting interest. It was, rather, the sort of document one had to study; it embodied a meticulous, academic approach to the problem of access and interest development.

The question of a Korean Christ who was going to establish the Garden of Eden by 1967 was totally absent. They were even reluctant to include their address, preferring to give only a phone number.

Amhurst College Lectures, March, 1961. Late in February the group learned of Amhurst College, which had a "School of Metaphysical Inquiry." Located across the bay and high in the hills of State U. City, this college was housed in a large, decaying mansion left over from the gold-boom days of the late nineteenth century. In the thirties, a granddaughter of the original owner had converted it into a liberal arts college, teaching the standard curriculum of such institutions, except for one course taught by the heiress herself, called "Creative Involutionalism." [1] Such unusual interests were continued by the next heir, who, though trying to continue the college, expanded these esoteric concerns through the School of Metaphysical Inquiry.

In order to understand the DP's relation to Amhurst College, it is necessary to digress briefly into the occult milieu.

Among the various subterranean worlds of American society, there are occult foci, the edges of which only occasionally expose

---

[1] The course description read: "A critical comparison of Platonic and post-Platonic methods of thought. A thoroughgoing study of Cora Amhurst's group consciousness idealism."

themselves to the view of conventional citizens. Across America, there are people who attend to what they variously call "New Age Knowledge," "occult learning," and "metaphysics." They typically refer to themselves as "students of metaphysics" who are "seeking enlightenment in the higher spiritual realms." Although adults of all ages and economic groups can be found among them, they are predominantly middle-aged and older, lower-middle-class women.

The content of the milieu is quite diversified, united only by a nebulous seekership. A definition like the following usually prevails at its gatherings: "We are all students of new things who must keep an open mind to new truths; there is some truth in what everyone says; take what one finds best in whatever the other person is saying." Terms such as "science," "students," "inquiry," and other terms typical of the quest for knowledge are used freely. There seems to be a rule that one does not argue with someone who is espousing something one does not believe, regardless of internal consistency, conceptual clarity, or empirical truth. This stance is actively proclaimed from the podia of the milieu; speakers do not challenge one another.

Amhurst College was a local gathering place of the occult milieu. A few titles of lectures given there will illustrate the milieu's concerns: *Do You Have an Astral Body?* (". . . the art of projection, viz., meditation, adoration, and illumination"); *Communication with Extraterrestrial Worlds and Intelligences* ("Attendants are invited to exchange experiences regarding interplanetary travel . . ."); *My Visit Aboard a 200-Foot Martian Spacecraft on February 14, 1960* (". . . he will tell what the great Master Kumar told him about coming events . . ." including: "Will another President ever be elected in the United States?"); *Great White Brotherhood of the Brotherhood of Light* ("The universal teachings and methods of the inner plane government of the great Cosmic Masters . . ."); *Celestial Music* ("Many will find these transmissions very healing as well as inspiring—cleansing the radius of much negation"); *Soul Mates* (the investigator ". . . has been gathering data through the scientific finding of the Theocrometer as to whether an affinity and a soulmate are one and the same").[2]

The present heir and president of the college was himself an occultist, and upon being approached by Lee he booked her for a lecture. (He also got half the one dollar per person "free will offering.") The school's mimeographed monthly flyer of March, 1961, carried the following announcement, embedded among topics such as those given above, but twice as long as any other. It read in part:

Wednesday, March 15, at 8:00 P.M., a lecture by Yoon Sook Lee, B.A., B.Th., B.D., of Korea on: *The Divine Precepts.* Miss Lee is a teacher of the New Age, giving principles from Divine revelation as taught and verified by her from a Master teacher (whom she will reveal in her lecture). She will give a history of her Master teacher and show his direct revelations pertaining to the end of this civilization or the last days of it and the ushering in in its place of the New Age. Miss Lee shows, as is explained also by her book, "The Divine Precepts" how her teacher reveals the Divine schedule of Cosmic restoration, including fallen mankind. He teaches that now is the time of Cosmic restoration and of a full Cosmic transition from the long, gloomy, Cosmic Winter of the Adamic age, having ended in 1960. From this year, Evil takes only a defensive position and is replaced by Good with an aggressive stand. From now on tremendous changes in all aspects of human life will take place. After 1960 the spiritual world unites with the physical one. The New Age is highly spiritual as well as scientific. The globe will not be destroyed—but many changes will take place on its surface. Within seven years a great change will come and within ten years a complete change. Within three and one-half years from last Summer, Mankind will see fulfillment of revelation (the last book of the New Testament). God is showing these signs in many ways. That is why all kinds of spiritual phenomena (flying saucers, teleports, dreams, visions, signs in the

---

[2] A serious, full-scale study of the occult milieu has yet to be performed. Existing treatments tend merely to satire and spoofing. Among the best are: Long John Nebel, *The Way Out World* (Englewood Cliffs, N.J.: Prentice-Hall, Inc., 1961) and Richard Mathison, *Faiths, Cults, and Sects of America* (Indianapolis: Bobbs-Merrill Company, Inc., 1960). See also H. T. Dohrman, *California Cult* (Boston: Beacon Press, 1958), Chap. 5, and H. Taylor Buckner, *Deviant-Group Organizations,* unpublished master's thesis, University of California, Berkeley (1964), Chap. 2, "The Flying Saucerians."

sky, precognitions, etc.) are appearing today. The New Age will bring one world, one religion, one language, and other unities, as well as perfect harmony of spirit and of body.

The most interesting items in the blurb are the mention of the "fulfillment of [the book of] revelation" within three and a half years (i.e., by the end of 1963) and a "complete change" within ten years. This was the last time these figures and specific predictions were publicly proclaimed. On into 1962 and 1963 the line to outsiders became "soon" and "within a few years," but no definite time was offered. Also of interest is the reference to phenomena on which the occult milieu is centrally focused ("flying saucers, . . . etc."). Although these things could be made explicable within the DP, most of them were not central to it. An attempt is made, rather, to show that the DP's were interested in such things and could explain them. Thus the line was molded to better fit the affinities of the potential audience.

Over fifty people appeared to hear Lee's lecture. It seemed to have been a success. Encouraged by this, the president consented to set up regular classes for her so that those interested might receive more "enlightenment." The April flyer carried the announcement:

Divine Law and Precepts:
Miss Yoon Sook Lee, B.A., B.Th., B.D., will conduct the following classes on Friday evening at 8:00; April 7, The Principle of *Creation*, The Fall of Man, The Mission of Christ; April 14, *Christology*, The Consummation of Human History, The *Resurrection*; April 21, The History of *Restoration*; April 28, *The Second Advent of Christ*, The Prolongation of the Providence of Restoration, The Completion of the Restoration. *When and Where will the new ruler appear? How is He different from others?*

Free Will Offering

"Those interested" had, however, apparently heard enough the first time. Not a single person appeared for Lee's first class, and the rest of them were cancelled. A proportion of the occult milieu was ready to listen to anyone new, but they apparently found Lee's message too much like traditional religions to try it again.

The Radio, April-May, 1961. The newspaper, door-to-door handbills, and lectures in the occult milieu were failing. Perhaps radio would work. Various stations were priced. Even among those that would take them (the larger ones will take only members of the National Council of Churches) there seemed to be a considerable difference in the cost of time. The one felt to be most reasonable wanted eighteen dollars for fifteen minutes. This was a local "religious station" with a largely Negro audience. Unhappy in broadcasting to such a limited population, they considered other alternatives, but stations generally charged at least fifty dollars for fifteen minutes. Reluctantly they bought time on the "Negro station." Their "slot" was eight weeks of 9:15 to 9:30, Sunday morning. Because Bertha read better than the others it was decided that she would record the eight thirteen-minute tapes. These consisted of slightly abbreviated, consecutive chapters of the DP book. The writing and reading styles were academic, a tedious consideration of the Bible from Genesis to Revelation. It omitted any reference to whom, where, or when the Messiah had or would come, and indeed it was only in the last broadcast that the messianic thrust became even dimly apparent. The text was adapted to radio only by cutting and interposing phrases such as "we will begin our lecture on the creation with a consideration of. . . ." This technique was hardly calculated to win the interest of the Negro working and lower classes.

There were also some problems with the station's service. On two occasions the preceding program ran over into their time, leaving only a few minutes for the DP lecture, which was cut off at 9:30. "The Age of Restoration," as it was called, ran its eight weeks (April and May) and was cancelled in disgust. The total result was two phone calls, one from a bedridden elderly lady some miles from Bay City and another from a Negro minister. Neither appeared at the DP Center.

Two Series of Newspaper Ads and Two Public Lectures, June, 1961. In June the DP's turned to the Saturday religion page of the *Daily News.* Somewhat less than half of a religion page in Bay City was composed of news articles on the mainline churches, their illustrious personages and activities. Interspersed among these were little articles on the perimeter religions that advertised on the bottom half of the page. The number and length of the news stories on perimeter religions appearing on the top part of the page seemed to be in direct proportion to the number of column inches of advertising they bought on the bottom half and the length of time for which they bought them.

In the bottom half, in addition to large blocks of advertising for various mainstream denominations, there was also a collection of boxes advertising spiritualist churches and other religions that felt they needed some distinctive mode of representation (e.g., The Salvation Army, Cultural Integration).

The Divine Precepts first entered this little world of newspaper religion on June 3, 1961, with a black-rimmed, one-column-inch box. Beside a box proclaiming Unity Temple and above one devoted to Applied Mental Science, it read:

THE DIVINE PRECEPTS
(A Complete New Age Revelation)
420 Ash Street. Phone WY 8-5147
Ash and Pine St. Buses 6,61,62
Maple 31
Free Lectures 10 a.m., 2 p.m.
7:30 p.m.
Monday through Sunday
Miss Yoon Sook Lee

This ad had a number of curious features. The headline is "The Divine Precepts," with the revelation in almost apologetic parentheses. They did not want to put people off by being bold, as is also seen by the use of "a," instead of "the." The stipulation of lecture times is interesting because few people actually appeared, and the DP's were prepared to talk to anyone at any time. The announcement of lecture times was calculated to convey the impression of large audiences, which would of course require scheduling. This impression was vitiated, however, by their announced willingness to give lectures three times a day, every day.

The ad appeared again on June 10 and then stopped. Lee had

found a better vehicle for access and a way to save money on ads. A spiritualist minister in her fifties, who advertised the Aquarian Gospel Temple on the same page, saw the blurb and went to see the DP's. Out of this meeting came an invitation for Lee to speak at the medium's church. This was duly announced in the medium's box the next week along with a seven-line item in the top half of the page: "AT GOSPEL TEMPLE, Miss Yoon Sook Lee of Korea, lecturer on the Divine Precepts (New Age Revelation) will speak Monday, 7:45 P.M., at the Aquarian Gospel Temple, 450 Broadway, Suite 102." Again the following week Lee was announced as speaker at the Gospel Temple.

With increased exposure, however, it became apparent that Lee was not talking about a New Age in the way the spiritualists meant it—a gradual spiritual awakening among the people—but, indeed, Lee had a new Christ. The minister would have none of it and cancelled further arrangements. Through the ads and speaking engagements some middle-aged and older ladies appeared at the DP flat, although none made many visits or was converted.

The DP appeared in the *Daily News* again the next week and then stopped, for the group had gone back to the *Times* classified section. Now they tried the personals section. Along with items on membership in a tennis and swim club, applied hypnosis, and an offer to "assist with life's problems, by appointment only," there appeared these lines:

A COMPLETE NEW AGE REVELATION
Free Lectures Daily
420 Ash St. WY 8-5147

This ran every day throughout June and produced only a couple of elderly ladies, a response they were now trying to avoid.[3]

Thus these ads brought to a close the first flurry of disembodied

---

[3] DP difficulties with elderly ladies are discussed in Chap. 8, the section on "Veteran Seekers."

access attempts.[4] This class of strategies was laid aside, not to be taken up again until May, 1962, eleven months later.

SECOND FLURRY: MAY-DECEMBER, 1962

The second flurry was not as compact as the first. It was much more sporadic, containing numerous periods of inactivity, but still it formed a set of efforts with a pattern and logic.

Announcing the DP Center, May, 1962. The first attempt in this series lasted only three days. By May the house they occupied was well on its way to renovation and suitable for viewing by a large public. It was felt to be proper to announce the existence of the DP Center. On Thursday, May 9, Merwin and Elmer hung a well-constructed wooden sign from the second floor of the house. Measuring four by five feet and neatly lettered in cream and black, it read:

> THE DIVINE PRECEPTS
> CENTER
> Proclaiming God's New Revelation
> Lectures Daily 2 p.m. & 8 p.m.
> Meetings Tues. and Fri. 7:30 p.m.
> 706 Columbus Ave. WY 8-5147

A Bay City building inspector appeared the next day and informed them that in order to open a public assembly hall they needed to install fire equipment, mark fire exits, and so on. Such measures would cost three or four thousand dollars. Perceiving a civil liberties issue, Merwin consulted the local American Civil Liberties Union, where he was told that places for public assembly had indeed to be safe. The sign came down the next day, and with it their fantasies of hundreds of people crowded into the building's long basement.

---

[4] There was one minor exception. In August an ad for the DP book appeared in a large-circulation occult periodical. The ad belongs to the first six months, because it was placed long before it appeared. On the ad and its consequences, see Chap. 12.

The three-story building had been conceived as a place where crowds would congregate to hear Lee preach the new words of salvation and where droves of converts would receive their training before going forth as missionaries, as was the practice in the Korean headquarters. Both intentions were effectively prohibited—the latter by a zoning ordinance forbidding boarding houses in that block. The value and attractiveness of the building diminished considerably in the eyes of the DP's.

Storefront Church "Bible Week," June, 1962. The DP's were now afraid even to hold their small, twice weekly study groups in the house. Fearing that the inspector would call at night to see if they were complying with his directives, Lee moved the study group from the front room to the back of the house and pulled the shades. The front room was carefully arranged to look like a living room, and Lee projected an air of secrecy around the study group gathering.

The next week Lee contacted a man known as "Brother Bob," who had a storefront church in a slum adjacent to downtown Bay City. Brother Bob lived in a single room in the back of his church and had a Sunday morning congregation of five persons (a single family, all female). He worked evenings as a janitor in a hotel and was more than happy to rent his hall to the DP's on weekday evenings.[5]

In physical appearance, the church was a stereotype: a store converted to a church in a slum area comprised almost entirely of bars, garages, and Negro and Mexican tenements. It had the disturbing feature of being next to a laundromat, the various gurgling and whirling noises of which were clearly heard through the thin walls during services. About eighty people could be seated in its straight-backed wooden pews within its yellowing, papered walls and before its pulpit, which was draped in worn purple velvet.

On May 18, Lee began holding study groups there. That eve-

---

[5] Brother Bob was under the impression that DP's were a standard Christian sect, albeit a bit more prosperous than his own. Desiring to use his church, the DP's put expediency before conversion and made no attempt to correct this impression.

ning she announced that beginning on June 12 the cult would conduct a Bible Week for Bay City and hold meetings in the church every evening. The relevance of these events for disembodied access is in the method chosen to assemble an audience.

The group had recently sold the pickup truck with mounted camper which they had purchased for Chang's use (he had been expected but had never arrived), and they then purchased a Ford bus. Some months before, Elmer and Merwin had taken out a permit to operate a sound truck. Elmer mounted two loudspeakers on the roof of the bus at each end of a five foot sign reading:

THE DIVINE PRECEPTS
390 Valencia St. at 15th

Proclaiming   For Informa-
God's New   tion Call
Revelation
7:30 P.M.   WY 8-5147

An inverter and tape recorder were installed by Elmer. The tape recorder was mounted with a thirty-second repeating tape of Bertha's shrill voice:

Ladies and gentlemen, we are proclaiming God's new revelation, the Divine Precepts. This message gives the answer to the worldwide turmoil and what will happen in the earth in the next few years. We have entered, since 1960, the Golden Age. Come and listen at 390 Valencia nightly at 7:30.

Beginning Friday, June 8, Elmer rode the streets of Bay City five or six hours a day. Their permit prohibited broadcasting in commercial sections, at a speed of less than ten miles an hour, and near schools, churches, hospitals, and libraries. Nor could one street be used over four times a day. Elmer concentrated on one of the poorest of the residential areas.

This was the only advertising. On opening night, Tuesday the 12th, twelve DP's and sundry hangers-on appeared at the storefront church. They far outnumbered the audience: an emaciated, working-class male who left after an hour; a fortyish Filipino male who sat reading a newspaper; a sixtyish working-class female who walked out within twenty minutes; and three small boys, aged nine or ten, who were ushered out because of loud play.

Elmer rode the streets of a single working- and lower-middle-class district all the next day. That evening five DP's went to the revival hall. They waited half an hour and no one appeared. Lee took down a sign reading "Revival Here Nightly" and bundled her charges off to witness at a spiritualist church. Bible Week had lasted two days.

This episode was the end of the line in Bay City. They returned to concentration upon strategies of embodied access for three weeks, and then Lee announced that the group would split up so that each adherent could start his own "mission field." Bertha departed for State College Town, Minnie moved to State U. City, and Merwin and Alice established separate residences midway down the peninsula. Alfred and Elmer were left behind to continue work in Bay City and to attend to Lee's needs.

Religion Page Ad and "Perfection Personal." A few days before this decision, Alice, with Lee's approval, had placed a newspaper ad that constituted the first use of covert presentations at the disembodied level. On Sunday, June 24, the following began to appear in the personals section of the *Times.*

For the key to perfection, call AN 5-1926.

People may not have been interested in new revelations, but they were at least intrigued by perfection. The phone began to ring regularly. Alice's ploy was to entice the caller by saying that this was an important new message from Korea. She tried to gain a commitment from the caller to appear at the Center to receive a full explanation of how perfection could be achieved. The religious content was held back but was admitted if the caller inquired about it.

Even on Saturday night there was a call from a man who invited himself over to see Alice. He was an unemployed radio announcer who said he was lonely, but who soon left when he saw what company was offered. This was the only person to appear in response to the ad, although many made promises. Most callers were curiosity seekers and many hung up when Alice answered.

By the end of the week the ad had more nuisance than access value. There was much phone ringing and much baiting and hanging up. For a fee, the *Times* furnished an answering service, which the DP's purchased after the ad had run seven days. This device successfully filtered out people who hung up, but failed to produce any interested enough to leave a name. But there was no time to think of that. Lee had by now announced the convert dispersion.

The perfection personal did bring one interested person of note—an early morning disc jockey who broadcast phone interviews with persons who placed personal ads that interested him. At 8:20 in the morning during the second week of the ad, the D.j. broadcast this tape recorded encounter between Alice and himself.

D.j.:   We have called the lady who placed the ad and here is the story behind the ad.

Alice: Well, the purpose of this ad is to tell people about a message which was brought here from Korea. We met the lady who brought this message to America several years ago in Northwest State. After we heard it, my husband and I, we realized the great importance of getting it out to the people —so—we had it published in a book—since that time we have been urgently giving people the book [laughs nervously] —[quickly] one way or another. That was the purpose of the ad.

D.j.:   Do you find people really are interested in achieving perfection?

Alice: Well—uh—what I found with this ad—I would say so— yes.

D.j.:   Just how do people react to such a tantalizing one-line ad as "for the key to perfection, call AN 5-1926"?

Alice: [giggles] I believe there has been all kinds of people—young —old—the curious—ah— And I've had the gigglers, obviously curious and yet embarrassed because they were curious, you know?

D.j.: How was the secret—the key to perfection—brought to light? Do you know?

Alice: Yes [nervous laugh], but I couldn't tell you over the phone [again same laugh].

[Questions and answers on the DP were cut here by the station.]

Alice: Oh, it started as a slick trick to get people to call. Actually I can offer people the key to perfection. I know that sounds like a very egotistical statement, but it's true, although it is too complicated to go into on the phone [nervous laugh].

D.j.: Have you found it actually has brought perfection into your life?

Alice: No, I can't say I have attained perfection. I say this: It is the *key*. This unlocks the door.

D.j.: And then it's up to you from then on?

Alice: That's right. It's up to the individual.

D.j.: [assuming announcer rather than conversational voice] Well, a little perfection could go a long way in this tired old world, and maybe there is a key to it. [Theme music swells up.] Alice says this message may be heard on a tape recording at 706 Columbus Avenue, right here in Bay City.

[Network theme noise, medley of electronic beeps swells up, show theme out.]

[loudly] And that's another of the savory aspects of life I encountered as I CALLED THE CLASSIFIED, right here at Station WXYZ, 789 on your dial.

The station estimated its listenership to be 150,000 at that hour, the greatest number a DP disembodied access attempt had ever reached. But *no one* appeared at the Center to receive the key to perfection.

Also at this time, Elmer convinced Lee that they should again advertise on the Saturday religion page. After all, it was a full year later in the course of cosmic restoration and people should be more aware of the vast changes taking place. A black-bordered, column-inch of the Divine Precepts appeared in the *Tribune* each Saturday from June 23 to July 28. By putting the slogan "God's

New Revelation" in large letters, this ad was less apologetic about revealed truth than the earlier ones had been.

The Proclamation of
GOD'S NEW REVELATION
"The Divine Precepts"

Completed Testament Age is here.
God has revealed new things and has
started a new work at this time.
For information, call WY 8-5147

The ads cost thirty dollars and resulted in contact with three people, none of whom converted.

It should be noted that the DP's placed short-term newspaper ads many times, but never for very long periods. In contrast, many perimeter religions sign long-term contracts for this sort of space and advertise year after year. The reason the DP's offered for not conforming to this practice was that it did not bring in a sufficient number of interested people.

Although this is true enough, another source of this reluctance might be considered. The DP's of course believed their system to be the one final and total explanation of human existence. In contrast to their felt uniqueness, when advertising they had to present themselves in a standardized fashion; namely, within a column-inch, black-bordered box. To assume the face of religions not so insistent upon their finality perhaps appeared to concede that they were a religion among religions competing for an audience in the conventional game of getting customers. Thus they never permitted themselves the conventionality of being listed in the more inexpensive church directory, which contained listing of both mainstream and perimeter groups.

Institutionalized action offers a limited number of "fronts" or materials from which to mold a presentation. Those available on the religion page, and in the mass media generally, did not offer a proper means of conveying their uniqueness, authority, and finality.

Speaking at Santini's, July, 1962. Toward the end of July, the Reverend Santini, a spiritualist medium who professed DP belief but made no commitment,[6] resorted to a common ploy among spiritualist ministers for keeping their congregations interested: he decided to present a weekly guest speaker at each service. Lee was invited to inaugurate the series. Santini was a long-term advertiser on the religion page of the *Tribune*, so he was able to get an item into the top half of the page. His patronage earned just over four column inches.

MINISTER FROM SEOUL
HERE MONDAY

The Rev. Yoon Sook Lee, minister from Seoul, South Korea, will appear as guest minister at the Temple of Spiritual Light, Studio 102, 450 Broadway, Monday evening July 30, at 7:30. Her topic will be "The Lord of the Second Advent."

The Reverend Lee, who is the founder of the Divine Precepts Association in Bay City, an affiliate of the Divine Precepts Church of South Korea, is the author of "The Divine Precepts."

Lee spoke on the failure of Jesus to complete his mission, gave various reasons for why the Kingdom of Heaven was not yet here, and stated that the new Messiah was coming. Her presentation was pedantic, much in the manner of an uninspired university lecturer. The audience was the usual handful of elderly ladies who attended Santini's services, and no new contacts came out of the news story or lecture.

This event was a telling reflection of the DP's relation to spiritualists a year and a half after arriving in Bay City. The first time Lee spoke in a spiritualist church there were a number of elderly ladies who visited the DP Center. This time there were none.

---

[6] Reverend Santini is discussed in Chap. 8 under "exploiters."

Social Problems Personals, September, 1962. In September, Elmer, who was particularly fearful of embodied access, suggested that Alice's attempt at covert advertising was a good idea and ought to be tried again. Lee agreed and worked up three one-line ads. They appeared one a week for three weeks in the personals column of the *Times.*

WHY the rapid increase of suicide today? WY 8-5147
WHY the vast amount of mental illness in Bay City? WY 8-5147
WHO can stop moral decay? WY 8-5147

The phone began ringing twenty to thirty times a day. About half offered nothing but the click of a phone hanging up when answered. By the third week, only four calls had produced people who appeared at the Center. None became converts or, indeed, came more than once.

So many calls, so few of which produced persons at the Center, became a nuisance. The phone rang so frequently (often in the middle of the night) that Elmer began muffling it under several pillows in order to escape it during study and prayer groups, meals, and at night. Lee's feeling that personal contact was the most effective way to institute access and gain interest was again confirmed, and the personals stopped.[7]

State U. Newspaper Personal, October, 1962. Taking his cue from these Bay City personals, Lester, in State U. City, thought the approach might stimulate interest within the university community. The last week of October he placed the following among the personals of the *University Daily,* a paper circulated among more than 25,000 State U. students and faculty.

MONEY ISN'T THE ANSWER. Sex isn't the answer.
Neither is politics or present-day religion.
What is? 850-4492

---

[7] In addition, Elmer reported that they were getting callers who said things that Miss Lee should not have to hear. Thus one offered to come listen to the DP if he could receive the message while nude.

The phone rang thirty or forty times the first day. Many calls were "wrong numbers" or silent on the other end. It was the regular DP meeting day in State U. City, so callers were invited to the evening meeting. Many callers promised to appear. Ludwig in particular became agitated. This was IT; the movement was really going to move. He dragged all the flat's chairs into the living room and called the Bay City Center to bring more.

Six students showed up. The entire gathering hardly made a dent in the chair-crammed front room. All six seemed slightly embarrassed and/or bored as the group droned on in serial reading about resurrection. Two walked out in the middle of the meeting; the rest were polite. None came back.

This first day was nonetheless the best. There were about thirty calls each day and many people promised to come, but only one more person actually appeared.[8]

Ludwig and Foreign Students, October-November, 1962. As an immigrant, Ludwig felt that the DP should be spread among foreigners and took the university foreign students as his mission field. Day after day during September and October were spent at the university going through some 25,000 cards in the student file, locating foreign persons by copying off the name, address, religion (if any), and nationality of anyone not from the United States,

---

[8] The Cuban blockade began the day before the ad started. That week the State U. campus was the site of demonstrations of various persuasions. "Food runs" on supermarkets were reported in some West Coast cities. A part of the interest in the ad may have been prompted by these larger events.

However, stimulus to call had other sources as well, as indicated in this report:

> Secretaries in a research center on the campus discovered the ad and delighted in conning other members of the staff into calling the number. The whole affair, which was seen entirely as a joke (as were the DP's, the odd and demented butts of the joke), produced six or eight calls the first day the ad ran. It did not result in anyone attending the meeting.

The favorite opening line of these calls was "I understand you've got something better than sex."

Korea, or Japan.[9] In this way he meticulously assembled a hand-written mailing list of about 2,000 people.

Ludwig wanted to send a letter to each person, but one that would appear to be a personal communication. A form letter, printed on the cult's multilith press, had such a personally typed appearance (if one did not look too closely and notice that the margins were justified). Ludwig signed each letter and hand addressed and personally stamped each envelope. The envelopes thus appeared to enclose personal greetings rather than to be bulk mail.

The letter itself was a masterpiece of studied ambiguity and covert presentation.

Dear Fellow Student:

This is not an advertising letter, but an important message.

An event has taken place for which mankind has been waiting throughout the ages, an event which will bring about great changes in this world within the very near future. This will have a revolutionary effect on you as an individual as well as on your nation.

I heard of this event a few months ago, and I value this information higher than all I have learned in my years in College and at the University. I am a foreign student as you are. When I realized the importance of this message for my country, I felt that I should inform you as well. You are one of the very few people of your nation who have at this time the opportunity to receive this information. You and your friends are invited to call me at 850-4492 or to visit me at 281 Ivy St., State U. City (entrance at the back of the house). I am generally at home on weekends and daily after 4 P.M. There is, of course, no charge.

To give you this information will require about one hour. I am not exaggerating when I say that this may very well turn out to be the most rewarding hour of your life.

> Sincerely yours,
>
> [Signed]
>
> Ludwig . . .

---

[9] Koreans and Japanese were omitted on the advice of Lee, who said that students from these countries were likely to have heard the scandalous stories told about the DP in that part of the world and thus were poor prospects in a missionary campaign.

Notice that no religious language is used, nor is the "Divine Precepts" mentioned. The only hint of millenarianism is the reference to the "event which will bring about great changes in this world within the very near future" and its "revolutionary effect." Emphasizing solidarity, the letter is addressed to Ludwig's "fellow student" and states that he is "a foreign student as you are," even though the thirty-five-year-old Ludwig was no longer a student.

There was some indecision as to whether to post them all at once or simply a few at a time. Lee advised that if they were sent all at once Ludwig would be swamped and unable to give adequate attention to each person. He should send a limited number at a time.

Ludwig began sending about a hundred letters a week. Still unemployed, he was always by the phone waiting to receive inquiries. Roughly 500 letters were sent out by mid-November. They produced many inquiring phone calls and many vague explanations in an attempt to get people to the apartment. Eight people appeared to be introduced to the DP. One of them, a Chinese graduate student in economics, became a convert.

The letters continued in December, only now at the rate of about 300 a week. Ludwig meticulously reported the final results in the cult's newsletter:

I have sent letters to over 1,900 students from practically all countries of the world, but the results are not very impressive. Out of an estimated 150 students who called me on the telephone, thirty-six came to hear the tape.[10]

Ludwig's German Parties, December, 1962. Ludwig saved his own national group until last and made use of a special ploy. Each German foreign student was sent a letter inviting him to a

---

[10]At least one foreign student thought the letter was a veiled overture from a political group and because of concern over his visa turned the letter over to the local police. The police asked Ludwig to come in for questioning. Accompanied by Miss Lee and Lester, Ludwig appeared and let Lee do the talking. She apparently made it clear that the DP's were strictly religious, and the matter was dropped.

party. The list of thirty people was divided into three groups, so that each gathering would be small. All married and Catholic Germans were invited last and in one group. (Married and/or Catholic persons were thought not to be easily convertible.)

The invitation was composed in German and hand written:

> [*Salutation*]
>
> May we invite you to an informal party? We are a group of young Germans in State U. City and Bay City. In the course of our studies we ran across information of extreme significance for you personally as well as for our country. We would be glad if we could see you [date and place].
>
>

[*Signed*]

Ludwig and Elsa . . .

Ludwig described the results of the first two parties.

On one evening three people came, on another, seven. Greta and my sister Elsa had come from Bay City, and we did everything to make our guests feel as a German family. As the result we found—besides the usual rejection—at least two people who were very interested to attend our study meetings.

As expected, the third group, the Catholics and married people, were not receptive. Despite Ludwig's glowing hope that the two "very interested" people would return, neither did. Both were graduate students in anthropology who were interested in primitive religion and millenarianism.

*   *   *

The second flurry of disembodied access attempts ended with Ludwig's German parties. Into early 1963 there was talk of again using the radio—the largest of the local stations—but the cost was felt to be prohibitive.

We have seen variations in the type of disembodied media employed (handbills, newspapers, radio, mailing lists, public signs, sound trucks, letters); in the target group (educational strata,

religious place people, secular place people); and in the definitional basis of presentation (overt and covert).

One fact about these strategies is inescapable: they consistently
failed to produce the results desired by the DP's. These efforts
were not only failures by external criteria (no matter how low
one's expectations), but, more important, they were perceived
by the DP's as truly abortive. The failures thus became an important source of threat to faith and hope that had to be managed. It can be seen that one way to manage such a threat is not
to engage in the strategy, a straightforward, if negative, maneuver
employed by the DP's from July, 1961, to May, 1962, and after
December, 1962. Other more interesting maneuvers will be considered in Chap. 12.

chapter 6

Embodied Access

RELIGIOUS PLACES

A systematic enumeration of all efforts at embodied access was not possible because of their sporadic and individual character and because of physical and social limits on canvassing the activity of each convert. It nonetheless did seem that embodied access was more frequently attempted in *religious* than in *secular* places.

It is of course presumably true that religious proselytizers are well advised to locate persons disposed to religious perspectives. There seem, however, to be additional factors that promoted concentration on religious gatherings. One has to do with the number and range of accessible public gatherings in a community. In terms of sheer numbers, religious probably far outnumber secular occasions at any given time. DP's were not averse to employing secular occasions. Religious ones were merely more available.

A second factor was perhaps more important. While there are of course many secular public gatherings (in streets, stores, bars, night clubs, etc.) and secular public occasions (e.g., sporting and theatrical events, political meetings, public rites), the rules of *engagements among the unacquainted* differ greatly between the secular and the religious. The rules of religious places offer an interesting contrast to those that prevail in secular places and at public secular occasions;[1] namely, the participants are open to

---

[1] On the circumstances and rules of accessibility in public places see Erving Goffman, *Behavior in Public Places* (New York: The Free Press of Glencoe, Inc., 1963), Chap. 8, esp. pp. 124-139.

engagements by whoever may desire to present himself.[2] Indeed, participants in religious occasions often feel obliged to create interaction for strangers. There is a propensity to envelop everyone and to make them feel at home. It is also appropriate for strangers to introduce themselves to others and to express an interest in the occasion. Access is even further opened by the assumption that strangers are sincere and of good will. Such a presumption is of course fostered by evangelical and ethical beliefs, which in the religious setting are doubtless more than normally activated. This is in contrast to secular places and occasions, where bad faith and ill will are presumed and strangers are treated in a guarded manner.[3]

In the secular realm, such circumstances of *universal mutual access* and *assumption of sincerity* are normally limited to gatherings that set limits on who can gain entrance—usually through requiring membership (as in a club) or personal invitations. This is one of the more obvious ways in which the world is made "safe" for interaction among strangers. Religious occasions stride a more hazardous road into a potentially more dangerous world of contact. People in religious gatherings more than normally expose themselves to strangers. They are therefore particularly vulnerable to those who would use this access for unanticipated purposes. This is their peculiar sociological interest and was an important part of their attractiveness for the DP's.

COVERT PRESENTATIONS

Most often the DP's practiced covert presentations in religious gatherings. They thought that this was necessary for the obvious

---

[2] This is at least formally the case, though there is the matter of class and race sorting that takes place among religious organizations. "Openness" is also limited by rules of dress (e.g., nudity) and demeanor (e.g., obvious intoxication).

[3] See Goffman, *op. cit.* From this perspective, "the city" is a complex set of places with varying rules of interpersonal access. One subset of these, the religious, allows strangers to meet one another quite easily. Upon recognizing this opportunity feature of social life, it is possible to suggest that the reasons for the variously deprived and lonely becoming active in religion have less to do with their deprivations than with their knowledge and mastery of rules of interpersonal access in given social places.

reason that open espousal was never wholly welcome and frequently led to ejection. By being covert they could stay in a gathering longer and thus be in a better position to find people who
might be sympathetic, and of course they could avoid being
branded as bearers of heresy. As with encyclopedia salesmen and
American communists, covertness is tempting when one's wares
are likely to meet strong resistance. They were also not without
sensitivity to being rejected by outsiders, and this stance kept
down the level of interpersonal conflict.

In addition, DP's wanted people to know them on a personal
level, to become friendly "as a person," before broaching the
subject of the DP. A personal bond was thought to create more
constraint to listen and seriously to entertain subsequent claims
about the DP.

Some less evident features of gatherings per se and the DP's
sensitivity to their rules can also be suggested as promoting
covert presentations, which might otherwise generally seem to be
cynical and dishonest manipulations of religious occasions. It
could be said that the DP's were acting in "bad faith," and in
one sense they indeed were: they declined to engage in appropriate self-disclosure. However, there is another sense in which
a covert presentation was the most honest position that they could
take. In an unlikely way, it represented a proper regard for the
occasions they infiltrated.

An occasion offers a set of procedural rules distributed among
a set of permissible roles that are occasion-specific. Upon entering
one of these little worlds of involvement, a DP encountered a
defined and limited number of ways in which he could present
himself in a nondisruptive manner. He had to choose between
fitting himself into an extant and permitted presentation and
breaching the occasion's order by presenting himself honestly.
To do the latter was to be a source of distraction and to have a
negative effect on the occasion's participants.

When a DP took up a permissible presentation—when he
came on[4] covertly—the occasion could proceed without hindrance.

---

[4] The slang verb "to come on" is used for lack of a more proper alternative that denotes the same process. "To come on" is "to enter or present one-

In so doing, he submitted to the power of immediate constraints and displayed a regard for the proximate involvements of others. This is the sense in which covert presentations displayed the highest regard for rules of occasions. One did not spoil the occasion or another's enjoyment but still had access. Of course paradoxically, being honest to the moment necessitated being dishonest to rules about truthful self-disclosure.

There were two main presentations that displayed an appropriate regard for the occasion: the *seeker-onlooker* and the *member*. Being a seeker-onlooker meant stationing oneself and announcing at the appropriate interactional points that one was "interested" in that religion. Others perceived this as contemplation of whether or not to take up their way of worship. Seeker-onlookers were accorded friendly interaction in order to impress them with the local system's merits. Member presentations were hazardous, demanding, and less frequently practiced, for they required movement into apparent belief and sustained participation.

A third presentation was also covert, but displayed less regard for the moment. This was the practice of coming on as a spiritualist, as someone who was looking for the meaning of phenomena such as teleportation, astral projection, and spirit communication.

Presentations also varied in the number of times a convert presented himself at a single recurrent gathering. Some were *rudimentary*, consisting of only one attendance or attendance over widely spaced intervals, so that the convert was still a stranger to the occasion. Other infiltrations were *systematic*, in that the DP presented himself with enough frequency to become known to a number of the participants as a regular attender.

Seeker-onlooker. The least stressful, productive, and most practiced DP strategy was the rudimentary covert presentation as a

---

self . . . ; to participate; to perform; to do these things with a purpose or specific attitude or skill, as if one were on a stage; always followed by an adjective telling the purpose, attitude, or skill of the one who has come on, or esp. of the initial impression of that person on those present" [H. Wentworth and S. Flexner, *Dictionary of American Slang* (New York: Thomas Y. Crowell Company, 1960), p. 117]. "To present oneself as . . ." and "to make a . . . presentation" are rough equivalents.

seeker-onlooker. This was the activity of converts on those days when they had nothing more systematic underway (a frequent circumstance). One perused the church page to find a religious occasion and went off to it. Or one might simply walk through a neighborhood having a number of churches and stop in where an occasion was advertised on a bulletin board.

At the occasion, converts looked for people who appeared, like themselves, to be newcomers. Although DP's were sometimes approached by real members, such persons were as likely as not to be avoided. One of the contingencies of the rudimentary seeker stance was that the people who were most likely to initiate interaction with a DP were those who were least likely to be interested in taking up other religious views.

Although these were places of proper engagements among the unacquainted, it did not always follow that DP's entered encounters. Whether they did or not depended upon the aggressiveness of the convert and the way he sized up the participants as DP material. There were many occasions during which converts did not enter into any spoken interaction. This was frequently the case with Merwin, Elmer, and Alfred, who were not aggressive initiators and were therefore more dependent upon the participants instituting access to them. Thus an unknown, but probably significant number of hours was spent *in* gatherings, but not *of* them.

Typically, however, converts would sit through the program and then make an effort to mingle in the post-program period. For this, the DP's had prepared phrases for making openings. Thus Alfred and others used the simplest and most innocuous opener of all—typically, "What did you think of the (program, service, speakers, discussion)?" If the person displayed reservations about the occasion, his affiliations and religious attachments would be probed. If this probing revealed disenchantment with conventional religions (a genuine seeker) or an open-minded conventional believer, the encounter would result in an invitation to stop by the DP's residence for a religious message he might find interesting, or to attend "a little study group we have."

When a participant initiated the engagement by asking for impressions of the program, the answer would be that it was indeed interesting, "but I wonder about. . . . What do you think about that?"—thus turning the probing back on the participant. When the conversation focused on the pleasing qualities of the architecture or interior decoration, which it frequently did, Alfred, for example, would forthrightly sort out participants with the comment, "I like a religion that is more ascetic than aesthetic, myself." Agreement vs. puzzled looks indicated the usefulness of further probing.

Miss Lee had originated the seeker-onlooker presentation, and it was she who first brought it to systematic application. She initially assumed it in the mainstream churches of Northwest Town in early 1959 by remaining after services to feel out people for receptivity to "new messages." She reported that this was not succssful because the good parishioners seemed always in a hurry to get home to their Sunday dinners or on to some other occasion. They were not interested in discussing religion, at least not at any length.

This failure in mainstream religious occasions continued for years, although the DP's persistently worked such places. This persistence is noteworthy because it was concurrent with a belief that mainstream churches were the abandoned rear guard of the old kingdom. They were filled with spiritually low people who were not receptive to new revelation.

Why, then, did they bother to spend so much time in them? Why not go where the seekers were more abundant, namely, to perimeter religious occasions? The DP's own explanation was that while *most* people in these places were unreceptive, there were indeed *some* open-minded people still seeking within the church, and they were looking for them.

While this is true enough, one other less obvious factor also seemed to be significant in their mainstream tenacity. DP's were quite aware of the invidious distinctions made between mainstream and perimeter religions. They had, in fact, a marvelously conventional disdain for "cults" and the like. While they recognized that people of deviant persuasions were "spiritually sensitive" and recruitable, they also recognized that the "far out" prior beliefs and typically undistinguished class standing of such people would not give them respectability. The conversion of Lester, for example, was a point of great pride and mentioned repeatedly in these terms to outsiders. Although mainstream religions were inhospitable, they were the road to respectable converts.

There was, then, a dilemma: conventional-occasion people were respectable but less frequently interested; deviant-occasion ones were unrespectable but more frequently interested. Both types of places were worked in an effort to make the best of both worlds.

In addition to her mainstream activity, Lee visited the perimeter religious gatherings of Northwest Town. Even though relatively small, Northwest Town had its quota of these: two mediums, an active flying saucer club, a theophilosophical library, a number of pentecostal and other "shouting" churches, and prayer and Bible study groups in the mainstream churches. In them, Lee presented herself as a foreign student interested in religion. She did not announce that Christ had returned and that she had come to save them all. She was, rather, a quiet, dignified little lady who, it was hinted, might be amenable to taking up their way of worship.

Because she was a Korean, Lee was in a particularly fortunate position in coming on as a seeker-onlooker. The university and the town happened to be unusually focused on the Orient, and Korea in particular. The university promoted Oriental enrollment by offering free tuition, and there was a local foundation dedicated to the adjustment of such students through arranging employment and "friendship families." (Lee's first DP manuscript was typed and edited through her friendship family.) The town had an active helping relation with its Korean "sister city," and a local resident was nationally famous for his work in placing Korean orphans with American families. (By the early sixties, he had placed over 3,000 in America, about 100 in the vicinity of Northwest Town.)

This climate gave Lee more accessibility than most strangers and made her more accessible to others. In spite of this, she was quite cautious and did not cast her pearls before swine.[5] She spent untold hours in religious occasions, very rarely gaining access to anyone judged sufficiently spiritually sensitive and open to new things. The degree of sensitivity she sought can be judged from the nature of the first people she attempted to interest. Among the very first was a garage mechanic who was first seen at pentecostal meetings and who frequently spoke in tongues. He was given a chapter of her manuscript on the DP, read it, and thereupon received in a dream a vision of the original sin (Satan and Eve copulating—in color). The Apostle Paul also appeared and informed him that Lee had the true message. Shortly afterward his family had him incarcerated in the state mental institution. Lee thought this a correct procedure as he had been seized by evil spirits (i.e., had turned against the DP).

The search for sensitivity was also manifest in a concurrent situation, where Lee felt obliged boldly to skirt the rules of appropriate access. Again in a pentecostal gathering, she observed a Mrs. Trude, a speaker in tongues who "received spiritually" and consorted with spiritualist mediums. Learning her name, Lee simply phoned her, told her name, and said that she also was a student of new things and had heard that Mrs. Trude was one of "God's gifted children" (i.e., was hallucinatory). With a covert presentation based on their mutual interest in spirit phenomena and Christianity, Lee sustained a relationship with Mrs. Trude for many months. Moreover, Mrs. Trude had a middle-aged lady friend who was also interested in such matters, thus making a trio.

In addition to Lee's own efforts, some of her early access resulted from persons initiating a relationship with her. Thus, while at a flying saucer meeting in late spring, 1959, a Mrs. Osborn, wife of a well-known local banker and politician, saw what she thought to be a beatific and glowing countenance in Lee. She is reported to have said, "I knew that woman had something I wanted." After the meeting, Mrs. Osborn initiated access by offer-

---

[5] Town folk who gained access to her were, according to Lee, "only interested because of my different color." Lee was quite conscious of race and sometimes wished aloud that she were a "white man," for then people would pay more attention and grant the DP more credibility.

ing Lee a ride home. Lee was at that time coming on as a poverty-stricken Oriental student and so defined herself to Mrs. Osborn, who was immediately sympathetic and began buying Lee clothes and food. She was soon invited to join Lee's Saturday afternoon Bible study class.

Another peculiar type of access was instituted by a Mrs. Quinby, a fifty-year-old practical nurse interested in spiritualism, flying saucers, and radical right politics. Early in 1960, Mrs. Quinby learned of Lee from a local medium, who told her that Lee was a very interesting woman. Always interested in the latest thing, she called on Lee at the Women's City Club. They talked for several hours, during which time Lee recounted her religious pilgrimage, including her conversion to Chang's group, "a new Christian movement in Korea." Mrs. Quinby also joined the Bible study group.

From the point of view of access to later converts, Lee's most important contact was initiated by Gladys, the domineering, obese wife of a meek accountant. After meeting Lee in a Methodist prayer group one day in the late fall of 1959, she invited Lee to her home. Gladys asked her what she thought of American churches. Judging her to be a good prospect, Lee took up the opening and asserted that "God has taken his hand off the churches." In view of the DP's boldness in later years, this may not seem to be particularly forthright, but it was the most challenging thing Lee had said in America to this point.

Gladys responded that she could not agree more; the churches were spiritually dead; all they talked about these days was psychology and sociology, not "things of the spirit." In the face of such responsiveness, Lee began to reveal the DP. Gladys joined the Bible study group, and her friend Bertha, a sometime participant in the same Methodist prayer group, was soon informed that she, too, should join. The Maple Hill odyssey had begun.

Spiritualist. As has been seen, DP's were fond of attempting access by using an interest in spiritualism as a presentation. However, until the advent of Lester, the practice had been confined to use for access in deviant religious places. Lester developed the ploy and took it into conventional religious places, after which it was adopted by other DP's and passed into their repertoire.

Lester's main mission field in the fall and winter of 1962-63 was the complex of some twenty churches and student religious centers clustered along the edge of State University. This was a lush growth that offered gatherings to be penetrated every day, all within a few blocks of each other. Lester's rudimentary attempts were most frequently directed to the one-time discussion groups that were convened for people who might be interested in something of current topical concern.

One such time was an evening "Conversation on Tillich," organized by a religious center to discuss a series of talks that Paul Tillich had recently delivered at a local church. The course of this "conversation" reveals the dynamics of rudimentary infiltrations.

The group was composed of five university students, a seminary professor, a staff member of the center, and Lester.[6] It was held in the lounge, where participants sat in cushioned chairs around a low circular table. The meeting began with a round of self-introductions, in which Lester followed the pattern and simply gave his name. The seminary professor dominated the discussion with answers to questions about Tillich's views: his theism, his case for Christianity *vs.* Christendom, his ontology, and the like. There was disagreement with Tillich on some points, but the group was basically in agreement with him. Lester was attentive and followed the conversation with sympathetic and responsive facial gestures. He gave the impression that he was much in accord, or, at least, seriously entertaining the points being raised. Aside from the observer, Lester was the only one who said nothing.

This went on for about an hour and a half, when the talk began to wane and the group lapsed into a moment of silence. The staff person leaned forward, looked at the seminary professor and was about to close the meeting when Lester made his move.

Erupting from his silence, he loudly addressed the professor

---

[6] Plus the author (the observer) who presented himself as a seeker-onlooker.

saying, "I would like to ask a question." The participants looked to Lester.

I have had experiences which I would like to discuss. I have had visions; my spirit has left my body when I am lying in bed, and I know other people this has happened to. I have read about these things, and I find that many people have had these experiences. I would like to know if others here have had experiences like this.

This was so dissimilar to the previous activity that the participants simply stared blankly at Lester after he finished, and several seconds of staring and complete silence ensued. Everyone was motionless. Finally the staff member shifted his body slightly and looked at the floor. Getting hold of himself, the seminary professor began with the words, "Tillich would . . . ," speaking loudly, presumably to recall forcefully what the occasion had been about. He made some not very understandable remarks which concluded that Tillich did not accept such occurrences as valid.

During this, the others had regained their social postures and responded with polite but open skepticism. As each participant brought up objections to the occult, Lester responded with an attitude of "you have a point there that merits consideration." Thus he mentioned the work of a British anthropologist who reported seeing Jesus and other religious adepts, people floating, and materializations and dematerializations while on an expedition in the Himalayas. With a skeptical smile, a student asked Lester if he had ever verified these reports. Lester, with a "that's a good point" look on his face, admitted that he had not. The staff person asked Lester how he could be sure that these things were not within himself, that they were not a projection of his inner concerns. Reflectively, Lester said that he had considered this, and then continued in a calm, positive tone that they seemed so real. Other people who had these sorts of experiences also said that they were so vivid, more real than the events of everyday life. He *felt* that they were not from within himself.

Lester was also asked if he had personally communicated with spirits, to which he responded that he had not, but that he knew persons who claimed to have done so. His emphasis was on the "claimed to have." He left the validity of the claims open.

Another student sarcastically told him that these phenomena might be of interest to biologists, but that he did not see that they had any religious relevance. Lester, again noncommittally, answered that he thought it bore on how one was to prepare for and face death. Spirit contact seemed to him to indicate that there was life after death.

This gave the seminary professor an opportunity to bring the occasion back to Tillich. He jumped in with Tillich's position that life should not be predicated on what happens after death. He put Lester down by further stating that belief in spirits was an improper way of dealing with the fact of death; one should live in the face of death, not in the face of belief that there is no death. This instituted a brief period in which Lester was pushed aside as the encounter turned to Tillich's views of eschatology, Christendom, and church renewal.

The cycle of Lester interjecting spirits, brief talk of them, and a shift back to Tillich repeated a number of times. The participants strove to keep the occasion within the official focus, and Lester worked to bring it back to spirits.

During the spirit phases of these cycles, Lester managed to mention that he had attended spiritualist churches and that Jesus turning water into wine was a natural thing that perhaps we could all do if we knew how. He also said that he *understood* that in the spirit world space and time were different, and that everything was done by thought, so that what you willed came true. You could, for example, travel and create objects by willing it in thought.

This alternation between spirit and Tillich foci lasted about half an hour, after which the Tillichians finally regained dominance and talked for another forty-five minutes. Lester was reduced to silence. After the meeting ended, some participants lingered to talk among themselves, but none talked to Lester.

It is clear that the ploy of the spiritualist presentation was to announce oneself as experienced in spirit phenomena. This was aimed at fostering access to people who had hallucinatory problems, and thus might be drawn to the DP, or who were simply intrigued by this little known and mysterious realm. To take up this presentation was to go on a fishing expedition with spiritualism as the access bait.

Such a fishing technique is simple and can be practiced almost anywhere. Perhaps its crudest form is illustrated by a "chance encounter" initiated by Lester one Sunday morning in the lounge of a religious center. Lester wandered into the lounge after the religious service in the adjoining church and found there a male undergraduate who sat reading the Sunday paper. Lester browsed in the lounge looking at the magazines and reading the bulletin board. He appeared to be waiting. Thinking perhaps he could help, the student asked Lester if he was looking for someone. Lester answered that he was.

> Student: May I help you find them?
> Lester: No, thank you.
> Student: Do you know what he or she looks like?
> Lester: No, I don't.
> Student: Do you know their name?
> Lester: No.

Perplexed but not put off, the student made small talk about the content of the Sunday paper. In his interpretative remarks on current events, Lester worked around to the subject of spirits. The student showed interest, and Lester came on about how the spirit world was now in a state of turmoil and very easy to contact at this time. Indeed, Lester went on, "all of a sudden," that very morning, he had received a spirit communication that he should go to this specific religious center to meet someone. Lester stopped and left the implication hanging unspoken between them—namely, that there they were talking by the preordained work of the spirit world.

Through attending a Sunday luncheon and discussion group of graduate students, Lester brought the spiritualist presentation to systematic application.

This Sunday luncheon consisted of a simple meal followed by religious talk, often centered around participants' personal testimonies. From the beginning, Lester testified to this group about his various spiritual experiences, including his spirit world travels, his vision of fiery red balls, and his spirit visits from a peculiarly effeminate man in seventeenth-century dress. He would sit at one of the tables during the meal but eat very little. Instead, he talked about the spirit world, how we can communicate with it as never before, and how someday life on earth would be wonderful when the spirit and material worlds came together. Needless to say, participants did not know what to make of him.

As weeks passed, he raised concern in the group that he was a "very mixed up kid" who needed their help, for he had begun to attach spirit phenomena more clearly to a Christian view of history and an imminent second coming. He casually began to invite members over to his flat to join a study group should they wish to know more about these things. Someone finally attended and reported back the messianic, and what was felt to be extra-Christian, character of the DP. It was becoming clear why Lester was among them, but still it was felt that they should try to help him by providing a place where he could "talk these things out." However, forbearance ended when it was discovered that Ludwig and Minnie had begun infiltrating an adult Bible study group in the same church. The graduate students might be able to stand it, the minister said, but he was less sure about lay adults. He asked Lester and his friends to stay out of his church.

Spiritualist presentations, then, tended to disrupt the moment for the participants and were in this sense less faithful to proximate rules, although more faithful to rules of self-disclosure.

Member. Member presentations were most faithful to the requirements for a smooth running occasion and most unfaithful to rules of self-disclosure.

Among the more humorous of such activities were Minnie, Ludwig, and Lester's efforts to infiltrate a tongues-speaking subgroup of a Presbyterian church in State U. City. The group was part of the tongues-speaking movement active on the West Coast at the time. Some fifteen core members of the State U. City manifestation held semiweekly prayer and Bible study sessions in one another's homes. Through coming on as prospective church members at the general religious services, the trio learned of this activity, showed interest, and began attending.

In these sessions, they prayed "in the name of our Lord," and in Bible study they offered interpretive discussions that seemed orthodox (i.e., fundamentalist). The DP's affective conduct was, in the language of tongues speakers, "loving." In this manner they fostered the impression of being fully in accord with the views affirmed and maintained in these living rooms.

After two months it was decided that the tongues group was sufficiently receptive and prepared for further information. The trio brought in Miss Lee, the master of this ploy, to work on the group. In her first meeting with them, Lee gave the oft-repeated story of her religious pilgrimage and finding of the Lord (who was not named as Chang, but left undefined and was perceived as Jesus). So far, so good. The tongues speakers were being promoted into strong, affective, religious ties to DP's without their being alienated by talk of a new Christ or by any particular apocalyptic conclusions.

However, the major contingency of this strategy emerged and abruptly ended the process. The group's leader learned who the DP's actually were from a minister in another town who had received similar treatment. He informed his church's minister, who then investigated for DP activities in the rest of his church and discovered the most charming of infiltrations: Lester was becoming a Sunday school teacher.

This was a very large church (2,000 members and six ministers) and had an elaborate group differentiation by age and marital status. Among its many groups were those for categories like married college people, parents "without partners," "mature women" interested in the Bible, and "The Young People—for post-college-age single adults, 18-30." Lester met the latter's specifications, and this was the group he had joined.

Before Lester began with the Young People, the group's president had seen him at a church in the area that was a center of activity for the tongues movement. Lester and Lee had given their "testimony for Christ" that evening (both took a covert, regular Christian line), and the president had been impressed with Lester as "a real solid Christian." He was therefore delighted to see him appear at the Young People and made a special effort to introduce him into the leadership core.

Although the group had over two hundred members (for dances, skiing parties, dinners, scavenger hunts, and athletic contests) and an average Sunday attendance of 125, there was a preponderance of females and a dearth of members with "real religious conviction." According to the president, most of the males in the group were "oddballs." Lester was therefore a prize catch. He had religious conviction, was not an oddball, and was willing to work. Although he did not participate in the group's social events, he did attend a small prayer and Bible class organized within the larger group, and he helped serve dinners for other groups' occasions. Most important, when volunteers for the program committee were requested, Lester responded.

Sunday programs of the Young People consisted of a talk, after which the audience broke into smaller, more intimate discussion groups led by members. At the time Lester joined the program committee, its task was to appoint discussion group leaders. Lester said he was interested in such a post and offered his two years of seminary study and linguistics training as qualification. The leadership core was duly impressed and decided to appoint him. However, he could not begin right away because older appointees were sufficient to fill the available posts in the immediate future. Unfortunately, before an opening occurred, the tongues group infiltration was unmasked and Lester abruptly withdrew from the group.

Withdrawing from religious places was, indeed, a pronounced DP pattern. In some places they were simply asked not to return. But forbearance was forthcoming in others, and still they rarely continued once some official knew their intentions. DP's thought that once the people of a place learned of the DP they had done their job, and there was no reason to shove it down the participants' throats. It was simply their tough luck if they rejected it.

Moreover, DP's often stopped going to places where they were merely playing the seeker-onlooker role and had not drawn any attention.

This swift pace of constantly moving on to new religious places was promoted by the pressure they felt themselves under to make new converts. If nothing turned up, or if they were ejected, or if people knew about them and did not become more accessible, then it was not worth the time to stay there. This conception ever drove them into different places, religious and secular, and seemed to be a factor in successive DP migrations and dispersions.

The Front Organization. One additional important possibility for the gaining of covert access in religious occasions should be mentioned. This is the phenomenon of the front organization, which refers to the operation of an organizational structure with seemingly unrelated purposes, but that actually exists for the sole purpose of gaining access to persons attracted to the front. Although the West Coast DP's did not employ it, they were not the only DP's in America. About two years after Lee arrived in the United States, another convert, a Colonel Kim of the Korean army, was assigned as an attaché to the Korean Embassy in Washington. He was a handsome man in his early thirties, had an excellent command of English, and had been an early convert to the Korean DP.

Not wishing to jeopardize his embassy position, he kept his DP involvement undercover and for more than a year did little to secure converts. In the spring of 1962, he contacted an old army friend, Jun Han, who he learned was no longer in the Korean army but was attending college in America. Kim invited him to Washington, and after gauging his receptivity to the DP, he let Han in on what was really happening in the world. Colonel Kim reported that he did not begin with biblical history, but with a vision of how Koreans were going to be the rich rulers of the New Age.

Han converted, moved to Washington, and became central to the East Coast DP. He was not merely a former army officer with some college study, but also a black belt karate champion.

He was the sort who could break boards and shatter bricks with a single karate chop. What was more obvious, Kim and Han thought, than to open a karate school in Washington? After all, karate is highly spiritual; its philosophy is amenable to the subtle introduction of the DP during instruction. For example, give and take is important in karate, and it is also an important Divine Precept.

The school opened in the fall of 1962 with a paying class of forty. The first class was graduated in March, 1963. The event was heralded by a feature article in a Washington newspaper, and it was reported that diplomas were awarded by the Korean Ambassador. The head of the Washington Y.M.C.A. addressed the students and guests. A local television station broadcast the news and passed their film on to the Voice of America in Korea. The front had gained public recognition and acceptance.

In a "Letter to the Master" printed in the Bay City DP newsletter, Col. Kim summed up the success of the school:

The Karate Institute has been established to play the role of a fleet steed for the Divine Precepts. In the past eight months it has passed the stage of a colt and has become an excellent horse who may run for a thousand miles.

The Institute's plant is not big enough, so we are looking for a larger place, which God will give us.

This fleet steed not only brought persons to them, but more important, provided the basis for covert presentations in religious places. In the same letter Col. Kim reported:

In January and February [1963], the churches were scheduled to study Asia and the Far East. I caught this chance and infiltrated into the churches as a speaker on Korea with brother Han as demonstrator of karate. I spoke rather broadly, but stressed the movement of New Truth in Korea and the unification movement of Korean churches and introduced the activities of our saints of the unification. I spoke of the bloody struggle of our members in Korea and of the heart of the Father which [Chang] taught us.

Br. Han captured the hearts of the audience with his fascinating art of karate. Then I attacked with testimony. We were welcomed and received praise everywhere we went.

In this way, the way was opened for me in many churches to speak on the Divine Precepts. Wherever I go, I advertise and also tell people they should see Br. Han's demonstration. In this way we are working as a team in a wonderful relation of give and take.

Colonel Kim also reported that this led to all manner of other speaking engagements. He was speaking in various parts of Virginia and frequently receiving expenses-paid invitations from Christian groups in other parts of the country.

The complexity manifest in this strategy far surpasses anything achieved by the Bay City DP's, but then they did not have such esoteric abilities.

OVERT PRESENTATIONS

There were three primary types of overt presentations in religious places: audience missionizing, literature distribution, and concerted proselytizing of professional religionists.

Audience Missionizing. The most frequently practiced overt presentation was quite similar to rudimentary covert presentation. The DP's attended religious gatherings but were not so shy about coming on as missionaries. Bertha and Minnie were specialists in this. Bertha, for example, would walk up to an individual to whom "the spirit led" (most likely a young male) and introduce herself as representing Yoon Sook Lee from Korea. She would straightaway invite the person to the DP Center to hear a very important message that explained how the world was now "entering the fourth dimension." If interest was forthcoming, she might go on to explain how the spiritual and physical worlds were going to unite and how all this had started in 1960, when the "balance of good and evil" changed. What exactly had signaled this shift would, however, never be revealed.

In such encounters, appropriately sympathetic persons would also receive a DP business card, which read:

THE DIVINE PRECEPTS
The Complete New Age Revelation
Lectures daily at 706 Columbus Ave.
South of Grant St. Phone WY 8-5147
Buses 6, 61, 62, 5, 55, 22, 32

The person receiving the card was urged to come to the Columbus Avenue address and was assured that no matter what time of the day or night he appeared he would hear a lecture, because people were coming at all times. (This sometimes gave the impression that thousands of people were coming and going all the time. People were indeed coming and going at all hours, but at the rate of less than one a day.) The tone of the invitation suggested a mysterious, gigantic assembly, not yet brought to public notice but soon to be widely known.

Religious discussion groups in particular offered an opportunity to missionize more than quietly with individual participants. They provided a platform upon which to be a more or less direct champion of the DP. This was difficult, however, because even discussion groups have a definite focus, typically some theological figure, problem, or incident in the Christian Bible. If DP's were to remain within the official channels of talk, the range of topics they could raise was quite limited. They sometimes imposed such restrictions on themselves. Thus, in a discussion group on original sin, the DP who was present persistently argued that the sin was Eve's sexual intercourse with Lucifer and Adam. Although a very old thesis, it was bizarre enough to mark the DP as a distinctive participant among this group of college students. The problem with this sort of harassing, however, was that when taken out of the total DP context, any single argument appeared to be standard fundamentalism, devoutly to be ignored.

A much bolder stance, infrequently assumed, was to attack the framework of the discussion directly. Bertha sometimes did this in adult Sunday school classes. No matter what the topic, she simply stood up during the discussion and announced that the group was quite out of date because the New Age was upon them. They should not waste their time in worn-out religion; God had taken His hand off the church. Needless to say, such breaking of the framework was never appreciated and Bertha was regularly asked to leave.

Lester even tried this before he had learned the wiles of witnessing. During a seminar in a State U. City church he arose and told the participants that he could no longer restrain himself.

They were going to think he was crazy and irrational, but he was compelled to speak: "Christ is here; I know him; and I am one of his workers." This effectively disorganized the flow of events, but the seminar leader managed to save the day by closing the meeting.

Literature Distribution. On a few occasions the DP's assumed the quite explicit evangelical stance of literature distributors at religious gatherings. The first effort, soon after they arrived in Bay City, was directed at spiritualist churches. Because of the vague, benign impression that they fostered of themselves, the DP's were initially welcomed into the spiritualist fold and accorded the "we-are-all-seekers," "live-and-let-live" treatment.

However, not being low-key occultists, but rather righteous truth dogmatists, the DP's soon began to distribute business cards and handbills en masse to spiritualist audiences. Such blatant "customer cadging" was resented by spiritualist ministers, and DP relations with the participants cooled.

After this experience, literature distribution was largely confined to passing out handbills at the city convention hall during religious conventions. These were very large gatherings at which other groups sometimes did the same thing. It was quite legal, and no sanctions came of it, nor did customers.

One other effort bears mentioning. Shortly before the new house was renovated, a new handbill was printed. One Sunday morning, three DP's stationed themselves on three corners surrounding the most prestigious, upper-class church in Bay City. They began passing handbills to the parishioners as they approached for the morning service. Most of them politely accepted the material and proceeded into the cathedral. Shortly thereafter a priest came racing out, ran to the closest corner, and grabbed the handbills from the DP. He told her in quite definite terms that she was unwelcome and that she and her friends had no right to be there giving out material. He then rushed to the next corner and repeated the performance. The disarmed DP's retreated.[7]

---

[7] It is of interest to note that this priest was a direct functionary of a nationally known cleric who officiated at that church. He was often publicly

Proselytizing Ministers. Professional religionists of the established churches maintain offices with secretaries and are to be found there much of their working day. They are religiously concerned men who are peculiarly open to approach by those who would like to abolish their jobs. Although the DP's had a good deal of incidental contact with this category of people, there were only two concerted attempts to proselytize them.

The first took place in April, 1962. At that time there was a renewed push to gain access. Lee set a vigorous example by calling on ministers of the Establishment. During the better part of April, accompanied by two or more followers, she daily placed herself in a neighborhood with a cluster of mainline churches and went from one to the other to see the minister. If he was not available, she would make an appointment and return. Happily, church secretaries assume that there must be a delicate reason for the stranger to insist upon seeing the minister, a reason that would preclude advance statement. This arrangement promoted access and made for many surprised pastors.

Upon entering the minister's office, Lee and her entourage would be graciously received and comfortably seated. Drawing out a DP handbill and handing it to the minister, Lee would say that this explained what they wanted to talk about better than they could do orally. The full page of single-spaced, typed text opened:

THE NEW AGE HAS ARRIVED!
The Dawn of the Golden Age, the Restoration of the Garden of Eden has begun. The New Era was initiated in the year 1960.

The world will be completely changed according to God's New Dispensation. The great universal tribulation has started. Watch the destruction of evil on one hand and the establishment of good on the other.

Most ministers did not seem to get beyond the first few lines. Although responses to this opening varied, most came to the same conclusion, and the DP's were quickly ushered out the door.

The second spate of proselytizing ministers was almost entirely

hailed as an enlightened, liberal Christian and was frequently associated with civil libertarian and free speech causes.

Lester's work. State U. City was unusually endowed with religious seminaries, at least five of them having set up shop within a few blocks of the university campus. Immediately after his conversion, Lester thought that seminary professors had to be informed that their teachings were obsolete, inasmuch as the definitive revelation was at hand. Returning to the seminary where he had been a student, he preached the good word to some of his old professors. No one was convinced, and he moved on to other such schools, where he approached only those professors who had a direct concern with biblical interpretation. Many listened, but none was interested. Lester exhausted this mission field and moved on to the student religious centers of State U. City with covert presentations.

*   *   *

Covert and overt presentations in religious places were, then, the DP's main strategies of access to outsiders. The focus now shifts to a field of less frequent attack: the world of secular places, their different rules and thus their different strategies of access.

Secular Places

Like much of their work in religious settings, DP strategies of access in secular places involved manipulation of institutionalized roles. I shall describe the manner in which they trifled with three such roles: employee, patron, and salesman.

Employee. DP's were relatively circumspect about witnessing while at work. Most people did not have the proper "awareness" to be able to recognize the DP's truth. Therefore mention of cosmic concerns would only make work more difficult, as it would alienate others.

Elmer, however, felt that he had a special set of co-workers and did attempt to interest them in the DP. In the spring of 1961, he began work as an orderly in the psychiatric ward of a general hospital and zestfully took up his task of being friendly with patients. Those who produced typically psychotic dream and hallucinatory material were objects of his special attention. Elmer explained to them that this material came from the spirit world and, in particular, from spirits who had a special affinity with that patient. These contacts were a rare gift, intended to inform the person contacted of the New Age. The content of the dreams or hallucinations had providential significance for worldly events.

Within a few weeks, patients began complaining to their therapists about this additional help. The complaints were passed on to the male supervisor of the nursing staff, who spoke to Elmer, whereupon the supervisor himself began to hear about spirits and the doomed world order. He allowed that it was all right to talk with the staff about these matters, but that Elmer was not to raise such topics with patients. If he was going to be a useful member of the team, he should simply be nice to patients, confining himself to conversation about trees, buildings, and so on. Elmer consented, but a bit later the same complaint once again reached the nursing supervisor, this time with a suggestion that Elmer's employment be terminated. The supervisor felt that psychiatric wards should work with everybody's problems, those of both patients and staff, and that Elmer was a good object lesson in tolerance and understanding. He again asked Elmer to stop, this time adding that he would be out of the hospital if there were any more complaints about interpreting the mystical significance of dreams. There were no more complaints, but the staff continued to hear of spirits.

After a few months, a certain equilibrium settled into the ward; Elmer was accepted by the staff as bizarre but harmless, since he had stopped upsetting the patients. However, aside from his preoccupation with spirits, Elmer had a much more "unnerving" quality, as one staff member put it. Unlike other orderlies and staff, he could never seem to mind his own business. He continually attempted to make talk with staff members and joined any conversational group in his vicinity. As the nursing supervisor put it "Elmer was omnipresent." This propensity seemed quite odd to the staff, since they did not know of his affiliation with a con-

versionist cult, but Elmer was simply striving to acquaint the
staff with spirits as much as possible before going on to talk of
the broader DP system.

Over a period of two years, Elmer did manage to get a handful
of staff members to a DP meeting. At least three nurses went
and reported to their co-workers that the affair was "far out." After
many evasions, excuses, and postponements, the nursing supervisor was induced to be a speaker at a DP party in the spring of
1962. He commented on those present: "I felt I had much less
sick people on my own ward."

Bertha and Minnie were also extraordinarily active in witnessing at work. They obtained their first employment in an outlet of
a chain of cafeterias, which I shall call the Mass Eatery. Their
job was to take orders over a counter, in front of which the customer stood, and to place the complete meal on the customer's
tray. These establishments, open twenty-four hours a day, represent the quintessence of mass society: semi-self-served, streamlined,
mass-produced meals eaten under hard fluorescent light.

Along with the requested food, Minnie and Bertha slipped
DP business cards onto the customers' trays. While this was
intended as simple religious proselytization, some thought otherwise. They understood the cards as sexual overtures. This activity,
in combination with Minnie and Bertha's propensity to sit down
and converse with strange men, fostered the strong feeling that
theirs was a cover for less than holy hustling. Customers wondered just what sort of Divine encounter and revelation they
might experience if they attended the free lecture.

The manager of the Mass Eatery learned of these cards and
the women's behavior and wondered the same thing. He called
them into his office and told them that their solicitation would
have to stop. Mass Eatery was, after all, a respectable place. The
girls of course indignantly denied that their hustling was anything
other than holy. Since they were both reasonably hard workers
and Mass Eatery had difficulty retaining employees (the work
was hard and the pay poor), neither was fired. Rather, there ensued a cycle of transferring them from outlet to outlet as each
manager encountered the problem and passed them on to get

them out of his hair. Though they always agreed to stop passing cards, they always, in fact, continued.

Patron. The rules of public places assume that patrons use them for the "usual" purposes, i.e., for those purposes for which they exist. The simplicity of these purposes, however, makes it possible to use the settings as a façade for irregular (or un-"usual") ends. Thus some derelicts use train stations and libraries not to catch trains or read, but to keep warm and sleep. And some homosexuals use selected streets and bars not as thoroughfares or for drinking, but to accomplish a liaison. So also one type of prostitute uses public places with access to strangers in mind.

Not surprisingly, the DP's engaged in the same sort of thing. The case of the prostitute is particularly instructive, because one of Bertha's favorite strategies was to patronize coffee shops and snack bars and to feign the appearance of the single girl lingering long over her coffee. By unabashedly making eye contact and acknowledging smiles, she invited men to initiate access to her. She recognized the sexual assumptions of these contacts and consciously sought to exploit them for the DP. She would explain the male's conduct to him in veiled religious terms, noting that many people were seeking for *something* today. This play between her and the erstwhile partner typically culminated in an invitation for him to come over to her place to hear "an interesting message." This was of course subject to various interpretations. Sometimes it would even be an invitation to dinner. The ambiguity of these overtures can perhaps best be judged by the occasion on which a young sailor appeared for dinner with a bottle of wine for two, only to find a rice-based meal set for seven, chaperoned by a Korean lady.

In the winter of 1962-63, Elmer and Alfred attempted access in libraries and museums. Elmer liked to station himself near the psychology section of a library, observe in what books people were browsing, and wander about the reading rooms noting what books were being read. Upon finding a person involved in a book imagined to be "cosmic" in concern (books on psychology, religion, or world affairs), he would stay close by the person, waiting for an occurrence that could bring about a conversation. Elmer did much looking, but he rarely found opportunity to talk and often complained about the difficulties of striking up a conversation with strangers.

Access was equally difficult in museums. While walking around looking at the exhibits, Alfred's ploy was to station himself next to a co-patronizer and hope for a likely opening. He complained that it was difficult to make such an opening. If you looked at a work while standing beside a stranger and said, "That is certainly an interesting bear," (or whatever) they tended to "look at you as if you are some kind of a nut" and walk away.

Salesman. A sometime convert named Earl introduced one of the more unusual DP strategies, that of utilizing the job of door-to-door salesman as a cover for selling the DP. Earl found the DP by means of a card from Bertha in the Mass Eatery in June, 1961. At this time he was selling Hopkins Products door to door, a type of work that is typically precarious and available to practically anyone who will take it.[8] Earl gave the impression of having converted and moved into the flat in July, 1961. He soon began complaining to Lee that Elmer and Merwin were slow, Minnie was ignorant, and Bertha was domineering. The group needed stronger leadership, and he was just the man. It was not very difficult for him to sell himself to the DP's. Indeed, they actually welcomed his offer to take over the direction of proselytization. After all, Earl was an impressive man. He said he was a college graduate and had attended a world-famous theological seminary for a year.[9] He spoke with the deep, knowing, well-modulated tones of a senior professor or man of the world. His conversation was studded with (frequently erroneous) allusions to giants in intellectual history and to renowned contemporary thinkers. His physical appearance supported his interpersonal style: he appeared to be in his late thirties, was of

---

[8] Hopkins Products is a far less polished version of Avon. It specializes in such items as extracts and cosmetics.

[9] This seminary's alumni office later reported that no one with Earl's name had ever registered there.

medium build, and had a slightly sunken scholar's chest and receding blond hair. His pleasant, mature face was that of a pipe smoker, although he was not one.

Earl promised that under his plan he alone would make two hundred converts within a year. All the DP's would go door to door selling Hopkins Products, and when they got inside and made a sale they would go on to bring out the DP materials. They could thereby work and witness for the Precepts at the same time. Enthusiastically, Bertha, Minnie, and Alice quit their jobs and were joined by the unemployed Alfred. Less enthusiastic and far more slow, Elmer and Merwin continued to talk to mental patients and carry mail, respectively. Within two weeks it was painfully evident that far from making a pitch after completing a sale, they were having trouble getting into homes in the first place. The group's finances began to falter without the contributions of the three women. They struggled along into September, when Lee halted the venture. Earl fell from grace but continued to live marginally in the flat and turned to selling Bibles door to door. He left the DP residence when the group moved in March, 1962.

In May, 1962, Bertha and Minnie proffered a somewhat different kind of salesmanship in public places. A certain traffic island in downtown Bay City was observed to be frequented by people who preached their message from there to the streams of passing pedestrians. The Salvation Army, among others, used it regularly, along with a prophet with a sandwich board announcing the end of the world and the desirability of immediate repentance. Bertha and Minnie proposed to join this sidewalk show as saleswomen for the DP. Lee approved the notion, and almost daily the girls appeared there for about an hour between five and six o'clock. One would harangue the crowd while the other passed out handbills.

They found themselves quite unable to snare an audience from the flood of pedestrians, who seemed more interested in getting home than in hearing about the last days. The prophet with the sandwich board was the only person to listen to them, and he had a distracting habit of walking back and forth in front of them yelling that they were anti-Christs. The situation was further complicated by another set of millenarians who sometimes got to the island before the DP's and pre-empted its use. After some weeks Bertha decided they needed a sign to make them more conspicuous. She and Merwin made up a heavy paper sign with a wooden frame, about seven feet long and four feet tall. It read "FIGHT COMMUNISM WITH THE DIVINE PRE-CEPTS." This was duly trundled out of the DP Center toward the local bus stop. Within a few hundred feet it was found that the persistent Bay City wind tended to make it more of a sail than a sign. (They had neglected to put holes in it to permit the wind to pass through.) It was wrestled back to the Center and deposited in the basement. With it went the street preaching strategy. Its demise was explained as due to "too much wind around that traffic island." People could not hear what was being shouted, and it was therefore a useless activity.

CONCLUDING REMARK

I should like to conclude the discussion of access with a general comment on what might be termed the split between moral belief and action.

One of the DP's running critiques of the satanic world was what they saw as omnipresent duplicity and feigning of emotions and feelings in everyday life. One of the points of their disaffection from the established order was the tendency of people not to be truthful to one another, to say nice things when they did not really mean them, and to "agree" when they really did not. DP's prided themselves on being able to see through people, to know what was "really" in their minds. They could do this of course because of their revealed truth, which allowed this special perception. This truth showed how Satan entered into people and caused them to act in this way. In the coming new order, however, everyone would be able to read everyone else's mind, thus making it impossible to misrepresent oneself and be insincere without others knowing it.

The split between moral belief and action lies in the fact that although they despised "insincere performances," they persistently engaged in them in their strategies of access. In recognizing this one can go on to ask what it says about the constraints and exigencies of a given type of action in the face of a lofty criticism of that very action. It would seem to reveal in a most dramatic way the powerful effects of situational constraints. Thus we have seen the channeling forces in the situations faced by the DP's. Given the situation and their view of it, covert presentations had a certain inevitability.

In finding such moral contradictions among those with the most intense moral commitments, perhaps it must be concluded that intense commitments are not sufficient protection from falling into the split between belief and action. Structural constraints may be so compelling that no matter how intense the moral commitment, all enterprises are subject to them.

Indeed, it may be that enterprises dedicated to the highest moral aims and manifesting the highest intensity are more liable to contradictions. Because they are a holy cause pitted against evil in a struggle where anything goes, harmony and honesty can wait for the New Kingdom. Rather than the split occurring *in spite of* ideological condemnation, it might occur *because of* ideological components that weigh more heavily in the formulation of action and because the enterprise can justify itself in the grandest of cosmic terms. Not seeing themselves as the ordained of God, or whatever force, more mundane enterprises caught in such a contradiction are in a less self-justificatory position. As a holy cause enterprise, then, DP's were especially vulnerable to the split between moral belief and action.

chapter 7

Promotion Vehicles

Strategies of access merely secured interested persons, or prospects. In the DP, access accomplished only the rudimentary first step, that of getting people to a DP residence. After this, the DP's felt they could get on with the real work of promoting conversion.

In this and the two chapters that follow, I shall describe and analyze their "real" work. This task is more difficult than is immediately apparent. While the DP's engaged in considerable promotion activity, their procedures were not systematized. Promotion was in many respects haphazard and dependent upon the inclination of adherents at any given moment. This variableness is most acutely indicated by the DP's extremely limited vocabulary for referring to differential prospect alignments, differences in exposure to and acceptance of their doctrines and promotion activities. Thus almost all prospects were lumped together as either "interested people," "new people," "students," "material," or sometimes even "prospects." [1] This is not to say that DP's failed to respond differentially to interested persons, only that their responses had not been worked up into much of a vocabulary and thus into conscious differences in response and treatment.

---

[1] This might be contrasted with segments of social life that have more elaborate vocabularies of contact alignments. Aside from conventional fields like salesmanship, attention should be called to the sophisticated promotion vocabularies of some criminal activity. See, for example, the excellent studies of David Mauer in *The Big Con* (New York: New American Library of World Literature, Inc., 1962) and *Whiz Mob* (Gainesville, Fla.: American Dialect Society, 1955, publication No. 24).

Likewise, discernible promotion vehicles and tactics often lacked designative terms. The enterprise was conducted more in the style of a group of amateurs haltingly but seriously playing the game of winning souls.[2]

Although there were significant vacillation, hesitation, and contradictory conduct, combined with distinct failure to apply tactics universally within categories of prospects, it is still possible to discern the developing outline of the DP's promotion program.

First, there were two concrete promotion vehicles, settings, or media through which information about the DP was communicated. One of these was what the DP's generally called "listening to the tape." I have conceived of it more generally as "the briefing session" in order to include equivalent ceremonies without or in addition to using a tape recorder. Ideally, prospects were put through the briefing session during their first appearance in a DP residence.

The other primary vehicle was the "study group" or "meeting." This was the setting in which DP's put their goods on guarded display, usually to prospects who responded sympathetically in the briefing session.

Second, there was a set of uncodified, repetitive "general promotion tactics" brought to bear upon prospects in and beyond the briefing session and study group. These will be discussed in Chapter 9, where they are classified in terms of their relation to the seekership, affective-bond, and intensive interaction steps of the conversion model.

Prospects varied considerably in the alignments they took to the cult, and these variations affected the treatment extended by DP's. It is therefore necessary also to consider the range and types of these stances and how the DP's coped with the peculiar problems presented by them. Presentation of these alignments in Chapter 8 will also provide the descriptive, or "ethnographic,"

---

[2] Compare the routinized and articulate access and promotion programs of the Jehovah's Witnesses, who require regular and written reports, follow-ups, and systematic canvassing. For a renegade's inside view, see W. J. Schnell, *Thirty Years a Watch Tower Slave* (Grand Rapids, Mich.: Baker Book House, 1963), esp. Chap. 15.

background for an understandable depiction of the more abstract general promotion tactics.

THE BRIEFING SESSION

SCENE CONTROL

DP's not only held back their doctrines for presentation in a briefing session, but also felt it extremely important to have exclusive control over the session. This necessity for control is seen particularly in those circumstances where it was problematic.

In Northwest Town, Lee was first a live-in housekeeper for a widowed mother of three. As the house was small, her movements were unavoidably watched and her visitors surveyed. She remained six months, but because of interruptions and concern over what might be thought of many of her visitors she left to become house-keeper for a working spinster and her elderly, ailing father. This house was larger, and she could come and go and receive visitors without being so easily observed or interrupted. However, the Episcopalian spinster observed Pentecostal women among Lee's visitors and made disparaging remarks about them. After only three months, Lee moved again and became housekeeper in the local Women's City Club, which was empty much of the time and which allowed her great scene control. She could receive in-terested people and hold her Bible study group, which was now a going concern. Finally, upon moving to Maple Hill her control was perfect, for she became mistress of her own house.

In Bay City, DP's ruled a flat, and after that a house. Scene control was no longer problematic. It became so again, however, when Minnie moved to State U. City. She rented a room and began receiving people in the landlady's living room at various times of the day and evening. Minnie had been invited to use the room, but daily use had not been expected. The landlady found it uncomfortable to discover a stranger in her front room almost every time she returned from work and asked Minnie to invite fewer guests. Unable to accept this interference with her scene control, Minnie moved to Lester's flat, where control was again established.

In these and other instances there was, then, a persistent effort to gain maximum leverage before introducing DP reality and initiating promotion of its acceptance. Given such leverage, the DP's could install the scenic equipment and presentational material, regulate the entrance and exit of actors, and make the rules of appropriate conduct.

THE SCENE

Location, housing, and equipment are important impression-producing features of all scenes. Some characteristics of DP premises may be described to indicate how they chose to define themselves through the physical aspects of their scenes.

Their second-floor flat in Bay City was flanked on the east by the downtown section and Negro and Mexican slums. A white working- and lower-class district was to the south, and to the north and west were white middle- and lower-middle-class residential areas. Their own neighborhood was a racially mixed, lower class transitional area. Its main street consisted of economically declining businesses and more bars per block than any other Bay City street. The flat itself was next to a large park and two blocks from the main street.

Ascending the grass-mat-covered steps to the flat, one emerged into a long, drab, dimly lit hallway. Prospects were led down the hall to a room featuring Victorian bay windows adorned with fading, flowered drapes. Standing at the door, one was presented with a center aisle formed by rows of second-hand wooden straight-backed chairs. These stood in two rows of five chairs on either side, facing the aisle. At the window end of the room were a small table and chair used by the leader. The walls were bare, except for a calendar and a cheap world map. One wall contained a fireplace, which had long ago been converted for use with a gas heater.

The scene created in the three-flat house in the same neighborhood was very similar. The room nearest the street was outfitted with furniture from the room just described. There were also bay windows (though with plastic drapes) and a similarly converted fireplace.

The State U. City flat was located in an apartment house district a few blocks from the campus. The DP's had the second-floor flat of a two-story building, the lower level of which housed a Chinese restaurant. One gained entrance to these quarters by walking down a narrow alleyway, past the restaurant's kitchen and restrooms, around to the rear of the building, and climbing the outside stairs. Many had difficulty finding it.

The State U. City scene was also outfitted with second-hand wooden chairs and devoid of any decoration. The overall impression was one of Spartan simplicity—an unfrilled, no nonsense approach to creating reality—and of poverty.

No DP premises were ever reasonably heated. The gas heaters were occasionally lighted to take the chill off, but most often the scene rooms, as well as the rest of the premises, were chilly.

Some symbol equipment was used in the scene room of the Bay City flat in that a large Bible lay on a small table in the corner, along with a slotted wooden box labeled "contributions." These were not, however, placed in the scene room of the house, leaving it devoid of religious symbols. In State U. City, a framed photograph of Chang reposed in a scene room cranny for a brief time. The picture was flanked by candles, creating a suspiciously altar-like impression. One prospect so commented, and the artifacts quickly disappeared.

Such were the physical features and atmosphere of the settings in which people were to be told about the new Christ and the world's end.

EARLY BRIEFING SESSIONS

In her role of seeker-onlooker in Northwest Town, Lee invited people to drop by and see her. These were social visits in which religion was the main topic, much in the manner that buffs of all types talk about their hobbies. Lee usually contributed her tale of long religious seeking and of finding the Lord (implicitly Jesus, but actually Chang) and a "movement of new truth" in Korea. She came on as a devoutly religious person dedicated to religious studies. She would then comment that she wanted to form, or else had formed, a Bible study group, and perhaps the visitor would like to join. Indeed, it just so happened that she had composed a text that could be used as a guide for biblical study.

The imminence of the Second Advent was mentioned, but with an air of mystery. Visitors were uncertain of her meaning, and Lee's offer to clarify the enigma if they attended her Bible study sessions formed part of the stimulus to attend.

After Lee created her little band of prophets, a rudimentary division of labor was instituted. Now her converts gained most of the access and induced people into DP scene rooms. Lee did little access work and became a specialist in briefing sessions.

After arrival in Bay City, she continued to use her religious pilgrimage and personal testimony as the style and content of the briefing session. However within a few months she began to feel that it was too great a burden to give a personal explanation to every prospect.

THE TAPED SESSION

Elmer still owned four tape recorders from his pre-DP life and suggested that the problem of repeated explanations would be eliminated if they simply played a tape. Lee, anxious to make certain that the initial picture given was an adequate one, abbreviated the DP book only slightly, and when recorded by Bertha it ran four and a half hours. Elmer set up a tape recorder in the scene room, where visiting prospects were taken and left alone to listen. Not surprisingly, DP's found that few people would sit four and a half hours listening to a tape recording. They tended to walk out without a word after an hour or so or to excuse themselves, claiming the press of other business. Sometimes the tape would finish and the DP's entered the room only to find the prospect sound asleep. Eventually the recording was split into two segments of about two hours each, and an attempt was made to have people come to separate sittings. This of course posed the problem of getting anyone to return.

The four and a half hour format endured eight months before it was at last agreed that the tape was too long. Lee had an intense fear of leaving out some important point but managed to reduce the tape to two and a half hours. Bertha was again the speaker, and prospects again tended to walk out.

Six months later, in May, 1962, it was again felt that the tape required shortening. By reducing the sections on Old Testament events and their significance, Lee was able to cut it to an hour and twenty minutes.

It was additionally thought that expecting prospects to listen to Bertha's voice for even this shorter period was asking too much. Perhaps a male voice should alternate with Bertha's intense intonations. But what male? Lee knew that none of the DP males could read rapidly, accurately, or authoritatively enough. Attending the study group, however, was a young man who appeared interested in the Precepts. He could read well, had a deep baritone voice, and spoke with authority. Although not a convert, his voice was sufficiently attractive to justify the request that he read for the tape. He agreed.

However, upon beginning to use this tape, Lee found many prospects overinterested in the identity of the male voice. Some wanted to meet him, and a few thought the voice was that of Mr. Chang. Unfortunately, Lee could not produce her speaker, for he was, in fact, an observer who had stopped attending DP functions. Prospect attraction to the voice was so disconcerting that Lee had the script re-recorded. This time she used Leo, who, while less polished than the previous speaker, could read accurately. Lee worked on the statement again and proudly sheared off six additional minutes. She now warned prospects that it was "dangerous" to hear such a short version, that it was very condensed and "only a summary." "Do not judge quickly."

After the dispersal of July, 1962, DP's were not allowed to have tape recorders for their briefing sessions. Lee forbade it on the grounds that they should learn to talk for themselves rather than letting a machine do it. (She continued to use the machine in Bay City, however.)

Nonetheless the mission field people kept alleging the need for a more efficient method of briefing and by November had persuaded Lee that a taped talk should be made available. Moreover, it was felt that even a one-hour session was too long. While some standardized introduction was necessary, more time should be available for eliciting the prospect's response.

Again laboring, Lee reduced the tape to thirty-four minutes. She cited this figure with pride; she had performed a feat that she had once thought impossible. Bertha and Leo were again the readers.

The tape still opened with an assertion of the necessity for a new revelation and stated how man, who fell because of a copulating Eve, should grow to perfection. The detailed review of the meaning of biblical incidents was entirely dropped in this version. The speakers instead moved quickly to relating that in 1960 the scale had tipped for good and the end of the world was at hand. Jesus had been sent to accomplish this but had failed. Therefore someone else must do the job. A new Messiah was necessary. "From what part of the world will the new Messiah come?" The answer was offered: "From the East." What nation, then, would be chosen to be God's People, and how would one recognize the "true Christ"? These questions were not answered except with the statement that the "true new" Christ would be he who would discover the "true nature" of Satan's sin and "subjugate" Him. The tape closed with Bertha melodramatically intoning: "And His kingdom will last forever."

Because the tape was fairly short, it was now felt reasonable to make phonograph records rather than tape recordings. A one-man record-making operation (discovered in the Yellow Pages) was commissioned to make a few records. These were used into the spring of 1963.

That spring it came to be felt that the briefing session *itself* was defective. It was simply not producing enough people who went on to study the Precepts. The session was discarded, and effort was directed toward getting people to commit themselves to an *initial twelve-hour session* in which they were not only briefed, but were taught *the entire book in one sitting*. That is, the DP's attempted to collapse the briefing session and study group phases into one period in order to avoid the heavy losses that occurred in moving from the former to the latter. This strategic change was predicated on the assumption that people were not coming back to study or convert because they lacked the *knowledge* that would make them do so. If prospects only knew the whole story, then they would convert. It was an approach to conversion that was intellectualized in the extreme.

The point to be made here has to do with the effect produced by isolating a person to listen to a long, dull, canned communication. One of the requirements of conversion is an affective bond between a prospect and one or more believers. Such bonds were given little support—and, indeed, were perhaps destroyed— through isolating prospects and requiring them to endure a tedious tape. Face-to-face contact is an obvious precondition of affective ties. It would be difficult to plan a more effective device to stifle such ties than the DP's early tapes.

There was some slight recognition of this in the progressive cuttings, but the main stimulus still was not that of getting to know the person. The aim was, rather, that of providing time to counter objections and to allay disbelief and hesitation. In fact, with the thirty-four minute spiel, Lee began sitting in the room with the prospect, stopping the tape after each major section, and asking for questions, objections, and points for clarification. Regardless of its aim, this tactic did appear to create more personal relationships and greater interest in returning to study the Precepts.

However, even with the first tape, DP's did attempt to forestall rapid exits. Someone would remain by the closed door waiting for the tape to end, then would enter and ask the prospect what he thought or if there were any questions. Visitors were also asked to sign the guest book, and almost everyone did. Lee especially might then begin her "sizing up," in which she probed the religious affiliations or leanings of the prospect in order to approach him in appropriate terms. The point most stressed would be that of course one could not understand the Divine Precepts in one sitting. The tape merely gave one a general idea. The person should attend the study group, which was described as informational in nature. Participation in a study group to learn this information in detail was merely *suggested*. DP's avoided conversional presentation. Prospects were not asked for their souls and fortunes or threatened with damnation; they were asked to delve into some materials that they might find of value.

Computations based upon the guest books suggest that between January, 1959, and June, 1963, the DP's induced more than 700 people into the briefing session. Something less than half that number probably attended a study group at least once, and a very small fraction of those went on to become converts. The briefing session was not a successful scene.

The Study Group

The study group was designed to lead a set of persons from the beginning to the end of the DP book. The ideal pace was to study one chapter a meeting, two meetings a week for six weeks. This projected course was rarely realized. Only a handful of people attended that often or that long. The course was frequently started for new people, who would then drop out; new people would come, and the book would be started over; they would drop out, and so forth.

It was felt that assertions as enormous as a new Lord of the Second Advent and the end of the world required considerable preparation. These conclusions had to be approached in small steps in order to lay out sequentially the fundamental beliefs or evidence leading to them. Lee explained it in this way:

We make clear statement after one reads through eleven chapters. It is very obvious in the twelfth chapter. So we ask everybody to find it out in sequence. Find out after reading in sequence, because it is not good for new people to hear the conclusion first. It only stumbles them. Why do we do that [viz., "stumble" them]? It is destructive.

Our intention is to reveal everything, but we want to prepare people to receive that statement [that the Lord of the Second Advent is here]. That is why, until we come to that point, we don't refer to it. It's . . . for the sake of [that person]. . . .

But if you explain logically why second advent must be fulfilled in such a way, then you can explain . . . the twelfth chapter.

So we . . . explain in the first chapter what was the purpose of creation, which had been failed. . . .

[Lee then gave a summary of the eleven chapters.]

Then we come to the present day and explain in Chapter 12 how in this forty years universal events, world events . . . there was providential significance behind world events. Then we explain, finally, who can be the third chosen people and nation for this last dispensation. There in the twelfth chapter, again, I only present as a formula. The Lord of the Second Advent must be the one who can fulfill the Old Testament and New Testament. He must be the one who can fulfill the purpose of all other religions. He must be the one whom whole spirit world can witness to him. He must be the one who can subjugate Satan.

I gave only formula. If this formula is acceptable then everybody use this formula and find out the right person using this formula. I said [in the book that] the Lord of the Second Advent, or the new leader of the new world cannot come from the West—western hemisphere. He must come from the East. There I explain why East. I explain how these two hemispheres make different contributions for this new world. So if this is acceptable, then you had better look for new leader in the Orient. This only formula.

Many people reading twelve chapters still don't know what it means.

So it only stumbles people; it only give stumbling block to people if I say everything plainly. That why I only give formula.

Not because I want to hide anything. No, time is here. I want reveal everything, but have to reveal in sequence.

Note the conception of the nature of the prospect that is built into this social arrangement. He is a person who will suspend his judgment for six weeks while attending study groups. He will not get ahead of the presentation or find stumbling blocks on any of the steps of the stairs to the Advent. And, as we shall see, he is a person who will not argue or ask for conclusions.

Because the study group was an instrument for the communication of a belief system and explicitly focused upon giving a good impression, it seems most useful to employ a dramaturgic perspective in describing it.[3] The study group was composed of a group of performers who took a line before an audience. The appropri-

---

[3] Erving Goffman, *Presentation of Self in Everyday Life* (New York: Doubleday & Company, Inc., 1959).

ateness of this perspective is suggested by the occasions where no audience appeared and the study group failed to "go on."

PREPARATIONS

The main problem in the production of a study group was to assemble an audience. I have discussed the ways in which an audience was gotten for the briefing, but there was the additional problem of getting them back for a meeting. The most frequent means of attempting this was to go through the recent entries in the guest book and, after the evening meal, call those who had not obviously rejected.

Most people failed to be activated by this. It seemed that a peculiarly large number of obligations and afflictions befell those who had contacted DP's. Spouses were ill, personal health was precarious, grandmothers were dead, water pipes were broken. In State U. City, Lester found that students who contacted the DP's had particularly heavy study and examination schedules that made it difficult for them to get away for the evening. Some were so unimaginative as to say they could not come because they had no mode of transportation. DP's offered them rides to and from the meeting and thus effectively trapped them. However, after one or two phone declinations, DP's made no further attempts with that individual.

While the phone tactic was being pursued, converts prepared themselves. The men donned suits and ties and the women combed their hair and put make-up on. Lee would retire to her room and pray for the success of the meeting. Sometimes other DP's would pray with her.

Shortly before the official beginning time of 7:30, DP's came into the scene room and attempted small talk with the waiting prospects. Converts and prospects usually had difficulty sustaining conversation in such a public place and faltered from topic to topic. Most often everyone sat in silent tension, assuming the pose of "waiting for church to begin."

PRELIMINARIES

Precisely at 7:30, Lee entered the scene room. She would give a general smile of recognition and sit at what was defined as the head of the room. This was the signal that the main performance had begun; bodies shifted, and all attention focused upon her.

Lee typically wore a long, gray flannel skirt, blouse, cardigan, and loafers. Her hose were of heavy cotton. She sat upright, often with her legs apart (apparently an Oriental posture, but one that looked a bit odd in a Western skirt).

Total attendance (converts and prospects) averaged around thirteen people per meeting. Attendance ranged from nine to twenty, with at least three DP's at every meeting. Most of the time at least six participants were DP's (almost half the average group).[4]

The proceedings would begin with a male convert passing out the hymnals and Lee announcing a hymn. Their hymnal was printed on the multilith press and contained sixty-five songs, mostly pirated from Protestant hymnals. None contained reference to Jesus by name, although the collection was heavy with reference to Christ and God. Lee had a marked preference for hymns praising closeness to God, such as "Nearer My God to Thee," as opposed to "distant" ones, like "Lead On, Oh King Eternal." Her favorite, and the most frequently sung, was "Call of the Reapers," wherein the "Lord of Harvest" is implored to "send forth reapers."

> Hear us Lord to Thee we cry.
> Send them now the sheep to gather,
> Ere the harvest time pass by.

The hymnal also contained eight songs written by members of the Korean group. These venerated Chang and the New Age. The verses were in Korean, but were of course transliterated. To the

---

[4] During most of the observation period, meetings were held twice a week in Bay City (Tuesdays and Fridays) and once a week in State U. City (Thursdays) and State College Town (Mondays).

unknowing they appeared to be strings of nonsense syllables and were not sung in the presence of new people who might not "understand."

The number of hymns sung varied with Lee's feeling about how much the "spiritual level" of the room needed raising. As many as six hymns—using all verses—were sometimes used.

Singing of traditional hymns may seem rather strange in a millenarian cult, but not if seen as a performance device. It was intended to provide some continuity with traditional religions and to give an initial impression of the performance as not so different from other religious bodies. Moreover, hymn signing was thought to drive away any Satanic spirits that might be lurking in the room; they could not bear to remain where praises were being sung to God.

With the spiritual atmosphere thus purified, Lee asked a DP to pray, after which she offered a prayer. These prayers usually first thanked the Father for his wonderful words and for the privilege that was theirs, even though they were so unworthy and could never repay Him. Second, they requested support and strength in witnessing. "Give us courage, strength, wisdom, love, that we may find those whom You find qualified [and] righteous." Third, the prayers pleaded for workers in the cause. "Bring Your spirit to those who are seeking." These entreaties sometimes became rather dramatic, as in this one by Lee:

Father, You have set the time; it is very close now. Where are the Americans? Tell me what I am to do with the Americans. Where are those who will come forward and stand on Your side in this most important time? It is Thy will to make this movement now. . . . Open their hearts, give them the spirit. . . . Lead them into Thy work. . . . Help them to take a stand now. . . .

This did not pass unnoticed by prospects as a kind of indirect plea, through God, for all those at the meeting to join up. Last, there would be a short discourse on man's sinfulness and rebellion. "We are the aliens of God. . . . All mankind has been wandering in the wilderness for all this long time. . . . Decadence and sin are all around us. Satan is the deceiver of all mankind."

The following prayer by Lee provides a fuller and more concrete appreciation of this part of the performance.

Father, we are the descendants of the rebellious. . . . We have no right to be called Your children. Our forefathers accumulated sins of rebellion, . . . and so did we. Nevertheless You have been seeking us [pause] with broken heart [pause] coming to us with so much tears and so much suffering. We are here in the price of Your tears. You are swift and blunt. You sent patriarchs. You sent prophets. You sent Jesus our Lord. And through many creatures You showed how much You loved us, but we, mankind, resented all of these people, denied our mistake, and crucified and persecuted them.

Father, You sent Jesus Christ to this earth, not to bring cheap peace but to destroy evil. Therefore, he had to destroy dead religions. He had to destroy all the Satanic ties in family, society, and all neighbors and communities. Therefore he appeared like a destroyer, a man who destroys this world. Naturally people could not welcome him. His coming was sharp, divided up and judged the evil and sin of this world. Satan hated him most, could not stand with him.

Father, today You have started new work. Because Jesus did not fulfill this work, somebody has to fulfill this work. Somebody has to accomplish this work. The one who accomplishes the work Jesus left cannot follow any other path but the path of Jesus, which was the path of rejection, being rejected, which was the path of the unwelcomed.

Father, we realize that our path cannot be easy one and we do not choose easy path, we want to follow the path You set before us. We are grateful with any obstacle Satan puts before us. Through this obstacle we will return victory to You. Satan doesn't want to be subjugated before us, but we must carry out, we must accomplish this task. Because Satan is the robber, Satan is the deceiver. Satan is the enemy to You, for centuries, for ages, and until now. We have to drive this robber from our walls, away, and take this world back to our God. We crave to see the day when You will reign this world with Your love and wisdom.

Father, we are here, tonight, to hear Your voice and to touch Your hand and to be embracing Your heart in the bosom of Your love.

Father, speak to each one of us and be present among us, open our ears so we may see You face to face, we may hear Your voice directly. Through each word we hear tonight resurrect our spirits from the fate of death that we may respond to Your love with gratitude, beauty, and love.

Father, we do not want to be like a stone, like a wood which doesn't have any sense. Father, we want to be like a human being. We want to be like beloved children to You that every action of love, every type of love flowing from You, may be sensed deep in our hearts, that we may feel Your love and we will be able to respond to Your love as a living, beloved child.

Father, I commit this meeting in Your hands. You alone lead our meeting and teach each one of us. And fill us with Your own spirit and power.

I thank and pray all these in the name of our Lord. Amen.

Lee's prayers were delivered with forcefulness and fervor. She shut her eyes and screwed up her face, giving the impression of great diligence. Minnie and Bertha prayed in similar fashion, although Minnie's Pentecostal background came through as she gasped between phrases and moaning crept into her voice. When the prayer had a strong element of salvation and cleansing, Minnie and Bertha squirmed in their seats and gasped softly, as though the Lord were indeed near and ready to cleanse them. However, these moments of almost Pentecostal fervor were brief, as other DP's were more restrained. In general, the meetings were sedate, middle-class performances, projecting a deadly seriousness.

SERIAL READING

The tone having been set, the main part of the performance began. This consisted of oral reading from the DP book. At this point, Lee had to decide where to begin reading. Because there were often first-meeting prospects in the same meeting with older prospects, she had to decide which to "sacrifice," as she sometimes put it. Most often she would continue with the person or persons who had been before, leaving the freshman prospect to come in on the story as best he could. The basis upon which she decided was her on-the-spot assessment of who appeared to be the best prospect at that moment.

Lee began the reading by saying, "Tonight we will study . . ." and then announcing the chapter number and title. The DP seated nearest her would be asked to begin reading. The amount Lee allowed any person to read varied with how well he read. She brought each turn to a close by loudly murmuring "hmmm" and beginning to speak. This process continued around the room, Lee reading when her turn came.

Upon stopping a reader, Lee usually asked if there were any questions. This was most often greeted with silence. If she was not interested in producing a particularly impressive performance, she let the silence stand, simply said, "next," and the droning went on. This was especially true for the chapters dealing with the DP version of the Old Testament.

Sometimes Lee would ask specific content questions. If no prospect responded, converts would offer answers. Typically, several converts offered successive answers, few of which Lee found adequate, and she would finally give the proper response. With the converts playing this role, some semblance of a discussion group was occasionally produced.

Most often Lee summarized, emphasized, and rephrased what had just been read. She would relate the content to current events, to prior parts of the world view, and to general problems of living. The "work of the spirits" figured very heavily in all these.

Often, very little talk was interjected between the reading of passages. Lee failed to talk or to promote talk, and the reading went on and on. Many prospects thought the procedure incredibly dull.

The reading and interpassage talk usually lasted about two hours. When it was finally concluded, more hymns were sung and the meeting was closed with a prayer by a DP and one by Lee.

"EXPRESSIVE" PERIOD

Post-proceeding activities varied somewhat. When first-meeting prospects who had not been sized up were present, Lee would engage them while the group was still seated. They would be asked what they thought of the chapter under study, and Lee would inquire into their place of birth,[5] religious background,

---

[5] Lee was always careful to determine nationality. Not only were twelve nations needed for the foundation, but she also required people to translate her book into other languages. Lee would even ask native Americans if they knew any foreign languages and what foreign-language speakers were among their acquaintances.

occupation, place of residence, and the like. She always remembered to have prospects sign the guest book and made certain she knew how to pronounce their names. She made a point of names by repeating them several times and receiving corrections until she had thoroughly mastered them. She remembered names and always addressed people by them.

If Lee had any announcements or wanted to make a particularly strong impression, she would hold the audience and give an additional talk. Thus, when she announced the revival in June, 1961, and was pushing for everyone to work on it, her post-proceeding talks ran on for an additional hour or more.

Before the dispersion of July, 1962, Lee generally dispatched Bertha and Minnie to serve coffee, tea, and cookies. Little groups would form as DP's circulated among them. Often people assembled around Lee as she held court, interpreting various topics in DP terms. This was a convivial period, in contrast to the starkness of the reading.

However, expressive periods were sometimes a problem. Many of the participants were strangers to one another, and most DP's were not particularly competent or aggressive interactors. Unless Lee held her little court and thereby engaged the participants, the mingling, on occasion, broke down into many people sitting alone and only a few holding conversations. Perceiving this "interactional supply" problem, she might then hold court or pass out the hymnals and gather everyone together to sing.

Such is the manner in which the DP's exposed their world view to a set of more or less interested prospects. There was of course a desire to present the product in its best light, to maximize attractive features and minimize unattractive ones.

This concern was manifest in their manipulation of the physical setting, performer dress, and method of world view disclosure. The expressive problems surrounding the physical appearance of the DP book and performer discipline in the study group additionally illustrate their dramaturgic concern.

PACKAGING

The appropriateness of the physical packaging of the world view—the DP book—was a constant source of anxiety. There were, indeed, four English versions of the book. All of them had the same structure, concepts, and interpretations. They varied in excluding or including subsidiary material and in overall literacy level.

Lee rendered the first English translation in Korea in 1956.[6] It was mimeographed on newsprint and paperbound with a green and white cover displaying the Yang and Yin. She brought several copies of this book to America, but did not use them in proselytization as they were manifestly Korean and written in imperfect English. She completely rewrote the book, with free editorial aid arranged by her friendship family. In this reworking, a number of empirically ludicrous observations were omitted, such as the following:

. . . The face, figure, manner, and skeleton are the representation of the internal man. One may judge the approximate tempers by the type of blood, because our blood represents our mind.

Direct references to Korea and translation problems were dropped (e.g., "In translating the Korean word TANGGAM I have chosen the word INDEMNITY, although it is not quite adequate").

Materials that linked the DP to authoritative Western opinion were added:

An English historian, Arnold J. Toynbee . . . has advanced the thesis that . . . a new form of civilization is needed before we can progress further. A new religion . . . would be a fusion of Christianity and major Oriental philosophies. With this new religion alone there will be generated new hope for mankind and the establishment of a foundation upon which a new civilization can grow. Such a new religion is now taking hold.

---

[6] Lee reported having compiled the DP in 1956. Before that, the only written version had been long, complicated, and written by another Chang follower. (Chang never committed his revelation to writing.) Even Lee had trouble deciphering this version, so she simplified and shortened the doctrines for presentation in English. Also, Chang had worked out the meaning of history only up to the death of Jesus. In order to complete the English version, Lee had to work up the detailed meaning of Western history since that time. She was uncertain of these interpretations, but said she would accept responsibility for any errors (during the accounting period at the beginning of the New Age theocracy).

The editorial work arranged by the friendship family did much to make this second version literate, and therefore respectable. However, when printed in the summer of 1960, Lee had only the Maple Hill people to edit and proofread the stencils. The book came out with a host of grammatical and typographical errors. In Bay City, many people noted these, and Lee spent untold hours going through almost 500 copies, pasting correction slips over large errors and rectifying smaller ones by hand.

These changes marred the book's appearance. In the fall of 1961, with the aid of a co-worker of Elmer's, a hospital orderly,[7] a more literate draft was produced and 750 copies printed. This version was thought to be appropriately impressive and literate until Lester became influential in the cult. Lester thought the grammar and syntax to be defective. He claimed the book's flaws had hindered him in studying the DP, and he was certain that scholars would dismiss the DP if its presentation were not more competent. Lee undertook to revise the book once again. After additional editorial work of some magnitude, Lee pronounced this fourth version as the final revision. Translations into every language of the world would be made from it.[8]

There was, then, a persistent (and expensive) concern with packaging the world view. It was important not only to omit information that would "stumble" prospects, but also to avoid being dismissed as illiterate and thus ridiculous.

DRAMATURGIC DISCIPLINE

The proper DP team role during scene room performances was to read when one's turn came and to answer questions if no prospect volunteered. Beyond this, one should remain quiet and let Lee manage the proceedings and prospects. As in all real-life drama, some performers were not entirely disciplined. Indeed, some DP's had difficulty turning in even minimal performances,

---

[7] This non-convert was said to have lent aid in exchange for the DP's later printing his book on how to win at betting on horse races. Politics is not all that makes strange bedfellows with religion.

[8] Ludwig and Greta had completed a German translation of the third version and had to go back and revise in terms of the fourth.

not to mention posing difficulties as active violators of dramaturgic discipline. A major problem was deficiency in reading. Elmer and Minnie were especially bad, and Merwin and Bertha were not overly adept. Despite having read Lee's book repeatedly for almost three years, they continued to be stumped by words like "treatise," "validity," and "Gautama."

Elmer still read in a slow, word-by-word, laborious manner. Lee never skipped him in serial reading, but she allowed him only very short passages. While he was reading, members of the team would try to help by greeting each stumble and silence with a chorus of correct pronunciations. In spite of Elmer's obvious incompetence, Lee demanded correct performance and often made his life more difficult by imposing the following sort of public discipline upon him.

Elmer: [reading] ". . . and thus invaded Jesuses disciples."
Lee: No, no. Jesus. Don't read as twice [i.e., as a plural]. Jesus' disciples.
Elmer: [nods head but continues to next sentence] "Truly, truly, I say to you. . . ."
Lee: [interrupting] Ummmmm . . . Elmer, say it again. You always say Jesuses. [begins previous sentence for him] "And Iscariot. . . ."
Elmer: [Repeats previous sentence correctly and reads on.]

Elmer was also a more active violator in that he sometimes tried to help Lee manage the performance. He tended to enter rapid exchange conversations between Lee and prospects, even though he spoke very slowly and it was quite a job for him to work up a sentence. At such times, Lee would sharply exclaim: "Shut up, Elmer." Sometimes she even repeated this to the group at large, followed by a comment such as "He is a very undiplomatic man."

On one occasion, Elmer entered the talk and wandered off about a druggist of his acquaintance who was interested in spiritualism. Lee waved him down and virtually shouted: "Elmer, be quiet. Can't you be quiet? You will ruin it." Elmer hung his head, put on a sad face, and Lee proceeded.

Such exchanges kept up discipline, but the audience seemed slightly embarrassed. It was as if they were witness to something they should not have been allowed to see. Prospects could also wonder if Lee was really the warm, friendly, motherly type she had appeared to be.

Elmer's lapses were brief, and he was responsive to Lee's anger. Leo was more forceful and less malleable. Although his faith vacillated, he was a devout and heated espouser in DP meetings. He usually assumed the quietness of his team role unless Lee encountered prospect resistance—a time when she least needed Leo's help. He would spring from his silence into a remarkably repetitive and heated tirade:

There is no faith in them. There has never been any faith when the Word of God's been given. When I first heard about this I wanted to reach back and change it all in the Garden of Eden. Ever since the prophets the people have never had faith.

This was the prelude to a recitation on Old Testament men of faith whom the people did not follow. If not restrained, he would give a complete account of history according to the DP. He often ran on for five or ten minutes. Before meetings he would promise to remain quiet, but he always forgot himself at the crucial moments. It was thus necessary to discipline him before the audience. Because he talked very loudly and rapidly and rarely noticed Lee's admonitions, the entire team would be required to put him down.

Thus on one occasion Leo was present while two Lutheran ministers of Lester's acquaintance were in attendance and a disciplined performance was particularly important. Leo was seated in a low chair in the corner. The ministers asked upon what authority the DP was given. The issue of faith cued Leo into his spiel. He bent forward as he waited for a pause into which he could jump. He found one:

Somebody asked by what authority this message is given. This is the same question that people asked Moses and Jesus. They say they believe in God, but they really don't because they doubt His word every time it is given.

Lee interrupted him: "That's all right, Leo; that's enough, Leo," and he reluctantly stopped. He tried again a few moments later, but Lee was again able to calm him. A few more minutes passed as Lee answered the ministers' questions. Again he started. Lee quietly put him back into silence. He was still bent forward, intently watching, his arms touching the floor as though he were about to spring up. He started to speak a fourth time. This activated the rest of the team. All six broke into a whispered, but loud chorus of "No, Leo," "That's enough, Leo," "Shhh, Leo." A flurry of hands waved him into silence. The ministers and other prospects who were present saw Leo as a "caged animal" to whom the DP's were saying, "Down, boy."

Aside from the problems described, DP's were rather well-behaved performers. Although it is difficult to estimate, comments by a variety of prospects suggested that these improper participants and their performance disruptions cast doubt upon the DP projection and detracted from confidence in their personal competence.[9]

The study group was, then, a peculiar type of performance that slowly disclosed the DP perspective. It and the briefing session were the major promotion vehicles.

After considering the prospect alignments encountered by these vehicles, I shall take up promotion tactics that were applied both during and after the briefing session and study groups.

---

[9] Other participants who cast doubt on the performance are discussed in Chap. 8.

chapter 8

Prospect Alignments

Prospect alignments may be arranged along a continuum of how close to or far from the "attitude," "spirit," or "stance" expected by the DP's particular prospects lie. As stated previously, "proper" and "close" consisted in being religiously concerned but "open-minded," suspending judgment for several weeks as the DP's slowly unfolded their doctrines. After all the evidence was presented, the prospect should enter an existential struggle and then accept the DP. As with most ideals, this projected propriety was rarely realized. Almost all prospects departed from this "closeness," some in rather spectacular ways.

The task of this chapter is to delineate the degrees of this departure, the ways in which it occurred, and the devices adopted to manage misinvolvement.

THE PATENTLY DISORGANIZED

Among the expected attributes of participants in social life is the capacity to attend and respond to the structure and content of ongoing interactional systems. Beyond the question of those holding a disparate view of a situation that necessitates activity to mask the disparity, is the question of those who find it difficult to formulate any view or to organize their relation to others. Such people are said to be "out of touch," and if they persist in their distance they are likely to be put in an asylum.

Although there were not many of these people—perhaps twenty—they constituted a conspicuous, if not spectacular group within the DP world. They ranged from the drunks who stumbled muttering into Bible Week and were quickly ejected to those so disorganized that they were soon put away. Among these last were a near suicide and a woman who wrote with her feces on the walls of her home.

Between the temporarily out-of-touch and the very disorganized, were a variety of prospects who somehow managed to negotiate their day, but their success seemed at best problematic. Thus for several weeks the DP study group was graced with Sonya, a German immigrant in her mid-thirties who always wore a muslin coverall over pedal pushers and an ivory god-doll on a leather thong around her neck. The yellow scarf that covered her hair produced a resemblance to the Virgin Mary of Renaissance paintings. She was said to have "received" some years before that she was Eve, while a male friend had received that he was Adam. When Abel was on his way, Adam mysteriously disappeared. This woman was now raising her son and persisting in the belief that she was Eve. During the expressive phase of the study group she sometimes spent a number of soulful moments conversing with the kitchen faucet and often stared into space in a way that prompted one observer to comment: "Man, she leaves the scene." When back in the scene, Sonya was quite interested in the males present, once attempting to press a young man into a Center bedroom for unquestionable purposes. Lee plied her with invitations to dinner and residence and tried to dissuade her from merely being Eve, suggesting that a much higher spiritual status could be achieved. Sonya, however, seemed to prefer being Eve and gave up DP company.

Other disorganized prospects made more trouble for the scene room performance. Among these was Elinor, a tall, emaciated woman in her thirties who dressed entirely in black. She sat looking straight ahead with a stony, faraway expression during study groups, and large tears would sometimes stream down her cheeks. She refused to read from the book, and once while sitting next to Lester she leaned over and fell asleep on his shoulder, snoring loudly. Everyone either ignored her or cast only furtive glances in her direction. More precisely, they engaged in "studied inattention"; for she was, in fact, the main object of attention, especially when asleep and about to slide in a slumbering heap onto the floor.

In some meetings she would suddenly come to and stalk outside to smoke a cigarette. While out, Lee would take note of her, saying she. was not good for the atmosphere ("She breaks the spirit") and would then have the group sing a hymn in order to restore the spiritual level.

Upon returning from a cigarette break at what was to be her last meeting, Elinor indicated that she was not as far away as had been supposed. She angrily demanded of Lee: "Who is this leader? Is this leader the Messiah? Is God going to wreak vengeance on all those who do not accept this leader?" Lee refused to answer, saying that Elinor had to find the answers for herself. Elinor shot back: "You are not going to tell me?" Lee said no, and Elinor got up and walked out.

Elinor's character assassination and neutralization followed. Santini began by giggling that Elinor was demon-possessed. "She is absolutely full of the devil. You can see it all over her face." (She wore heavy make-up and looked as though she had been beaten around the eyes—or had slept not at all.) Lee announced that Elinor had a "silly problem." She had come to her a number of times and asked her to pray for the return of her boy friend who had deserted her. As was Lee's wont, she used the case as an object lesson on another point: Elinor had brought her own personal problems into the meeting. She should not do that. "You all have personal problems, but you do not bring them to the meeting." Elinor was also made the prototype of the person to whom not to witness: "Do not cast your pearls before swine."

In their anxiety to make converts, DP's even invited out-of-touch people to live in the Center. Pierre was among the most bizarre of these. He was jobless and about to be evicted from the Y.M.C.A. when he received a card from Bertha in the Mass Eatery in January, 1962. However, he was French, and Lee was always interested in people who knew foreign languages. The DP's paid his Y.M.C.A. bill and moved him into the Center.

Pierre was raised in France before and during World War II

and was brought to America at age fifteen by his father, a well-known French socialist and professor of Romance languages. He was too disorganized to attend school, and instead worked as a bus boy (in various establishments, as he was repeatedly fired) until finally in 1955 his father paid his passage to Israel, where he was to start a new life. He worked as a translator in an import office but soon grew tired of Israel. He became hallucinatory and was incarcerated after authorities discovered he had lain in a field for five days while experiencing repeated views of Christ on the cross. He remained hospitalized for two years and was eventually assigned to daytime work outside the grounds. Officials had persistently refused his request that he be returned to America, so Pierre decided to take matters into his own hands. After leaving the hospital one day, ostensibly to report for work, he stowed aboard a freighter, where he was eventually discovered and put ashore in Italy. Making his way to Paris, he located an aunt who paid his passage back to the United States and Bay City. His father was then a visiting professor at a nearby university, but he refused to assist his son financially. Then Pierre met the DP's.

Now thirty years old, Pierre was a short, but well-built and presentable man. His single costume consisted of a tweed coat, tie, white shirt, and dress pants. He was the slightly ragged European intellectual. In most first contacts he appeared to be aware of situational requirements; however, in any sustained interaction it became apparent that Pierre was not always "tuned in." One basic rule of interaction is that a person makes a reasonably relevant response upon being addressed, that one at least acknowledges receipt of a communication. Pierre often seemed incapable of this. Instead, he received a remark addressed to him as an occasion for discoursing disconnectedly. His "oral stream of consciousness" typically touched upon how bad the Nazis were, how bad the Bomb was, and why science should be abolished. Insofar as he made sense at all, he expressed unhappiness with what he felt to be *gesellschaft* society, often mentioning French peasants as the ideal people. Since he was almost never even remotely coherent, he was rarely taken seriously.

Soon after he took up residence, Lee asked him to do a French translation of the DP book, but he could not get beyond the first few pages. Neither could he get a job. First he was selling shoes door to door, but he rarely went out to work at it. Then he planned to sell an oilless skin cream and hair dressing (made from Arizona rocks) door to door, but he did little more than keep various creams smeared on his face and hair. His black hair was dull gray for some time. Daily Lee shooed him out of the house to look for a steady job, and daily he returned without one. After three months, he found work as a carpenter for a yacht builder, but that lasted only one week. Later a language-teaching company hired him to teach French to children. Again within a few days he was fired.

As he was around the house much of the time, he became a general nuisance. It took him more than an hour to shave in the morning because he kept running out of the bathroom to free associate with whoever was around at the moment. Breakfast in the Center was not communal, as residents worked at different hours; but Pierre was on hand as each person ate. Bleary-eyed and tired, DP's were subjected to sudden and shouted admonitions, such as "You shouldn't drink coffee; it's bad for you" (Pierre was also a health food fan) and "Don't use that milk; its got strontium 90 in it."

In study groups, Pierre continually brought up the Bomb, the Communist threat, the sad state of society, and the like, and never perceived the issues that could be joined or problems solved with the DP world view. He was a nagging distraction and cause of disruption in the scene room performance. Lee had to tell him repeatedly to "shut up."

His single saving feature was that he brought many people to the DP Center. None of the prospects he turned up came more than once, but he was at least adept at gaining initial access. He worked at this, he said, as a gesture of appreciation to the DP's for taking him in when he had no money. (He was building up quite a bed and board debt.) Because he was oblivious to rules of access in public places, he simply accosted people on the street with handbills and invitations to the Center. Mostly, however, he worked his old Y.M.C.A. haunt and the local French Club.

By April it was felt that it was impossible to convert Pierre. He was so open to evil spirits that he was nothing but a burden. Lee wanted to evict him but procrastinated, until an event occurred that brought the matter to a head. During a scene room performance in the first week of May, Pierre removed his shoes and shirt and wandered aimlessly in and out of the room. Such ruptures in the public front could not be tolerated and he was asked to leave.

Pierre begged to stay on, saying: "I will starve to death if I leave. This is the only group that is receptive of me." He looked for a place to live but seemed unable to locate anything. He lingered, and DP's worried that they would never be rid of him. Lee told him that he should be able to care for himself; Pierre threatened to sit permanently on the front steps if they put him out. Finally, quarters were found, and Pierre moved. Lee justified his dismissal with an analogy: "We are like an army. If one soldier drops, we cannot stop. We cannot have any weak persons among us."

In this and several other cases, the DP Center appeared to function as a "halfway house" for what might be called the mentally ill. Indeed, in one instance it functioned literally as an outpatient residence.

This was the case of Leo, who had joined the navy at eighteen, just after Pearl Harbor, and served eight years. Afterward he married and worked in a naval shipyard as a fork-lift operator, the job he held at the time of his conversion. In the late fifties he was badly injured in an automobile accident and was confined to bed with a neck and back injury for almost two years. He became religiously concerned during this time and oppressed by guilt over the sins of his navy days. He was also confused about his religious identity, since his father was a rabbi who had married out of the faith.

In May, 1962, a co-worker who was a sometime DP gave him a DP book. He read it and went to a Friday meeting. His performance that evening and weekend forecast his DP career. He was silent throughout the regular serial reading, but immediately after the prayers he suddenly began an emotional and disjointed address to the group on his religious pilgrimage. He told of seeing lights behind people's heads, and, indeed, much of his talk concerned "circles of light within circles of light" and "the eternal circle of all being." The group was silent as Lee answered him with nods and "uh-huhs." After more than an hour he concluded by saying that the meaning of all he had said was that he was a disciple of the Lord of the Second Advent. After this, Lee and the DP's were warm and accepting of him but rather cautious in encouraging his desire to move in with them.

He went home that evening, but at four the next morning he called Lee twice and rejected the DP as being of the devil. That morning he went door to door among his suburban neighbors, telling them the Lord of the Second Advent was here. He reported for work Monday, witnessed to his co-workers, and when his superior notified Leo's wife of his behavior, she had him committed.

He was released three weeks later and took up DP residence. Back on his job he was angry and fearful because a co-worker contained an evil spirit that was after him. He was again delivered to the asylum. After two months of confinement, he began receiving weekend passes. A month later he was released altogether and returned to the DP residence.

Leo was hardly more appreciated than Pierre and, indeed, was frequently referred to as "our English Pierre." He not only talked too much about biblical history in study groups, but also bared his soul too much by publicly lamenting his struggle to believe:

Everything in me tells me that I should leave [the DP]. There's no love in me. I swing between belief and unbelief with every paragraph I read [of the DP book]. The Devil is after me now; I walked with Satan all my life and loved it.

Like Pierre, Leo constantly wandered about the Center trying to start conversations and kept converts up until all hours of the night. He slept very little because he suffered from an oversupply of insulin, which made him hyperactive. A special diet to prevent insulin shock was required, and the necessity for Lee to prepare his meals separately was a further point of irritation.

Leo's three months of residence in the fall were a study in the problems of inducing a recalcitrant to act normally. He was daily counseled not to talk about the DP on his job, but he thought it necessary to tell his co-workers about the meaninglessness of their lives and how the end was at hand. Lee repeatedly warned that he would be sent back to the hospital, where he was still an outpatient. Although the DP's lectured him that it was a waste of time, he even tried to convert the psychiatrist during his therapy sessions.

In November, Leo's faith grew even less secure as he became more concerned over his wife's belief that he was crazy. Finally, he had a crisis of faith and began to pack his things. Lee warned him that if he left he could not come back. He would be cut off from the New Kingdom. She also confronted him with more proximate considerations: Where could he go? His wife would not take him back. If he lived alone, he would surely do something that would cause him to lose his job. Boxed in, Leo relented and regained his faith.

However, two days later he left the DP and returned to the asylum, where he remained until January, 1963. After that he continued to go back and forth between the Center and the asylum.

In general, although some who presented themselves to the DP's had been extensively mangled by society, the DP's were not averse to attempting to rebuild them in their own image.

COUNTERMISSIONARIES

The patently disorganized had difficulty grasping and abiding by social rules and were in that sense the furthest removed from DP—or any other—reality. Countermissionaries had a relatively firm grasp on some other religious reality and sought to show DP's the true way of regarding the world. They tended to be Christian fundamentalists, among them Mormons and Jehovah's Witnesses. But even they did not persist in efforts to win DP's. They quickly came to loggerheads with DP's on their disparate sources of revelation and soon went away.

At least one such missionary, however, took the DP tactic of defining the study as an open discussion of the Bible and came around to give out his words of salvation. This was Winton, a plump youth in Ivy League dress who presented himself as a scholarly fundamentalist. In meetings he would usurp Lee's role and teach the group what was "really" revealed in the Bible. Lee of course felt she knew more about this than Winton. In order to keep him quiet, she would say, "A student of truth must be slow in making conclusion" and "We did not invite you to teach us; we invited you to study with us." In spite of considerable rhetoric about an open discussion, Lee was not about to relinquish her role of indoctrinator.

Winton would be only momentarily silenced. As each new point was presented, he quoted what he felt to be discrediting scripture. Finally, after some weeks of being pushed into silence, he became exasperated and during a meeting challenged: "You reject Jesus Christ as God?" Santini shot back: "Of course we reject Jesus Christ as God." Winton replied: "O.K., that's it. Goodbye." He grabbed his briefcase, and with a flourish and a mocking smile he walked out.

Lee then engaged in a neutralization ceremony, telling how Winton had come to see her privately with a Bible and con- cordance and spouting Greek. She had "put him down" by telling him that she had taken Greek for five years (with an A +) and didn't need him to inform her. Converts commented that he probably did not know Greek anyway. Lee also used Winton to make a general point about witnessing: People who are sophis- ticated about the Bible are not readily convertible. One should find those who feel, not those who work with words and want to be intellectual about religion.[1]

Even though countermissionaries were open and complete un- believers espousing disparate doctrines, DP's were ready to spend a good deal of time with and displayed great interest in them. They, at least, saw the world in religious terms and thereby dealt

---

[1] This was of course only a line to fit the occasion. DP's were actually quite interested in gaining intellectual converts, as witness the role of Lester. However, they wanted "feeling" and intellect in the same person.

with the same sorts of superempirical issues. Unlike with liberal religionists, DP's at least shared a universe of discourse with fundamentalists.

EXPLOITERS

Countermissionaries attempted to exploit the DP in order to win over believers. They openly avowed this aim and set about achieving it. A number of "prospects," however, were not so forthright and attempted to extract some nonreligious benefit from the DP's, such as inexpensive room and board, money, power, customers, or sex.

Because the DP's had a propensity to extend co-residence to people with some minimum of open-mindedness, they at times became involved with people whose primary interest in the DP lay in the utilitarian matter of the modest sixty-dollar-a-month charge for bed and board.

Walter, the occultist, was without doubt the most enchanting among these cases. Thirty-three years of age, he possessed a large, protruding stomach and wore thick glasses, through which he peered with wide, bulging eyes in a slightly vacant stare. He wheezed loudly, his straight hair was usually uncut and falling over his forehead, and he had several blackened and missing teeth.

He was born in France of a French mother and a United States diplomat. After graduating from an exclusive military academy and spending an abortive year at an élite Ivy League college, he served four years in the air force as an electronics technician. He settled in Bay City after his discharge and worked as a warehouseman in a navy shipyard. At the time he met the DP's, he had lived alone for eight years. Although trained in electronics, he worked too slowly to hold employment in that field.

He was discovered at a flying saucer convention in August, 1961, and after attending meetings, he took up residence in December of the same year. DP's thought him an excellent prospect, for he appeared to be in full agreement with them and was thoroughly attuned to the religiously unconventional. He was, for example, a member of the board of directors of the Bay City Flying Saucer Club and served as Director of Communications (i.e., he set up and dismantled the public address system). He was also a long-time member of the Rosicrucians, as well as treasurer of their local lodge.

For many months the DP's regarded him as a member and accepted his excuse that he was not the type to go out and witness. Given his appearance and halting manner, DP's felt this to be a reasonable position. His good faith appeared to be demonstrated by the contribution of an additional fifteen dollars a month and by his regular appearance at the Tuesday night study group.

As the months passed, however, there developed a growing unhappiness over Walter's lack of commitment. Rather than spreading the word, he retired each evening to his room to read and listen to music and FM radio. He attended his Rosicrucian lodge meeting every Friday as well as the less frequent Flying Saucer Club gatherings. In later months, he frequently dozed off during the study group and sometimes even snored loudly.

In the minds of the DP's, Walter was serving too many masters and, more seriously, he was not serving *their* Master. Complaints began that Walter was interested only in their cheap bed and board, and he was soon told that he need not attend study groups if he did not feel like it.

The DP's hypothesis regarding Walter's motives received support from his consumption of unbelievable amounts of food. A typical breakfast consisted of a quart pan of oatmeal. At dinner, he literally heaped his plate with rice, soybeans, salad, and meat. He shoved food into his mouth nonstop and generally finished a meal before anyone else. His second helpings rivaled the first in size. Estimating conservatively, he consumed three to four times more than any other male at the residence. During and after meals he frequently grunted, belched, moaned, and rubbed his swollen stomach, apparently in pain, although upon inquiry he always claimed to feel fine.

By the spring of 1962, Walter had become increasingly uncomfortable around the DP's. Although subtle, their pressures were making the alternatives open to him crystal clear: become a deployable agent or get out. In August, he departed.

While other bed and board exploiters were nonbelievers whose rejection and even contempt of the DP's eventually became apparent, Walter's stance presents a somewhat more complex picture. He was actually quite tolerant of their views. In order to understand how it was that he did not fall into either rejection or full belief, it is necessary to ask about the way in which he conceived reality.

For Walter, vibrations were the basic unit of reality. Everything had a "vibratory level," and persons at one or another such level sent and received the same kind of vibrations. Thus people who liked one another were said to have vibrations that harmonized. He spoke of his relations to the DP's in terms of their mutual vibrations being different; his of course were higher than theirs.

All worldly problems were actually due to the earth itself being out of tune with the universe. There was too much "negative polarity" at the moment, and the earth was therefore being "bombarded" with "positive polarities" to bring it back into its correct polarity. This was an impersonal and automatic process that functioned in the same way that a sick cell in the human body is worked upon by bodily processes to restore its proper order.

Because people are at different vibratory levels, they have to be sent signals that they can receive and understand (in the same way that an AM radio can receive only AM signals). Religious movements differ from one another because they are receiving vibrations appropriate to their particular vibratory level. The DP's were part of this general changing of polarity on earth, although as fundamentalists they were at a fairly low vibratory level. Higher levels did not take the Bible so literally.

Because of these differences, all people should not be in the same group. Higher types like himself, said Walter, were suited for the open, permissive rationality of the Rosicrucians, while lower types needed groups like the DP that imposed strict authority and operated on faith. Thus one can understand why

Walter told the DP's that he agreed with them and how he could be so tolerant and accepting. While they espoused a world view that explained him, he espoused one that explained them. (He never revealed these views to the DP's.)

Walter's image of himself, his views on basic human problems, and some of his activities should be further noted. They are testimony to the infinity of human belief.

For Walter, death was a change of vibratory level. The "real" person was a set of vibrations that resided in bodies now and again. Walter was incarnated in his present condition because in his previous life he had been a man of money and power who began to think he was the sole repository of truth. Because of this he was brought back into an environment where most people thought they were the sole repositories of truth, so that he would learn that this was an improper attitude. However, in spite of his present low estate, he was definitely part of the spiritual élite and above the common man in his understanding. He and the Rosicrucians were tuned into some of the highest vibrations.

Walter was convinced that before his incarnation as a man of means he had been a resident of the planet Venus. He had determined this by the following deduction: "I must have come from another world; otherwise I would not have been so confused as a child." In childhood, he had wondered what his parents were like in his previous incarnations and what they would be like in later ones. Since no one had told him about reincarnation at this tender age, he felt that he must have remembered it from an actual bodily sojourn.

Against this background one can understand Walter's reading and listening habits. He studied all manner of occult publications and was at the same time a daily reader of the *Wall Street Journal* (on the basis of which he talked intelligently about the events of conventional reality, particularly stock market fluctuations). *The Listener* and *Signs of the Times* (Seventh Day Adventist) were among his magazine subscriptions. Educational FM was his main radio listening, and to exercise his mind, as he put it, Walter worked out trigonometry problems while riding the bus to and from work. His place in the text was marked with Manual Number Three of the Master Level of the Rosicrucians. In short, Walter ingested all manner of information that might, from a conventional point of view, seem dissonant—if not downright contradictory. But armed with his vibratory conceptions, he could passively accept anything as being a part of the truth and go happily through the day seeing himself as one of the inconspicuous vibratory élite. He was a true son of the Twentieth Century.

The Reverends Stein and Santini were exploiters of a quite different type. Although promoting the impression of having converted to the DP, they were, in fact, on a devious quest for customers for their spiritualist church. Their association with the DP's began in June, 1961, and ran until late 1962, when, as the DP's caught on to them, their interest waned.

Santini, who was twenty-five and a native of Bay City, always dressed in a baggy black suit and floral tie. He plastered his black hair straight back from his thin face. His throat muscles seemed perpetually in a state of tension, highlighting a scar that ran from his right ear to his Adam's apple. The effeminate character of his body style was exaggerated by a slightly spastic left arm and leg.

He seemed to have spent considerable time in local mental hospitals. He sometimes told anecdotes about conditions in these hospitals, and particularly about his personal experiences, such as being strapped to a bed in a violent ward. Born a Catholic, he was "saved" in his late teens by a Pentecostal group and missionized for them before leaving the church to become a medium and spiritualist minister. Among his numerous claimed credentials was ordination by Billy James Hargis. However, the ordination certificate that hung in his church was issued by a Florida diploma mill, and was available for the modest fee of thirty-three dollars. Stein, the senior member of the team, was in his mid-sixties. His sagging face was marked by a mouth and eye twitch. His costume never varied: loud and slightly outdated sport coats and bow ties. Most of his life he had worked as a night watchman. While Santini claimed complete faith, Stein proclaimed the accomplishment of "ninety per cent" faith.

This pair formed a team of aging master and talented protégé.

Their one night a week spiritualist church was located in a decrepit office building. The room, already outfitted as a chapel, was used on six other nights by people with similar enterprises. Santini worked as a night clerk in a rundown hotel, but in this room he was the minister who delivered "spirit messages" and conducted "healing." Stein acted as the associate minister, delivering sermons and performing custodial functions.

There were more than fifteen of these one-night churches in Bay City, and mediums circulated among them as guest speakers and guest mediums. Stein and Santini were highly involved in this circuit. Attendance at these various services averaged six or seven people, although it sometimes ran as high as twenty when other mediums were present.

Like most spiritualist ministers, Stein and Santini were running a deficit enterprise. The DP's often attended their church as a means of proselytizing Stein and Santini, as well as of finding new prospects. The pair were most interested in having DP's at their services, for it gave them one of the largest congregations in the spiritualist milieu. In addition, prospects discovered by the DP's sometimes went on to attend Stein and Santini's services, thereby boosting their business even more.

This arrangement remained a mutually satisfactory one for some months, but the activities of Stein and Santini both in and out of the study group eventually led to disenchantment on the part of the DP's.

Upon entering the DP residence for a meeting, the pair made a grand show of affection, calling Lee "our little mother" and referring to the other converts as "brothers," "sisters," and "our family." (This was appropriate when DP's were among themselves, but Stein and Santini violated the rule of not flaunting it before prospects and other strangers.) In addition, Santini's actions patently contradicted the team's efforts to appear as members. He laughed and snickered, nudged, gestured to, and engaged in giggling byplay with Stein. Written notes were exchanged, and Santini often carried on gleeful, whispered conversations with his partner over some passage in the book—this while the rest of the study group was attending to the reading in dead earnest. Instead of bowing his head during prayers, as was the approved stance, he leafed through his book or gazed about, grinning at any others he might discover who had also failed to bow. (In contrast, when *he* prayed, his eyes were tightly shut, his palms clasped together and held high, and his prayer shouted forth with Pentecostal fervor.)

Stein attempted to remain unresponsive to Santini's invitations to editorialize on the scene. He ignored him or responded with disapproving glances. The rest of the group displayed great inattention to these antics, although they most certainly did not pass unnoticed.

Santini also felt it necessary to dominate discussions and to come on as an infallible expert. He virtually shouted down opposition, even though the approved (i.e., Lee's) style called for calm (albeit firm) reasoning and explanation. Although Santini was sometimes guilty of rather large doctrinal errors, he often acted as though he knew the DP better than Lee. His initial assertions were so firm that it was nearly impossible for him to retreat gracefully when Lee corrected his errors. He extricated himself by claiming the question was poorly stated and confusing or by insisting he had addressed a different aspect of the question. That these ploys were clumsily performed in response to what were, in fact, clear-cut issues did not escape notice among DP's.

Stein's forte was pontification. He was the wise old man. He always stood when speaking and intoned loudly but slowly, as though his were the authoritative last word. Gazing intently around the room, he seemed to dare anyone to interrupt his drone of wisdom. The character of this wisdom may be judged from the following, delivered on an occasion when Pierre was disrupting the study group.

There is a statement. You have probably heard it made very often. BE STILL AND KNOW. BE STILL AND KNOW. This is the first statement I make. The second one is to withdraw into your closet, retire into your closet, into your own secret place. This is another statement. I give you only two. Just be still and know, and to withdraw into your closet.

You know, uh, I have often thought, and I've told Rev. Santini of asking Miss Lee's permission to talk to this group, especially to several here, for a short length of time anyway, to give an exposition of my own faith. Permit me, Miss Lee, for a few moments to give an exposition of my own faith.

Uh, if we can, I'll go back to the same thought, be still and know. You can be still. Hold your tongue, if you can. Keep your peace, if you can. Withdraw into your closet, if you can. This is difficult for the impetuous youth, I know. It is very difficult. It is a test also. It is one of Satan's tests. For a purpose.

Lee defended against these defective participants by attempting to speak herself or by abruptly calling on the next person to read. But in contrast with her treatment of Elmer, she never insulted them into silence, if, indeed, that was possible.

In the early months of their association, DP's wanted to pressure Santini especially into moving into the DP Center and joining the cosmic battle. Efforts to accomplish this were minimal, however, because the group viewed the situation as a sensitive one. The two men shared an apartment and, the DP's said, slept in the same bed. For this and other reasons, they were thought to be lovers. And according to the DP's, this relationship prevented Santini from leaving Stein and becoming a full-fledged convert.

Santini did, however, take and pass the difficult DP exam required for full membership,[2] and he continued to make strong

---

[2] One of the requirements of full discipleship was a thorough mastery of the DP book. This mastery was determined by three three-hour written examinations. To help aspirants prepare for these, Lee had drawn up a study list of 192 questions. Each of the three exams consisted of ten questions drawn from that list. Lee graded the responses quite strictly against a standard of how close each came to regurgitating her text. (She employed a finely cut scale of one hundred on each answer.)

This examination was no mere formality. Lee did not hesitate to fail anyone and, in fact, flunked Elmer, Minnie, Bertha, Merwin, and Alice on their first set, although they all passed on the second try.

Some of the more interesting questions from that list dealing with minor doctrinal points will further suggest the DP's scope and elaboration possibilities.

professions of belief. During the time of the July, 1962, dispersion, DP's urged him, with considerable insistence, to take up residence. Sorrowfully, Santini refused. The spirits in the hotel in which he worked were so low that he became ill when making abrupt transitions to the Center, where the spirits were very high. Daily changes of such magnitude were too much for his constitution. In addition, he counseled people of very low spiritual levels, and he could not have such types coming to the Center and polluting it. DP's accepted his excuses, while privately noting them to be just that. They did not suggest the obvious option open to him: to quit his job and spiritualism. They felt that if he did not care enough to make these changes on his own initiative, he was not worth having. In the fall of 1962, both Stein and Santini were pressured to move in, but to no avail. They explained that they were teaching the DP in their church and spreading the word quietly in their own way.

The DP's were unconvinced, and by early 1963 had become thoroughly disenchanted with the pair. The idea that Stein and Santini were interested only in using the DP's as a source of people for their own spiritualist church was discussed openly. At their now infrequent appearances at the study group, they were given cool receptions, but nevertheless continued to gush with their standard family rhetoric and (now seen to be) phony affect. In January, 1963, Santini produced a manuscript that he claimed to be the rewritten and real book of Romans. The Apostle Paul had clairaudiently dictated it to him in order to tell the world what he, Paul, had really meant to say. The manuscript not sur-

---

How do you prove that God has the duality of male and female in His essentiality?

How is energy produced?

How do the planets maintain their positions and motions?

What is the purpose of marriage?

Why do people sometimes receive the name of a person who has passed away?

When will heathen religions be fulfilled?

What are the twelve events of resemblance in the lives of Jacob, Moses, and Jesus?

What is the significance of the [nineteenth-century] missionary movement?

prisingly proved to be entirely supportive of the DP. The DP's, however, received this document with polite, but passive interest. Santini, it was said, was merely attempting to re-establish himself in the group so as to use them further. In response to the increasingly cool and unsupportive DP attitude toward them, Stein and Santini soon gave up participation altogether.

As mentioned previously, Minnie and Bertha sometimes used the pickup façade as well as vague invitations as a device to bring men to the DP Center. It is therefore hardly surprising that among DP associates there were men whose interests were more sexual than religious. During their first year in Bay City, the women witnessed to many young men in military uniforms who were to be found wandering downtown. These invitees found themselves innocent exploiters of the DP scene. For the most part they were well-behaved, absorbing their disappointment gracefully and departing with little ado. A few, however, made passes at Bertha or Minnie anyway, although the situation was never allowed to get out of control. One such brief episode involved a priest, who appeared late one night to confess his loss of faith and to make sexual overtures to Lee. Such aggressively sexual men were ordered in no uncertain terms to depart.

In a few instances, however, Bertha and Minnie took an interest in men who were known to have sexual motives in the hope, it was said, of transforming their interest. Feeling there was an explosive potential in such activity, Lee usually terminated the relations as soon as she learned of them.

In one prolonged instance of sexual misinvolvement there was a reverse sequence of perceived motives. That is, the male began with more or less religious concerns, which over time were supplanted by sexual ones. This involved Minnie's pursuit by Trouver.

Trouver, in his early sixties, was an investigator for the aid to dependent children division of the district attorney's office. He claimed to have once worked with the F.B.I. on "subversive activities" and was wont to present himself as a detective. A longtime spiritualist, he was a frequent guest speaker in spiritualist churches of the type run by Stein and Santini.

He first learned of the DP's in March, 1961, from an Amhurst

College lecture announcement. Upon attending study groups he appeared quite interested and became enough of a believer to consider leaving his wife for DP residence. Although he did not do so, he did help the group in various other ways. Fancying himself a public speaker, he provided the DP's with free lessons in the art. He also began to insert DP views into his own speeches at spiritualist churches, although this practice was not appreciated by his audiences and led to a decline in invitations to speak.

It was he who suggested and arranged for the DP's to organize as a corporation as a basis upon which to secure a permanent visa for Lee. The original corporation documents of September, 1961, listed him as a director.

However, as early as mid-summer, 1961, Trouver had begun to show too little interest in DP doctrine and too much interest in Minnie. When she got off work at midnight he was there to drive her home, and when she began a shift at four in the morning he was on hand to deliver her. Trouver was to be found in Mass Eatery extraordinarily often and at all manner of unusual hours trying to engage Minnie in conversation. Noticing his rather odd hours and large blocks of time away from home, Trouver's wife learned of the DP's and called Lee to complain. Lee reported having attempted to restrain Trouver and instructed Minnie to discourage him. He persisted, however, and even went on to offer Minnie various expensive gifts and, indeed, to propose marriage.

Lee was quite unhappy with the situation, but felt constrained to keep Trouver around because of his demonstrated value in corporation matters. She counseled Minnie to be kind but firm in her resistance to sexual overtures. Perhaps his ardor would diminish in time.

That time was not long in arriving. One morning toward the end of September, Minnie left the Center en route to her early morning shift. She found Trouver waiting to give her a ride. She accepted his offer, and, upon arrival, as she was about to alight from his car, he leaned over and kissed her. The restaurant was but a few blocks from Trouver's residence, and at that moment his wife, who was in search of him, arrived to behold this romantic scene. She began screaming various uncomplimentary phrases and lunged toward Minnie with what one informant described as a "sharp cutting instrument." Minnie scurried into Mass Eatery, screaming, "You're the instrument of Satan," and managed to lock herself in the toilet. Thwarted, the wife retreated, but she had gained the final victory. Trouver had no further contact with the DP's and, indeed, even gave up speechmaking in spiritualist churches.[3]

CONVENTIONALS

The alignments described thus far were displayed by relatively few people but involved DP's over extended periods. The category of conventionals was occupied by relatively large numbers but involved DP's for very short periods, typically one, or perhaps a few, meetings.

Conventionals were people who operated within and were attached to conventional perspectives yet, for one reason or another, temporarily situated themselves in a scene produced and sustained by another kind of reality.

Most conventionals were casual acquaintances of some DP. From experience in familial, work, religious, or other settings, they became curious or concerned about the DP and its effect upon the person they knew. They knew little about the religiously exotic and did not display existential orientations; they became briefly involved only because they were confronted by the DP as someone with whom they happened to have dealings for other purposes. Thus, for example, there was a slow trickle of people from Elmer's hospital, and whenever Bertha or Minnie changed

---

[3] Due to space limitations, two other exploiters whose association was concurrent with that of Walter and Trouver can be mentioned only briefly. One was a thirtyish commercial seaman and apartment house handyman who was raised in South America of Dutch-Indian parents. He exploited the DP's for bed and board for some five months. The other, a Southern Rhodesian Anglo-Saxon in his middle twenties, who worked next to Minnie at Mass Eatery, likewise took advantage of the DP's. His numerous affairs with extra-DP women and a final sexual entanglement with Bertha led to his expulsion.

jobs there came a renewed set of one-time study group attenders. After Lester's conversion in State U. City, there was a string of acquaintances from the student religious centers, from the university chorus (of which he had been a member), and from his former seminary.

Only a few conventionals found the DP through a disembodied message or from being approached in a public place. Those who came to the DP in this fashion were usually on a lark.

During study groups, conventionals typically projected themselves as polite and neutral silent participants. They read at their turn, asked few or no questions, and maintained an emotional blankness. Neither approval nor disapproval was detectable. If a conventional happened to escape Lee's sizing-up ceremony, he quickly withdrew after the meeting.

Most often such people did not get away so easily and were forced to undergo queries as to who they were, what they did, and, most important, their impression of what they had just "studied." Typically, these ceremonies provided fascinating sociological studies in how people with disparate world views manage to get along together, at least for brief periods. Conventionals managed to exercise considerable tact and to withhold their actual opinions and impressions. In this way, the world was made safe for both the DP's and themselves. Through innocuous, vague remarks ("It's very interesting"), conventionals avoided the embarrassment of appearing radically displaced in the setting. In response to questions such as "Does this conflict with your belief?" conventionals might reply, "Not overly, no." This tact was perhaps a species of the humoring process that sometimes obtains between people who are radically at odds. One party simply goes along for the sake of getting past an otherwise hopeless encounter.[4]

While DP's sometimes recognized merely polite and tactful treatment for what it was, more often they formed the impression that conventionals were interested. Since the DP's had a hap-

---

[4] As has been seen, DP's also engaged in extensive humoring because many people "just wouldn't understand." The overt-covert access dimension could be conceived of as a systematic implementation of humoring.

hazard way of following up on prospects and in any case did not believe in pressure beyond a few telephone calls, the consequences for the conventionals of such misunderstandings were minimal. The consequences for the DP's themselves were much greater. Most of the time they believed that there were more prospective converts than was, in fact, the case. Failure of a tactful conventional to display further interest merely indicated that Satan had worked on him. This was part of the cosmic game; when "things" became more obvious, such people would quickly come around. Thus tactful conduct promoted an exaggerated conception of the pool of latent converts.

Although most conventionals successfully sustained polite neutrality and emotional blandness, a few had problems with "breaking up" or "flooding out." [5] The propensity to flood out was especially high among those who had attended a study group in the company of other conventionals. As the tension mounted, such people found it necessary to avoid eye contact with their companions in order to stifle a laugh.

Some who experienced acute flooding out tensions attempted to cope with them by intently fixing their attention upon the reading and the remarks of the speakers. This defense against impulse expression may be seen as the situational version of the more general strategy whereby exactly those who are furthest from a given reality feel most obliged to appear closest to it.

Once safely away from the DP Center, conventional companions released their tensions in peals of laughter and uncomplimentary remarks about their former hosts. Such delayed flooding out was a form of the quite general practice of treating others' faces relatively well and their backs quite badly, the latter process functioning to dissipate the sense of concession, compromise, and pollution generated by the former process.

The reverse role, that of the open scoffer, was quite rare. Countermissionaries directly challenged DP's but *were* attuned to religious issues, and in that sense shared in DP reality by

---

[5] Erving Goffman, *Encounters* (Indianapolis: Bobbs-Merrill Company, Inc., 1961), pp. 55-61.

taking it seriously. Open scoffers who happened into the DP Center—mostly State U. students on a lark—denied the relevance or rationality of religious systems per se. Rather than merely disputing the exact character of God's will or of the mission of Jesus, they struck at these notions themselves. Thus one evening two male undergraduates treated Lee and her doctrines flippantly and were aggressively hostile to DP "stupidity." One of them concluded his visit with the definitive declaration of pseudo–rational man: "I base my life on logic." The DP's allowed themselves overt anger with open scoffers and repeatedly tried to silence them with: "You came here to be told; you should be listening, not criticizing." They knew, of course, that they were observing the work of Satan.

VETERAN SEEKERS

Almost every community in America has a stratum of middle-aged women who avocationally attend to the religiously exotic and occult. Rarely committed to any religion, they instead carve out a career of studying each religious fad that arises. They are the first to listen and perhaps lend some support to new religious movements and the first to move on to even newer ones. Wherever one finds a spokesman claiming some esoteric new synthesis, wherever one finds a spiritualist church, there one discovers veteran seekers.[6] Although they may be active in conventional churches, they feel such organizations to be lacking in spiritual nourishment. Veteran seekers are afflicted with metaphysical lusting for such proper food as "higher understanding," and "deeper knowledge."

Contrary to the famous biblican dictum, these seekers never seem to find. They believe everything and nothing, for no new

---

[6] See, for example, W. R. Catton, "What Kinds of People Does a Religious Cult Attract?" *American Sociological Review*, Vol. XXII (October, 1957), 561-566. Relative to the historical and cultural universality of veteran seekers, consider Paul's experience at the Court of Areopagus in Athens. "The Athenians in general and the foreigners there had no time for anything but talking or hearing about the latest novelty" (Acts of the Apostles 17:16-21 NEB).

system makes any difference in how they live. If married, they go on keeping house; if maiden or widowed and working, their vocation goes forth. They simply accumulate miscellaneous religious information. Veteran seekers may be likened to scholars who collect data but never get around to organizing an assessment or analysis of them.

Whenever DP's arrived in a community, veteran seekers were predominant among their first audiences. Lee was inspected by most of the veterans in Northwest Town and even promoted five into an association that lasted almost a year. While living in Maple Hill, Lee ventured into occult groups forty to a hundred miles to the north and again snared a network of veterans with whom she worked for over six months. And upon setting up shop in Bay City, the DP's were active the first few months with the city's numerous veterans who came by to hear this latest dogma.

The fact that these three streams of prospects produced no conversions forced the DP's to conclude that this kind of person did not have, as one DP put it, the "oomph." Veterans enjoyed study groups and contemplation of the ethereal, but they were uninterested in dedicating themselves to remaking the world. Their conception of revolution was a genteel one: people would gradually awaken spiritually, and the world would change. But, as has been mentioned, such world awakening would not in any way interrupt their seeking.

DP's disparagingly referred to veteran seekers as "religious bums," who were neither coming from nor going to any place in particular.

By the end of 1961, Lee was teaching her converts to avoid anyone over forty, which meant avoid veteran seekers. In their anxiety to interest someone, however, converts continued to bring in a few such people, but upon sizing them up, any warmth or encouragement to return was withheld.

Beyond their failure to convert, there was an equally cogent reason for avoiding involvement with veteran seekers. In Northwest State they did not simply inspect the DP and move on, but learned the DP's insider portions, defined Lee as a communist, and called in the F.B.I.

In her first Northwest State efforts, Lee had not yet learned that veteran seeker interest did not indicate propensity to convert, and thereby she misjudged what should and should not be revealed. Thus she went beyond the DP text and shocked the veterans with the statements that Jesus was no long important and that there would be no churches in a few years. Church buildings, she said, were to become social halls after the one universal religion emerged. The good ladies were likewise taken aback by Lee's observation that in the near future they would have to leave their families if their spouses did not accept and follow the D.P.

Lee held a party for the study group in early April, 1960, and toward the end of the evening circulated a sheet of paper for the guests to sign. She explained that this was an attendance record, and that while they did not know the importance of what they were doing, this was a great day both in Korea and in world history. Vast changes in the world would begin from that day.[7] She displayed a portrait of Chang and venerated it to such an extent that one veteran later remarked: "I could see she was putting that man up as a God." This lady, the Mrs. Quinby mentioned earlier, had read Kenneth Goff [8] on the plot to institute a "red world ruler" and suspected Lee was part of it. She aired her suspicions to another veteran in the study group, and they jointly concluded that Lee was indeed a communist agent trying to build a front group and infiltrate the churches. Had Lee not said she wanted to get important churchmen interested in her teachings so they would lead others into a new faith that would destroy all present religion? Had she not said that someday they would realize why she had come to America? Was she not claiming to be a Christian, while at times saying that Jesus and current Christianity should be forgotten? Had Lee not said that they lived communally in Korea? Had she not predicted that the government of that fine Korean Christian, Syngman Rhee, would fall,

---

[7] This was the first "Parents Day," the day that Chang married his divine consort. This day and its functions are discussed in Chap. 11.

[8] Among Goff's numerous pamphlets, see in particular, *One World A Red World* (Englewood, Colorado: Kenneth Goff, 1952).

and had she not been happy when it happened? The evidence
was overwhelming; Mrs. Quinby contacted the F.B.I.

Likewise—and independent of Mrs. Quinby and her group—
a network of four veterans in a community north of Northwest
Town subjected themselves to Lee's teachings for several months
and finally concluded that she and her budding converts were
at best anti-Christs, and at worst subversives. This group's oldest
member expressed their sentiments:

I think its a subversive movement, definitely. There's too many signs
in the way they operate, their methods of living and doing things.
It's not in their [book or in] anything that could be detected, but it's
in what they are doing and what they tell that's not written down.
You know the more I think about it the more I think the F.B.I. should
be called in on this. It's subtle. They come in the name of religion
and compromise people's souls through fear and curses on their families
and sin and immorality. . . .

They don't tell much to anyone following until they've been thoroughly brainwashed and they think they have them thoroughly caught
in their snare, and then they tell them about the curses and dreadful
things that will happen to their souls if they don't continue on, and
if friend husband won't come, then he's the devil and an evil spirit.

I don't want any part of this new organization, new government, new
schools, new way of life under Master Chang's rule, "The Christ"
come in a new body.

They intend to take over and destroy our family, community, and
governmental way of life, and they say so and [are] ruthless in their
tactics, too. [They are] plenty tough [and] instill such fear. We got
that far along to get a good taste of that and find out that much, but
of course we faced them with the truth and the scriptures to back it
up, and they fled from us.

Although veterans were wont to condemn moral laxness in
modern life and although they thought of themselves as above
politics, they nonetheless eschewed participation in definite efforts
for collective regeneration and even retreated to a curious kind of
patriotism.

FRESHMEN SEEKERS

Freshmen seekers are junior versions of veteran seekers. Typically younger, less knowledgeable, and less fully imbued with an

occult-spiritualistic world view, they are embarking on a career that might lead to veteran seekership, radical religious espousal, or, under changed conditions, a return to more conventional world views (or possibly into other types of deviant activity).

Freshmen seekers came closest to the sort of ideally prepared people whom DP's sought. Indeed, pre-DP's were at least freshmen seekers, although they seemed to have gone somewhat beyond the incipient seeking that was the distinctive mark of the freshman.

I am hesitant to classify all freshmen seekers as religious seekers. Their seeking always possessed a religious element, but in many instances it coexisted with other kinds of concerns that could at any time supplant the religious ones.

The most conspicuous cases of this multi-directioned, tentative seeking were found among the DP's "Evangeline contingent." This was a changing set of unmarried women who lived in the Evangeline residence of the Salvation Army in downtown Bay City. They were classic portraits of the lonely working girl in the city: high school graduates working in menial office positions, usually far from home. Typically in their early twenties, their lives were devoid of eligible males and opportunities for marriage. Such women trickled through the DP because Greta, Ludwig's German friend, lived in Evangeline and regularly invited fellow residents to the Center. They had little else to do with their evenings so two or more Evangeline people were always at DP meetings, although as many as eight or ten were present on occasion.

Most Evangeline women attended one or a few of the DP meetings and returned only sporadically, if at all. In addition, they visited spiritualist and other offbeat churches, as well as the more conventional types. Many, indeed, appeared less interested in religious dogma than in (religious) places where males were to be found.

Two of them, however, became fixtures at DP gatherings, although they were never converted and became something of a problem. These were Dagna, a file clerk employed by the state, and Lucy, a keypunch operator for a large corporation. The short, fat Dagna's most notable feature was convulsive giggling in the presence of males, irrespective of their attractiveness or marriage-ability. Her close friend, Lucy, had conspicuous buck teeth and spoke in a very slow, lazy manner. Although less obviously stimulated by proximate males, she was nonetheless highly interested in them.

Dagna and Lucy attended DP functions for more than a year and a half. They assumed the stance of the very interested, if not, indeed, the near convert, although they declined invitations to DP residence. They and other Evangeline women seemed content with two visits a week and appeared to define them as social nights out. After all, at the DP's one could discuss religion while in the company of young men.

The DP's had not anticipated this use of their gatherings, but having defined them as a place to "just come and study" they had, in fact, laid themselves open for, and defenseless against, it. DP's frequently told new prospects (in the presence of people like Dagna and Lucy) that the DP's *only* desired one to attend their groups. Dagna and Lucy thus had a firm basis on which to attend study groups month after month.

Moreover, Dagna and Lucy did not appear to be consciously misinvolved with the DP's. It seemed, in fact, that neither of them really understood what it was all about. Each claimed to have read the DP book at home; each had been through it many times in the study group; each had heard most of the insider portions; each had many times heard Lee and others speak of judgment by 1967, the Lord being on earth, and all the rest. In spite of this they retained some vague notion that Lee was running a small occult study group. Thus, for example, no new prospects were present one evening and Lee explicitly and at length told how The Leader was going to restore the world in two or three years —maybe sooner, maybe later. Toward the end of Lee's discourse, Lucy, who had at this time been participating in study groups for fourteen months, asked in good-natured puzzlement: "Oh, where did you get that idea?" Lee was aghast and snapped: "You find out."

Dagna had attended DP functions for seven months when she was startled to realize that DP's were propounding "the overthrow of the United States government." The thought of such a thing scared her, she said, but not very much or for very long apparently, as her DP social life continued for many months thereafter.

DP's were prepared to wait patiently for a few months for people to convert, but they were quite unhappy with those who turned their premises into a setting for extended sociability. They were warm, permissive, and attentive to Dagna and Lucy for many months. In talks with the girls, Lee emphasized that everyone was lonely, but marriage was not the answer because the real cause was being "cut off" from God. In any event, in a few years marriages would be made in the movement (heaven?) so there was no reason to be concerned about men in the present. Lee had sized up her prospects and was offering the DP's strongest appeal to these deprived women.

Upon dispersion in July, 1962, Dagna and Lucy were pressured to live in the DP Center (in part, for the very real reason that the group needed the money). They declined, but continued to come on as "almost" converts. After this, DP's either ignored or spoke bluntly to them. Thus Lee threatened on numerous occasions:

You girls had better be careful; God will not respond to you because you are taking so long [to start] to work for this movement. If you respond to God quickly, God will respond to you quickly.

"Respond" meant that the women should at least witness for the DP. Lucy and Dagna maintained that they were trying to witness at Evangeline, but their co-residents thought the DP's were crazy and refused further association. (Evangeline was, after all, a "good Christian" women's residence.)

Lee also threatened them with unusually harsh judgment in the New Age accounting because God particularly frowns upon those who know about the DP and do not work for it. Such threats had no discernible effect. Like thousands of not-too-intelligent, frustrated women they continued down the road to veteran seekership.

Except for lack of affective bonds with the DP's (which in

spite of all their participation they definitely lacked) and except for not being at a turning point, Dagna and Lucy were excellent candidates for conversion. One can, in fact, speculate that had there been DP males to whom they were strongly attracted and had they come to a turning point, they would indeed have converted. Both women did entertain the DP with some seriousness; slightly changed situational conditions would likely have won them.

Most other freshman seekers who flirted with belief likewise failed to convert through lack of development of the proper situational conditions, especially through lack of affective bonds. However, in one unusual instance, a convert was lost through a peculiar reduction in acutely felt tensions.

This occurred with Alvin, who was well-built from the waist up but whose legs were so very short that he was hardly more than four feet tall. He failed out of a Bay City Catholic college after high school but continued in its night school, hoping to gain readmission to full-time study. Unable to obtain steady employment, he lived at home and occupied himself as a volunteer leader in Catholic youth activities. During an athletic contest sponsored by one such group, he injured his legs and was hospitalized. The ward orderly was Elmer, and since Alvin had already dabbled in the occult, he responded to Elmer's invitation to study the Precepts. Although on crutches for some months after his release from the hospital, he came to the Center frequently (often overnight) and under Lee's warm tutelage was coming close to conversion.

Alvin was at the same time bashfully aspiring to success in the entertainment field, having been a high school and church vocalist. A local television station conducted a talent show, in which weekly winners were decided by postcard ballots from the audience. Every few months, the weekly winners vied on a single program for "grand winner." Alvin was accepted as a contestant and in May, 1962, was voted weekly winner.

His parents were devout Catholics and became quite worried about his frequent visits with the DP's. After he had won the talent show, they announced that they would buy him a new car.

Driving lessons and special hand controls would of course be provided. They demanded, however, that he give up his visits to the DP's.

His conception of himself as an entertainer was now greatly strengthened, and he began to seek that kind of employment. Local public transportation was limited, and the car greatly increased his independence from his parents, who had formerly had to drive him about. These conventional, solid supports of his personal worth abruptly decreased his acute tensions, and he dropped the DP's. And, as in the classic account, "he went away with a heavy heart; for he was a man of great wealth." [9]

---

[9] (The Gospel According to Mark 10:22 NEB).

chapter 9

Promotion Tactics

Having discussed the characteristics and problems of both prospects and promotion vehicles, it is possible to describe the more important promotion tactics.

Promoting Affect: Warmth and Permissiveness

Despite disdain for false friendliness, the DP's consistently engaged in self-conscious affectation of affability. They pretended warm and friendly interest in a peculiar and faltering Carnegie-Peale effort to "win friends and influence people." Thus, on one occasion, after having watched Elmer perform a spate of affectation, I commented: "You're certainly a friendly person." He replied: "You have to be if you are going to win people. You grit your teeth and smile anyway." Minnie once related during a reflective conversation on the problems of witnessing at Mass Eatery that she tried to make each person she served feel as though he were the only person in the world. In this she said she was following the teaching of Miss Lee, "who told us that wc arc all actors and actresses for the Precepts, and that we have roles to play and we should play them to the hilt."

Lee had a particularly warm style. She greeted prospects with broad smiles and gentle bows and continually initiated conversations with them. While inquiring into matters of background and current well-being, she projected an impression of genuine personal concern. This elaborate warmth and inquisitiveness was, at times, not only inappropriate but embarrassing, for prospects were at best mere acquaintances. Thus Lee felt it proper to greet one male prospect who had attended a few meetings by holding his hand and warmly asking how he was. Later in the meeting she sat beside him, placed her hand on his knee, and stroked it while she again inquired into his intimate life situation. While shaking hands upon meeting or parting, she was prone to make such comments as "My, what warm hands you have." And of course she was always very interested in the prospect's past, present, plans, dress, and the like.

As might be expected, not all prospects were taken in by this solicitude. Thus on one occasion Lee sat beside an Evangeline resident and, stroking the young woman's knee and smiling affectionately, inquired: "Are you in good health?" The girl responded with silence and a cold stare. Finally, after more queries, she replied: "I do not want to be a disciple of this movement." Smiling weakly and withdrawing her hands, Lee muttered: "That is all right." But a look of dark anger had momentarily possessed her face.

During study groups and informal post-session gatherings, Lee's explanations were inconspicuously but unmistakably directed to new prospects, who were thus made to feel that she had a secret and special regard for them. While she appeared to address the group as a whole, her looks and smiles were most frequently directed at them. Her animated and confiding manner, combined with her pleasantly accented, though rapid English, produced a flattering and impressive performance. If prospects asked respectful, direct questions, she was likely to dispense such flattering comments as: "I like your sharp questions." [1]

Permissiveness was also practiced in patient listening to prospect reservations and in maintaining that DP's had no prohibitions in such "moral" matters as smoking and drinking (though such things were, in fact, disdained). Prospects were urged to

---

[1] Lee sometimes even engaged in flattery that embarrassed and deprecated her early followers. While quizzing a bright and well-studied State U. student on his knowledge of the DP, she commented: "It's so good to be working with intelligent people again." (Lee once told me that in Northwest Town she had gotten the impression that Americans were not as intelligent as Koreans. Her first converts learned so slowly, while Korean believers were articulate and "quick to learn.")

take their time in deciding about the DP; no need to feel pressured. Thus when one prospect wanted to drop the DP's after Lester had worked intensively with him for three months, Lester could still respond: "I am not asking you to accept it. I just want you to be with it, to associate with it." In this early stage, DP's avoided mentioning the dire consequences of rejection so as to avoid upsetting people. Their job was merely one of offering information.

However, such permissiveness existed only during the early phases of association. I shall later discuss how the line became much tougher for those who failed to respond.

Note that these calculated displays of warmth and permissiveness revealed at least some awareness of the necessity for affective ties in effecting conversion. DP's claimed at times that people were "prepared by the spirits" to accept or not and that it therefore made little difference what converts did. However, when it came to actually dealing with prospects, this notion was laid aside in favor of a more mundane and intuitive trust in the connection between interpersonal attachments and truth.

THE MORAL FRONT

Conduct calculation extended into concern over the group's "moral image." Smoking, drinking, and sex were opposed for religious reasons, but these prohibitions had, in fact, a much more practical basis. As the vanguard and leaders of the New Age, DP's had to refrain from activity in which outsiders might find fault. There would be tremendous public opposition to DP's before they finally ruled the world, and during that period "the tools of Satan" would search for every DP misdeed in their efforts to discredit God's hosts. If the victory was to come quickly, DP's could have no moral blemishes.

So too, before this great conflict it was necessary to be faultless, the better to impress prospective converts. Thus there was some concern over what people might think about bisexual households without marriage. When first in Bay City, DP's worked out brother, sister, and in-law relations to account for themselves and to allay moral misgivings among prospects.[2] In State U. City, Ludwig and Lester made it a point to be absent whenever Minnie was visited by prospects, lest they wonder about the propriety of two men living with one woman.[3]

Smaller matters were also subject to control. Thus there was a strict rule that passengers could not smoke while accompanying Elmer in the sound truck during the advertising for Bible Week. (This was an issue because Leo and Santini smoked and liked to ride in the sound truck.) In a study group that had failed to attract new prospects Elmer blurted: "I get so *damn* mad to think of how proud this nation is at this moment." Lee called him down and made him apologize to the group for his profanity. She then delivered a long, extemporaneous lecture on how "we have to be careful" because of what "new people" might think.

OPENING TO INTERACTION

Related to warmth and permissiveness was the marked degree to which converts promoted interaction with prospects. As is evident, DP's were hardly "nine to five" functionaries. Within limits of job demands, they tried to make themselves available at any time to anyone who was interested. Unlike the ministers' Monday off and limited office hours, DP's had no life apart from their religion and were ever approachable.

This was manifest in a variety of ways. Invitations were of course issued for study groups. There were also frequent additional invitations to come early and have dinner with the DP's before the meeting and to come over anytime during the day or evening simply to talk. Prospects who appeared unannounced were warmly received, and other matters laid aside in order to

---

[2] They found that in the "big city" no one appeared to care very much and within a few months dropped the pretense.

[3] According to Minnie, co-workers at Mass Eatery were divided on the question of whether she was a nymphomaniac or all three of them were homosexuals. DP's did not care about the opinions of what were felt to be the morally reprehensible and sexually loose types who worked at Mass Eatery.

give visitors full attention. During post-study group interaction, prospects were told that there was no hurry to break up, and they were welcomed, indeed urged, to talk far into the night. On occasion, Lee even suggested that all present stay and "talk until tomorrow morning." These all-night invitations were almost never accepted, although during his conversion Lester spent most of several nights talking with DP's. A variation on this was to invite the prospect to stay as late as he pleased and not to worry about getting home, for the DP's would put him up for the night. Alvin, whom we met at the end of Chapter 8, accepted such invitations on a number of occasions.

There was often an exaggeration of the social position and educational accomplishments of the group in order to make such interaction more attractive. Due to the way Lee dominated the study group, prospects would often have little notion of what the other participants were like. Lee was aware of this, and just before dismissing the session she would often point to each participant and detail his occupational standing. Nonbelievers were included in the accounting, giving the impression that everyone mentioned was a DP. Lee was likely to say offhandedly that members in State U. City were all graduate students. After saying this on one occasion, she pointed around the room in the following manner: linguistics (Lester), sociology (the observer), electronics (Elmer), engineering (Ludwig), economics (a Chinese graduate student), political science (Alfred). She skipped over Minnie, who happened to be at the end of the circle. Then she mentioned that two other absent members were in physics and mathematics. (One was, in fact, a skeptic and the other a pontificator who used the meeting as a place to put everybody down. Neither was, or became, a DP.) At other times, Dagna, Lucy, and Walter especially were represented as members. (The observer was also always described thus.) By thus exploiting the double meaning of "member" (attending study groups vs. believing) and being loose with occupational titles, DP's could quite nicely upgrade the composition of the membership.

A similar concern for respectability was manifest in the way followers always mentioned that Miss Lee was a trained theologian and a former university professor. With such a back-ground, she must know that the DP was rational and responsible, else she would not be involved in it.

After the July, 1962, dispersion, DP's played up the number of cities containing missionaries in order to give an impression of a large membership and to minimize the embarrassment of small study groups. A sense of solidity and untold interaction possibilities was promoted through the declaration that "our people" were in six neighboring cities, making no mention of the number in each group.

Suggestions of cult residence were of course the ultimate invitation to interaction. As was seen in the preceding chapter, these invitations were extended to almost anyone who displayed sympathetic interest (or even noncommittal politeness) and made more than one visit to DP's. The casual suggestion to move in was most quickly proffered to young, middle-class people not suspected of "sexual interests." The array of unconverted, mis-involved, renegade types who actually accepted these invitations provides some notion of the lack of discrimination exercised in inviting people to move in.

One final, peculiar tactic for promotion of interaction needs to be reported. In May, 1962, after the decision to hold Bible Week, Lee responded to the complaints of Greta, Dagna, and Lucy, who alleged difficulty in getting Evangeline girls over to the DP's merely to hear a lecture and study the book. More girls would come around, they said, if the DP's had social affairs. Lee accepted the idea and planned weekly parties, using the rhetoric that "young people are interested in the opposite sex" and that this was a way to get them to the Center. Having thus gotten them there, DP's could promote interest in their doctrines.

Four Sunday evening parties were held in May and June, and after the dispersal, three limping affairs in July and August. Attendance ranged from seventeen to twenty-five people, with an average of about twenty. In addition to DP's, there were a few conventionals and veteran seekers. The largest element were freshmen seekers from Evangeline, most of whom were much like Dagna and Lucy.

DP's had a curious two-part conception of a party. The "party" was held ·first, followed by the "after-party," in which refreshments were served and participants engaged in spontaneous conversations.

Partygoers arrived around 7:30 and sat in the hardbacked chairs, which were ranged around the room against the walls. Most of the people in attendance did not know one another very well and were not very aggressive, so the room tended to be quite silent. Participants perched on their chairs, stole glances at one another, and otherwise occupied themselves by appearing to look out the windows or at the floor. New arrivals were introduced around the circle by the DP host (usually Alfred), but the room lapsed back into silence after they were seated. Judged by the pre-party silence and tension, this seemed indeed to be, as one observer commented, a party to which only the wallflowers came.

Lee entered the room after about half an hour, her presence signaling the party's beginning. The master of ceremonies (Alfred, Merwin, Dagna, or Elsa) stood up and gave a short and embarrassed welcoming talk, after which participants had to introduce themselves.

Then came the first part of the "real party," which consisted of playing "sing along" records of American "folk songs" (borrowed from Walter). Alfred passed out copies of the lyrics so that people might know the words to American favorites, such as "The Blue Tail Fly." The recorded chorus was louder, if not better, than the group that was singing along in a faint and faltering manner. Almost everyone appeared to be acutely self-conscious, especially the Evangeline girls, who giggled nervously at having to sing.[4]

Having been subjected to thirty or forty minutes of embarrassment, participants were ready for the party's main event—the speaker. DP parties had to have a speaker; if one was not found, no party was held. This requirement arose after the first party, which had no speaker and which went so badly that subsequent

---

[4] The similarity between this and the first parties of early adolescence was striking. In those parties, too, boys and girls are acutely aware of each other as sexual objects and are hyperconscious of, and faltering in, their roles.

parties were only scheduled on dates for which a speaker was available. Over the course of time six speakers addressed the parties. Two of these were Elmer's superiors at the hospital: a doctor, who thought he was to address a Unitarian-minded group (for he had seen Elmer at his Unitarian Church), and a male nursing administrator whom Elmer badgered into coming. Another was a customs director, a family friend of Dagna, who, like the doctor, did not know what he was getting into. Two others were offbeat phony experts from the intellectual fringe and occult milieu: an "expert" on the United Nations and a "Doctor of Metaphysics" out to expose the Rosicrucians, from which he had defected.

The speeches were innocuous, and after perfunctory post-speech questions and answers, sections of the DP briefing session tape were played. Presentation of the tape was not announced, explained, or its content discussed. It was simply inserted here, listened to, and ignored, much in the manner of commercials over radio and television. At its end, the master of ceremonies arose, announced "the party is over," and invited everyone to partake of the refreshments. Elsa and Dagna were in charge of this, and the refreshments were rather elaborate, consisting of punch, various kinds of cookies, cake, and some hors d'oeuvre-type items. By now the ice had been broken sufficiently, and the speaker had provided enough "interaction supplies," for interaction to proceed fairly smoothly in multiple, cocktail party-like conversations.

One feature of these parties should be emphasized. DP's and their guests were not the types who could trust themselves simply to get together and talk. The party had to have a predetermined, orderly sequence with a *single* focus of attention: the uncertainty of spontaneous encounters and unfixed topics of conversation could not be tolerated. (Especially, one supposes, in the absence of alcoholic lubricants.) Speakers arrived late on two occasions and not at all on one. The expectation of lacking such a single focus caused great tension in the gathering, and considerable relief was expressed when the speakers did arrive or when a stand-in was recruited.

The party ploy achieved no discernible promotion results and was abandoned with the rhetoric that the only people who attended parties were those who simply wanted to attend parties. We find, then, DP's employing a tactic of the mainstream churches and encountering a homely truth also forced upon these churches: promoting religion in the name of sociability promotes only sociability (if that).

Promoting Congruence

Because some prospects were not knowledgeable about or did not believe in active spirits, DP's felt it necessary to provide them with evidence and experiences that would promote such belief and the possibility of conversion.

Such attempts at education typically included convert tales of personal encounters with the spirit world and descriptions of area mediums' continuing spirit communications and materializations. The latter were intended to indicate that concern with and knowledge of spirits was, in fact, not at all uncommon.

Although DP's used locally generated tales, they recognized the marginal and suspect authority and prestige that were attached to mediums (and to DP's themselves). In order to offset this marginality, there was frequent mention of Sir Arthur Conan Doyle's spiritualistic activities and, especially, of Emmanuel Swedenborg's lengthy musings. As we have seen, Lee was a student of Swedenborg and frequently related his secular and worldly achievements at great length. He would first be established as a man of great learning, respect, and power, after which his bizarre spirit communications and spirit-world travels would be detailed. The strain for respectability was also manifest in the oft-repeated claim that a well-known Bay City medium had made regular trips to the White House to conjure up the spirits who advised Franklin Roosevelt.

Prospects were also proffered magazines and books that explained and "proved" spirits. *Fate, Search,* and *The Chimes* were the more frequently used monthlies, and Wickland's *Gateway to*

Understanding and Borgia's *Life in the World Unseen* were continually loaned as highly recommended reading.[5] There are hundreds of books like them, but these two (and a few others) were preferred because of their authors' conventional respectability. Wickland was a doctor of medicine, and Borgia claimed his book to be the "spirit dictation" of Monsignor Robert Hugh Benson, English author and private chamberlain to Pope Pius X.

Of course the best evidence for spirits was direct contact with their world. As previously mentioned, most spiritualist churches in Bay City were financially insolvent, physically decrepit, and run by mediums who were more glib than spiritual. However, one establishment, the Pacific Spiritualist Church, stood in sharp contrast to the others. Its plush mansion in a high-rent district housed a thriving complex organization that conducted numerous services and meetings, including Sunday School, women's circles, and other accouterments of conventional religion. Not surprisingly, DP's took prospects there, rather than to the dingy spirit chambers, to make ectoplasmic connections.

The rotund, female minister of Pacific Spiritualist (Roosevelt's alleged spirit conjurer) was, without doubt, the most accomplished and theatrical of local mediums. Before the service, audience members wrote out questions for spirit persons and put them in envelopes. The medium was heavily blindfolded and the sealed envelopes were poured into a large pile on a table in front of her. With the aid of her spirit guide she invariably read the external identification (usually initials) and often appeared to know the written questions addressed to spirits through her. This performance was conducted in a brightly lit room, without curtains or discernible sleight of hand, and made for a very impressive and (aside from spirits) inexplicable accomplishment. DP's felt that such an obvious demonstration of spirit contact should be instrumental in promoting prospects to revise their conception of the real and the possible.

---

[5] Dr. Carl A. Wickland, *Gateway to Understanding* (Los Angeles: National Psychological Institute, 1934); Anthony Borgia, *Life in the World Unseen* (New York: Citadel Press, 1954).

In talk with unknowledgeable prospects about evidence for spirits, DP's took a sympathetic, I-was-like-you-once line in granting that they could understand how it seemed fantastic and incredible. They, too, had felt that way when first encountering the spirit world. But if the prospect seriously considered the evidence, then he would see its inherent rationality and incontrovertible truth.

Acknowledgment of difficulty in accepting the spirit world was often combined or equated with reservations about the DP world view. In discussions with prospects about spirits and their credibility, DP's were likely to say that when they had first heard "this message" they did not accept "sixty or seventy per cent" of it and had difficulty overcoming previous training in religion. Ludwig was perhaps the most forthright on the credibility question in frequently telling prospects: "If I had heard [the DP] a year before I did, I would have said, you're nuts to believe such things." By explicitly acknowledging the legitimacy of such an initial response, the DP's were not only defining disbelief as an impermanent response, but were also undercutting any tendency to regard them as psychiatric cases.

THE POVERTY OF ADVANCED PROMOTION

DP's expected prospects who underwent these promotion tactics to enter, on their own volition, a period of struggle and then accept the DP. Of course only a handful stayed around long enough to receive more than minor efforts at promotion, but a few maintained their association and did not enter an existential struggle. (See Chap. 8, the cases of Walter, Dagna, and Lucy; and the Appendix on the observer's role.)

The DP's were not prepared for this, for they expected prospects to reject and leave or else proceed steadily, though perhaps slowly, to conversion. Their promotion program was geared only to the initial weeks of acquaintance.

It was on the assumption that people would spontaneously take up the DP once they had a full understanding of it that DP's practiced their rhetoric of "It's your own decision" and "We are only offering information." Once a prospect had a full understanding, he would be moved to follow the example set by the total converts. What a person should do with his life in view of the DP was so obvious, they thought, that it need not even be spoken.

Therefore, when confronted with prospects who had all the information and were still disinclined to give themselves over, DP's were at a loss as to what to do next. As seen in the case of Walter, for example, little or no action was taken beyond some private carping over his failure to respond.

DP's were likewise at a loss in dealing with verbal converts. These people knew the situation and apparently believed in it, but inexplicably held back. Greta, for example, attended meetings for two years, displayed thorough knowledge of the DP, and spoke as a convert. But she made only minor gestures of commitment, and DP's did little to promote her total participation.

There was, however, another significant reason for the poverty of the later stages of promotion tactics. DP's were quite aware that compliance is unreliable if not freely given. "If it is not in your heart," Lee would say, "then there is no use in doing." That is, activity for reasons other than an inner sense of obligation and necessity was not "spiritually correct" and did not build up status in the new kingdom.

Translated from theological to sociological terms, we thus find considerable sensitivity to the power differential between normative and coercive control.[6] DP's intuitively understood that normatively granted power was, in one sense, the most coercive. Thus Lee disdained simply doing without feeling it and would not abide it in her total converts in everyday tasks. Put another way, DP's wanted complete consensus and were reluctant to browbeat and thus acquire unwilling and ambivalent participants.

Relations with advanced prospects were, however, mixed. On the one hand, cordiality, warmth, and attentiveness were reduced, although there were few attempts to cut people off altogether.

---

[6] Amitai Etzioni, A Comparative Analysis of Complex Organizations (New York: The Free Press of Glencoe, Inc., 1961), esp. Chaps. 1-3.

Advanced prospects could continue limited participation, but they were more fixtures to be ignored and treated casually than objects to be pursued. They were the dead who still walked in the land of the living.

On the other hand, and in spite of the dominant laissez-faire attitude, there were minor expressions of hostility directed toward advanced prospects. These took the form of more or less explicit threats of the dire consequences of knowing all and doing nothing. In study groups lacking early stage prospects but containing advanced ones, Lee would discourse at length on the perilous state of knowing but not doing. Such people could be struck down by God at any time and in any number of ways. It would also be said that everyone had to go through judgment, either now or later. It would be much harder for those who went through later. Churchgoing advanced prospects would be informed that those who remained conventional Christians were doomed. "Since you have come this far, you should know this."

Such threats were sometimes applied personally rather than categorically.

You might start having peculiar thoughts and dreams. Dark thoughts might enter your mind.

Prospects who said that they would most likely not accept the DP were treated with a vicious pity.

I feel so sorry for you. There is so much suffering ahead of you.

As last, desperate attempts, such threats seemed even to get out of hand and undo themselves. Thus one advanced prospect, who was a veteran seeker, was told by her spirit guides that the DP was "of the devil." Lee countered with the claim that low spirits were misleading her and she had better leave them alone:

Otherwise they will only confuse you and command you very abnormal things to do, requesting a price for what they have helped you.

You are now at a crucial stage. You will either progress or decline helplessly, depending on how you treat the spirits with you.

The veteran seeker only became angry and more convinced that Lee and the DP were of the devil.

Likewise, threats deriving from the DP's stern conception of God seemed to generate more anger than fear because of its contrast with the dominant "God is Love" motif in America. The following threat by Lee to Dagna and Lucy was perhaps less productive of fear than of alienation.

God is not all-loving and all-love-giving. That is a complete misconception.

When you meet God, the first question He will ask you is what have you done for Me? How much have you suffered for Me? That is what you will receive.

In general, such little threats were the ambivalent terminal ploys of an impoverished program for promoting advanced prospects.

Concluding Remarks

In spite of the fact that DP's correctly conceived the communication of their world view as a sensitive project in need of careful management, they evolved only rather ineffective devices for it. The progressive shortening and final abolishment of the tape, combined with the effort to merge the tape and study group, was in reluctant recognition of this ineffectiveness.

Correspondingly, the tactics of promoting affect and of mutual opening to interaction indicated the DP's operational (if halting) recognition of the extra-intellectual and social nature of truth.

The range of DP promotion vehicles and tactics did not provide sufficient data for making controlled contrasts, but the materials available suggest that they would have been more successful with a briefer and more affect-girded initial presentation. Despite the number of dispositionally available people being quite small on the West Coast in the early sixties, one must conclude that many amenable prospects got away because DP promotion vehicles were sterile and use of tactics was haphazard. DP's would have especially profited by occasions that sustained more interest than mere serial, oral reading (such as dynamic lectures).

A final point. The DP's covert motif and the exploitive prospect alignments point up a general pattern in social life to which sociologists might be more sensitive. Whenever any set of goals is organizationally implemented, people external to that implementation will seek to exploit it for unanticipated and disapproved ends. Although a universal social phenomenon, it is particularly germane to the study of disapproved roles and organizations, because they seem to be both more liable to it and more likely to engage in it. The former is suggested by the DP's considerable problems with exploitive prospects, and the latter by their propensity to covert presentations. Exploitation by outsiders appears to go hand in hand with exploitation of outsiders.[7]

---

[7] A helpful discussion of this phenomenon may be found in Edwin Lemert, *Social Pathology* (New York: McGraw-Hill Book Company, 1951), pp. 65-68.

part three

Faith and Hope

Put on all the armour which God provides, so that you may be able to stand firm against the devices of the devil. For our fight is not against human foes, but against cosmic powers, against the authorities and potentates of this dark world, against the superhuman forces of evil in the heavens. Therefore, take up God's armour; then you will be able to stand your ground when things are at their worse, to complete every task and still stand firm. Stand firm I say. Buckle on the belt of truth; for coat of mail put on integrity; let the shoes of your feet be the gospel of peace, to give you firm footing; and with all these take up the great shield of faith, with which you will be able to quench all the flaming arrows of the evil one. Take salvation for helmet; for sword, take that which the Spirit gives you—the words that come from God.

*"The Letter of Paul
to the Ephesians"*
(6:11-17 NEB)

Let us . . . exult in our present sufferings, because we know that suffering trains us to endure, and endurance brings proof that we have stood the test, and this proof is the ground of hope.

*"The Letter of Paul
to the Romans"*
(5:2-4 NEB)

chapter 10

Faith and the
Encompassing Culture

The conversion analysis sought to specify the dispositional and situational factors that accounted for people taking up the DP role. It is reasonable to assume that the factors that caused this were not necessarily the same as those that supported continuance and ensured faith in the world view's viability as an instrument for decoding reality. In this and the following chapters, I shall address this question of how and why it is possible to maintain faith after conversion.

Most lay discourse on how deviant groups maintain their faith displays a remarkable propensity to emphasize the inadequacy of such world views as cognitive systems. Correspondingly, it highlights those arrangements that function to shield believers from recognition of their cognitive and empirical lapses. The common sense response is, in effect, "My God, how can they believe such obvious nonsense?"—the premise of which is that deviant views struggle with severe cognitive contradiction or strain in squaring their views with the facts.

Sociological observers also pride themselves on their positivistic common sense, and it is therefore not surprising to find that common sense response reworded and incorporated as a premise in sociological writings. Consider, for example, a contemporary analysis that undertakes to contrast the common sense outlook with radicalism and to demonstrate that the organizational features of radical movements are dictated by the character of radical ideology.[1] It is argued that, in contrast to the common sense outlook, a radical world view attempts "to impose a unified, internally consistent schema of interpretation upon a world of heterogeneous meanings."[2] Because experience is, in fact, "an ambiguous environment of objects and events . . . which . . . do not have unequivocally stable meanings . . . , . . . all efforts to live by an internally consistent schema of interpretation are necessarily doomed to fail."[3] Again, a radical schema is "necessarily disconfirmed in practical experience."[4]

The premise here is quite clear: radical views are wrong. The entire argument is, in fact, that the organizational features of radical movements are functional devices to protect the adherents from seeing their gigantic error.[5]

Consider in the same light another analysis, which proposes to delineate "the means employed by deviant groups in maintaining their beliefs in the face of a divergent and more or less disapproving larger society."[6] This student mentions, in passing, that "*all* belief systems are, to some extent, arbitrary and . . . the same mechanisms are involved in maintaining them."[7] But the analytic thrust is clearly directed to specifying mechanisms that "facilitate the maintenance of divergent beliefs." These mechanisms are said to include selective attention to congruent facts, con-

---

[1] Egon Bittner, "Radicalism and the Organization of Radical Movements," *American Sociological Review*, Vol. XXVIII (December, 1963), 928-940.

[2] *Ibid.*, 939.

[3] *Ibid.*, 934.

[4] *Ibid.*, 939.

[5] Bittner does not consider an equally plausible explanation of radical movements' organizational features; namely, that radical movements are strongly disapproved by the encompassing culture and evolve their organizational features in response to and as a means of coping with the stigma and negative sanctioning they must face. Where the encompassing culture is radical and a minority espouses the common sense outlook, we should expect to find the common sense types displaying the organizational features that Bittner attributes to radical movements.

[6] J. L. Simmons, "On Maintaining Deviant Belief Systems," *Social Problems*, Vol. XI (Winter, 1964), 250-256.

[7] *Ibid.*, 252.

trivance of supportive situations, confirmative interpretation of ambiguous evidence, association and identification with co-believers, and ambivalence on the part of the encompassing culture. All five devices are said to avoid what is otherwise discrediting and inconvenient experience. If these mechanisms were not operative, the intake of cognitive materials would throw doubt upon the deviant belief system.

The role accorded cognitive materials is further indicated by the observation that one kind of argument that can be made "against a . . . belief system" is to "point out events in the real world which challenge the beliefs." [8]

We see, then, one popular imagery for conceiving radical or deviant world views. It is an imagery or set of assumptions that posits high vulnerability to experience and the necessity to engage (unwittingly) in careful selection of permitted experience through extraordinary control over actual experience.

It may be true that some radical or deviant perspectives must laboriously engage in sustaining a delicate make-believe reality and that the mechanisms adduced by the above students function to support this make-believe and reduce cognitive contradiction. However, I am more impressed with the way in which this approach underestimates the cognitive, explanatory, and confirmational capacities of certain radical or deviant perspectives.

An emphasis upon cognitive inadequacies may be useful for some purposes, but it can produce a distorted picture of the very formidable capacities of these reality constructions. I would, indeed, suggest that in the DP case at any rate, one finds a structure that is logically impossible to confront with disconfirming or negative evidence, at least in the short run. It was designed so that all experience, all counterarguments, would only produce confirmation (at least before 1967).

Although the sorts of supportive devices mentioned above might be found among DP's (or any group for that matter), this should not deflect attention from the structure of their cognitive

---

[8] *Ibid.*, 255.

system as a vehicle that possesses enormous explanatory scope and confirmational possibilities

High protection against discrediting and disconfirmation is, however, a peculiar quality and is perhaps found only among certain types of deviant world views. Leaving aside the question of how world views might be typified in a general scheme, we are here concerned with the DP as an instance of a single type, the fundamental characteristic of which is that its postulates are, in significant measure, super- or nonempirical. Reduced to its simplest propositional outline, the DP might be said to consist of the following:

1. There is an active, superempirical reality beyond or behind empirical reality; that is, reality is split into a spirit world and a material world.
2. The spirit world is populated by spirit persons who are aligned either with God and Good or Satan and Evil.
3. Since the Fall, these camps have fought for the control of man and the material world, and today they are locked in a final, decisive struggle that will be won by God.
4. All events in the material world are caused by actions of the spirit world, which cause events for a *purpose* related to this struggle. No event is in any sense accidental or random.
5. Satan's spirits hinder and God's spirits help those in the material world who help God in the struggle. Satan's spirits help and God's spirits hinder those in the material world who help Satan in the struggle.

The major implication of these primary postulates is that the meaning, explanation, or significance of any empirical object, event, or experience is not to be found in antecedent empirical reality, but rather in their significance to the superempirical cosmic war. It is not denied that one can find empirical antecedent causes (e.g., a nail in a flat tire), but these can be understood only by reference to the working of spirits (i.e., Satan's work).

This conception of causative, purposeful spirits radically transforms the significance of empirical reality. It decisively undercuts the methods, arguments, and verification paraphernalia of world views which assume natural events have natural causes. A radical revision of this sort perhaps makes it meaningful to speak of "another world" that possesses its own system of truth.[9]

The primary postulates derive their cognitive force from application in a simplified, everyday interpretive schema that is not subject to disconfirmation and that, if conscientiously applied, yields a continuous flow of confirming experience. The schema has two propositions involving but a small addition to the fifth primary postulate:

1. Anything that hinders or hurts a DP or the group or an outsider who is assisting is an attack by Satan's spirits.
2. Anything that helps a DP or the group or an outsider who is assisting is an act of helping or leading by God's spirits.[10]

The elegance and power of this view reside in the fact that whether plans go right or not, whether expectations are fulfilled or not, the believer cannot lose. He derives confirmation from any outcome. Everything is somebody's move in the cosmic battle.

A person who accepts the primary postulates and uses the everyday schema finds that reality is enormously transformed: everything becomes meaningful and understandable, more understandable perhaps than to those who rely on common sense.

It is the task of the following analysis to demonstrate the way in which thoroughgoing schema application produces endless evidence and confirmation and avoids disconfirmation and discrediting. It may then be possible to see how users can get locked in this kind of perspective simply from being overwhelmed and amply supported with the immense amount of confirmative cognitions it provides.

To suggest that the maintenance of faith was not a pressing

---

[9] By means of the terms "ideational" and "sensate," Pitirum Sorokin has made essentially the same argument for this fundamental difference between world views. See his *Social and Cultural Dynamics* (New York: American Book Company, 1937), esp. Vol. I, pp. 32-35, 65-72; and Vol. II, pp. 3-18.

[10] The logical structure of this conception.is of course far from unique. Eric Hoffer, among others, has observed that every body of true believers has its battle between good and evil, entailing a worked up "devil theory." See *The True Believer* (New York: New American Library of World Literature. Inc., 1958), esp. pp. 87 and 115.

problem is not to say that DP's escaped it entirely. They were, in fact, periodically faced with a large threat arising from an empirical prediction that was part and parcel of their belief—a belief that otherwise protected them so well. The DP system, having been so adept in managing experience, had gone on to predict a membership of 144,000 and the earthly millennium by 1967. In their own eyes, failure to make sufficient progress toward this membership goal was the most pressing problem. This date provided a spur to work and to work hard, but their very minimal success—in their own estimation—was a source of chronic despair and concern. They feared that they were not making sufficient converts in America to be worthy in the sight of God and to earn much temporal reward in the New Kingdom.[11] Individual DP's were subject to despair, and the entire group sometimes fell into a state of desperation.

Repeated or prolonged despair very often causes doubt. The DP's major problem was therefore the task of keeping up hope, a sense that success was imminent even if they were not successful at a given moment. In Chapter 12 I shall attempt to show the circumstances in which despair became an overwhelming threat and to specify the mechanisms through which new hope was generated.

Let us first turn to the matter of faith and doubt and the remarkable manner in which the DP perspective decoded raw reality. The discussion will proceed from the most distant sources of encompassing culture (the mass media), through face-to-face contact with outsiders (the perimeter), to internal cult events.

The Mass Media

Contrary to radical groups that attempt to isolate themselves from the perspectives and events of the encompassing culture (presumably to avoid "corruption"), DP's followed the larger

---

[11] America's quota among the 144,000 necessary converts was never very clear, but was spoken of as "several thousand."

world with great interest.[12] In Bay City, although they were too frugal to make constant expenditures on papers and magazines, Merwin frequently brought home batches of undeliverable ones from his post office job, and boarders also purchased daily papers, which were widely read by members. DP's in State U. City subscribed to and read *The New York Times*. In short, they fed—as do most of us—upon the conventional mass media.

DP's expected world events to manifest the cosmic battle through progressive deterioration of the national-international situation. Strong maintenance of faith required, then, a plethora of events manifesting disorganization, unrest, and deterioration. The mass media are well designed to provide just such material. News is *news* precisely because it is disaster, setback, and disorder, and it thereby nicely dovetailed with the DP's constant sensitivity to signs. The latest crisis mentioned in the newspapers was subject to at least brief mention by the DP's and often was an object of sustained conversation.

Some events of 1962 (the year of observation) may be reviewed concretely to indicate the wealth of material available and the method of decoding. The year began with massive demonstrations and a coup and countercoup in the Dominican Republic and great concern on the part of the Department of State. Terrorist activity in Algeria brought death to at least 500 people in four weeks. There were more than ten disasters of major note, including an avalanche in the Peruvian Andes that killed some 3,000 people. God and Satan were hard at it.

February's news was dominated by John Glenn's space orbit (which showed the ascendance of Good), but Satan still managed to come on with a strong set of disasters, including high winds and floods in Germany that killed over 300. (This last was caused by Ludwig's verbal conversion during that month. Under "the law

---

[12] Among many instances of deliberate ignorance of the encompassing culture, attention should be called in particular to Mother Ann Lee's delightful, explicit "Millennial Laws." See the appendix in E. D. Andrews, *The People Called Shakers* (New York: Dover Publications, Inc., 1963), pp. 249-289, esp. Sec. XI: "Orders Concerning Books, Pamphlets and Writings in General."

of indemnity," God's act in "leading Ludwig," provoked Satan's retribution on his nation.)

March manifested Good and Evil blows through coups in Burma and Argentina, a coup and countercoup in Syria, and demonstrations and civil strife in Guatemala. Two jet airliners crashed just after takeoff, killing all aboard. The Atlantic Coast was swept by violent storms, causing $300 million in damage.

April had no new major crises because it was the month of Parents' Day, the DP's equivalent of Christmas. God restrained both Satan and Himself for the occasion, but they redoubled their efforts in May, and the stock market plummeted the week of May 21. This boosted the expectation among DP's of imminent civil disorder, especially when on May 28 the market took its sharpest one-day break since 1929. While most of the nation stood in fear of another depression, DP's rejoiced over the wonders of the spirit world and the imminence of the end.

The stock market began to recover in June, and the previous month's difficulty was thought to be merely the first of many dips that would become deeper and more frequent as the end drew near. Because these were unprecedented times, DP's expected public events to be record-breaking, as was a June jet airliner crash that killed 130 people, a record for single-plane disasters.

July and August were punctuated by military rebellions in Peru and Argentina, as well as plane crashes, earthquakes, train derailments, and floods, including a flash flood in Sunchon, Korea, which killed 160 people. Satan was at work hindering the work of restoration in the Motherland.

Domestic disorder was furthered in September, it was thought, when James Meredith's enrollment at the University of Mississippi necessitated federal marshals and troops being called in to quell rioting.

The Pacific Coast underwent an unusual storm in October that killed forty-six and put out the lights during a DP meeting. The latter was an obvious hindering act of Satan. The confrontation between Russia and the United States over missile bases in Cuba was the highlight of the month. Most of the world may have been anxious about the United States quarantine and how the Russians might respond, but DP's were serene, confident, and, indeed, jubilant. For them, this was just one more move to make people more insecure and better prepared to accept the new truth. The first public notice of the crisis coincided with the first day of Lester's "money isn't the answer" ad in the *University Daily*, a coincidence that was of course arranged by the spirit world.

In November and December there were more disasters, a prolonged newspaper strike in New York City, and a New Year's Eve riot in downtown Bay City. Local newspaper headlines quoted the chief of police as saying that these riots were "the worst ever."

The mass media reported the winter of 1962-63 to be "the worst winter of the century" in Europe and North America. Many new weather records were set, and papers ran interviews with experts asking if and why weather was changing. DP's of course *knew* that weather was changing. It had to. The nonhuman material world was constructed in the image of man; man was changing; ergo, the nonhuman order was changing.

Decoding of the mass media was hardly confined to major events. A host of minor news items were grist for the mill, such as a blurb deep in *The New York Times* reporting the inexplicable collision of two ships during a fog in New York harbor. Lester came upon this and read the item to those present, commenting: "Hmmm . . . since they have radar that shouldn't have happened." Obviously Satan's spirits were fooling around at the controls.

Sensitive attention to the mass media also revealed direct spirit possession by increasingly active spirits. Thus late in 1962 a bay area doctor mutilated his wife with acid and knife, causing her death. The defense pleaded insanity and sought to establish the doctor's "two co-existent personalities" that fought for control over him. DP's knew he was sometimes possessed by an evil spirit. A few weeks later "a lonely forty-year-old secretary, driven by what she [had] described [to a neighbor] as the voices of evil spirits, jumped to her death from the sixteenth floor of a hotel." And not many weeks later a deputy sheriff accompanying a prisoner to a hospital inexplicably shot and killed a stenographer and weepingly explained: "I had to kill somebody; God told me to."

Local external events were also juxtaposed with DP activity as attacks of Satan. Thus a State U. City rape occurring on the same evening as a DP meeting was seen as Satan's retribution for God's occasion.

DP's are not alone in predicting doom, and the mass media fed them material that was already more or less decoded. One among many lamentations read by DP's was found in a May, 1962, U.S. *News and World Report,* the cover of which asked: "Is There a Decline in U. S. Morals? Interview with Dean of a Divinity School." Bold captions, such as "Is something basic happening to morality in this country?" and ". . . the impact of religion in America has been diminishing," led into the story.

Scandal, of late, has piled upon scandal, causing officials and citizens, too, to ask this question: Is a breakdown developing in U.S. morals?

The divinity school dean (Liston Pope of Yale University) provided an inconclusive answer, but DP's happily pronounced a resounding "yes," morals were breaking down and even conventional types were becoming aware. Conventional society did not know why yet, but soon they would.[18]

In general, any allegation of increase in deviance was an item of note. Divorce, suicide, mental illness, alcoholism, pregnancy without marriage, unemployment, or any condition reported with concern pointed to the end.

DP's were particularly happy to read charges of religious decline, and they drew upon conservatives and liberals alike for material. The Jehovah's Witnesses' *Watch Tower* was standard reading, and Elton Trueblood's lamentations in *Company of the Committed* was quoted with approval:

Bishop James Pike . . . and Bishop Gerald Kennedy . . . have had the courage to use the popular press to make our people realize that in large measure the contemporary church is in retreat.

---

[18] See also "What Has Happened to Law and Order in the United States?" in *Look,* Vol. XXVI (July 3, 1962), 13-17. This sort of lamentation and viewing with alarm is the stock in trade of today's magazines.

Many astute observers . . . are suggesting seriously that our Christian faith is now in essentially the same condition as that of the popular religion of Greece four centuries after Plato.[14]

Finally, DP's fed upon the abundant pulps and books of the occult milieu, all of which abound in mysterious happenings and New Age foretellings. Such literature's ostensive purpose was the education of prospects, but it also provided underpinning for the DP's.

In summary, rather than constituting a "pernicious flow" of disconfirmation, the mass media seemed only to furnish supporting data.

THE PERIMETER

DP's were, in general, in face-to-face exposure to conventional and discordant perspectives a significant proportion of each day. How, then, was such exposure managed? Let us examine some of the primary sources of DP perimeter experience.

THE RHETORIC OF RELIGIOUS GATHERINGS

Spending a large, continuous amount of time in competing religious places might seem to have a corrosive effect on DP faith. In fact, it appeared to be a potent source of support and confirmation. If a service was ill-attended, people were falling away from the churches in these last days; if well-attended, people were seeking for truth, but not finding it there. If it was housed in a new building, the church was resorting to external appearance to compensate for its inner death; if in an old building, people were falling away. If there was emphasis upon social religion, people were far from God in these last evil times; if the emphasis was biblical and apocalyptic, people were seeking for truth and needed only to be awakened.

Even modulated churches sometimes refer to "our changing

---

[14] Quoted in the *DP Newsletter* (March, 1963).

times" and "new era." DP's would silently affirm such references and increase their effect through retelling.

This past Sunday we [Bertha and others in State College Town] attended an Episcopal Church. It was very interesting to note some of the things the minister had to say concerning the New Age.

He quoted from a Catholic bishop's statement in Germany, and I quote as follows:

"The modern age has ended and we have entered the New Age. We do not know what will transpire at this time, or what the church's role will be in this age, or even what this New Age will be called, but we definitely know it has arrived." [15]

In some respects, DP doctrine was similar to some versions of orthodox Christianity. Because of this, DP's sometimes thought they heard their doctrines preached in the churches. However, they felt this to be due to God's spirits acting upon ministers and subtly infiltrating their thought. Ministers exposed to the DP were of course particularly susceptible to this influence. Minnie related:

[A Presbyterian minister] took the [DP book] to read, and after many phone calls and much urging he read [it]. The next Sunday night, after reading it, he gave the lecture. His subject was "The Creation of Man and The Fall of Man." He spoke from the Precepts. After the lecture I went up to him. His first comment was that he had read the book and it was most refreshing—and shocking in part. Then Ludwig, Lester, and I all went to visit him at his office. We talked for about two hours. He seems to be interested and did not fight us. Last night, November 4th, I went to the church. He gave another lecture, in which he said that Jesus was a man even as we are men. He was the true man, and we are the fallen men. Many statements were from the Precepts. Later I went up and talked to him. He had many questions on the spirit world and said that he wanted to come to our group meeting some Thursday.[16]

---

[15] Bertha, in the DP Newsletter (December, 1962). This produced not only confirmation, but also a comfortable feeling of superior knowledge. The Catholic bishop and the Episcopal priest did not know about the New Age, but DP's did.

[16] Minnie, in ibid. (November, 1962). Upon reading the passage quoted, the minister exclaimed: "That's a bunch of . . . baloney." In a calmer tone, he went on to say that his lectures were not taken from the DP and that in talking with them he had merely tried to be polite.

DIRECT SPIRIT MANIFESTATIONS

The work of the spirits was for the most part "hidden," in the sense that DP's had to define it as spirit work. However, some perimeter happenings were defined thus by outsiders, the most conspicuous of which were of course spiritualist churches. However, local spiritualists did not always produce directly supportive material. In one extreme instance, the minister of Bay City Spiritualist even told Lester that the spirits said the DP's were an evil group. DP's obviously needed a doctrine with which to handle such resistance. This was accomplished by the doctrine of spirit world levels or stratification—and of course good and evil spirits.

Most spiritualist sessions were concerned with answering audience questions to spirit friends and dealt primarily with the parishioner's life problems and general greetings from dead relatives ("Should I change jobs?" / "A message from my husband, please."). According to DP's, these were "low spirits" in the pyramid of the other world. As yet only the high spirits knew about the New Age. One therefore had to expect the lower spirits to reject or be ignorant of these larger matters. Mediums could contact spirits only on their own spiritual level, and since most mediums were low, their spirit information was defective. Further, mediums who claimed contact with high spirits might merely be conversing with a masquerading evil spirit. One could tell the difference between actual and spurious contact with high spirits by whether or not their messages supported the DP.[17]

However, by their very existence, spiritualist and other fringe groups supported DP faith, for they further fulfilled a Christian and DP prophecy. As the DP book stated:

The aggression of the spirit world will appear in such various ways as the awakening of people through diverse spiritual manifestations, an outpouring of the Divine spirit upon all people, as prophesied in·

---

[17] Cf. "The First Letter of John" 4:2-3 NEB: "This is how we may recognize the Spirit of God: every spirit which acknowledges that Jesus Christ has come in the flesh is from God, and every spirit that does not thus acknowledge Jesus is not from God."

Acts 2:17-21, and the instruction of prepared people through revelations.

Thus the insurgence of tongues-speaking groups across the country, especially on the West Coast, provided important evidence of the beginning fulfillment of their prophecy.

The spirit world is becoming more active, as is evidenced by the increase in "speaking in tongues" in the churches of [the Bay City area], and even other parts of the United States. But we must be wise in contacting those who have experienced this spiritual phenomenon, for most believe it to come from the Holy Spirit.[18]

WORK EVENTS

Obtaining and holding a job was governed by the action of spirits. Thus Elmer reported it took seventy days for him to find work in Bay City because he had to pay indemnity to Satan for becoming a DP. Ludwig searched for work for four months in the fall of 1963 for the same reason. Minnie was fired from a waitress job in the spring of 1962 because Satan acted upon her boss. Bertha also lost a job about this time, but she explained the event with a happier version of the same logic. God was taking her out of that job and putting her on another one where she was to meet someone whose identity was known only to God.

Work itself was a hard testing ground. After converting, Lester reduced his course load, but subsequently restored it when informed that Woodrow Wilson Fellows must be registered fulltime in order to receive their stipend. DP's felt that Satan was playing a mean trick on their star missionary. When another convert told Lee that he had failed his Ph.D. examinations, she instantly replied: "That is all right. There is purpose. There is purpose. You will stay in this country longer." Thus not all reversals and hardships were Satan's hindrances. God could be testing the convert or guiding his long range plans.

Minnie underwent a particularly poignant period of this type of testing while a waitress in State U. City in the fall of 1962.

---

[18] Lester, in the *DP Newsletter* (February, 1963).

The student population had returned in force, but the restaurant did not enlarge its staff to accommodate the increase. Minnie found it difficult to handle the influx, and this, combined with the unruly types she sometimes faced, produced considerable strain. Minnie shamefully related the not uncommon waitress blow-up that occurred as a result.

[On Sunday evening] a guy asked for oil and vinegar on his salad, and I by mistake put roquefort on it. When I took it over to him he said: "Sister, you'll just have to eat that one yourself." I picked up the salad and drew back to throw it at him and said: "You eat this, God damn you." I must've looked mean 'cause he dove under the table. I said it so loud that ever'body in the restaurant turned around and looked at me.

Monday night was the same busy, crowded scene:

A boy left a note by his plate saying I was the worst waitress he had ever seen and that I ought to give *him* a tip. I ran after him and threw the note at him and yelled terrible bad things at him.

[Later that evening] the manager told me to keep the line [of people waiting for tables] around the corner from the dining room, and I said to him: "I'll do what I please as long as I'm running this floor." I had a strawberry milkshake in my hand and drew back to throw it on him. I put it down, told him I quit, and ran crying into the back room. The manager came back and talked me into staying.

Minnie did not define these incidents as resulting from system-induced stress or her personal capacity to do the job. She was instead ashamed that she had cracked under the pressure of God's testing. Working in this restaurant was, as she put it, part of "God's basic training for the new order." It was one of the trials she had to go through in order to win His love. However, her outbursts were not her acting; they resulted from her weakness, which allowed Satan to take her over.

Moreover, this was her legitimate suffering; otherwise she would not be able to appreciate what God had already given her or the love she was to get from Him. Minnie felt she had particular and additional cause for her shame in that her basic training was easy compared to that of Chang, for he had undergone prison, starvation, and torture, and to that of the rest of the world's population who, in the last days, would have to endure disease, famine, earthquakes, and the like.

As previously discussed, DP's had considerable difficulty gaining and holding the interest of prospects, much less going on to make them converts. Such massive reticence was a lush field of spirit activity. Much of this definitional work has already been seen in previous chapters. A few amplifying observations will suffice in the present context.

Attendance at study groups was almost always below DP expectations. They perpetually lamented that Satan was very active in keeping prospects away.

An amplification of this, the "Satan's front line" dogma, strengthened the DP's position when it was most weak. According to the "precept of indemnity," Satan worked hardest against DP's when they were really striking a blow for God. Therefore if it appeared that Satan was really attacking them—e.g., if few prospects were appearing—that must mean that in some way they were really getting close to a victory for God.

Likewise, prospects' failure to return was the work of Satan. As mentioned above, DP's believed that those who knew the message and rejected it, or did not return, were in a worse position than those who were ignorant of it until the actual restoration. Early rejectors would not only be at the bottom of the New Age stratification system, but God would strike them down in the present. Thus the DP's were highly interested in the excuses prospects gave when declining further association. As reported, prospects were inordinately afflicted with bad colds, broken water pipes, fractured legs, dead relatives, and the like. These happenings were not seen as excuses, but as truths and evidence that God or Satan had acted on the rejectors. However, one could not expect all rejectors to have immediate misfortune. Everybody has a certain amount of good in him, or "credits" that he has built up with God. The rejector was safe until he had used up those credits.

DP's could not know how many credits the rejector had in "God's bank"; therefore they could not predict when a given rejector would get his water pipes broken or suffer whatever form the judgment might take.[19]

In general, DP's could not lose. If prospects came along, God was most active. If they did not, Satan was most active. It seemed, however, that Satan was most active most of the time. This meant that God's agents had to work that much harder. Minnie exhorted:

Now as we meet and talk to people and tell them this wonderful news, some are afraid, some say it is all false, and some say it sounds nice, but do nothing about it. Very, very few will listen, and even those who do study are always fighting with doubts and fears. Satan is always there to try to take them away. We have to be there helping these new children fight this battle until they are strong and can fight alone, using this Divine Precept as their weapon. My brothers and sisters, we are in a real war. We have to be strong to win. As our Leader's words for 1963 say: "Let us be victorious rulers" with God's blessing.[20]

EXCURSUS ON THE MANAGEMENT
OF PERSONAL REJECTION

DP's expected rejection and opposition, but they were not entirely impervious to it simply because it was a natural part of the struggle to win the world. They remained sensitive to repeated

---

[19] Compare this happy work reported to the American DP's in a letter from a Korean DP:

There are some people who still oppose and even persecute our group. Then the heaven works for us. A man broke his leg because he opposed us. A person got a twisted mouth, another was paralyzed, and in various ways the Father's mighty works were manifested. If you pray a lot, then the heaven will also work for you in the same way.

See also "The Second Letter of Paul to Timothy" 4:14 NEB: "Alexander the coppersmith did me [Paul] a great deal of harm. Retribution will fall upon him from the Lord."

[20] DP Newsletter (March, 1963).

dismissals, condescending politeness, insinuations and charges of mental illness, and anti-Christ allegations. Their primary plight was inattention and unimpressed attention, although like most people, DP's preferred to be liked and respected. How, then, did they accommodate themselves to this discrepancy between actual and desired treatment? Rhetorical management, at least, appeared to move along the following lines.

First, rejection and suffering were not only part of the cosmic battle, but were necessary and good for one's spiritual development. Witnessing and rejection were absolutely necessary in order to have a favorable position in the New Age. According to Lee:

Our hearts must be one with God's heart. We must experience God's broken heart of being rejected, rebelled against, and betrayed by mankind through the ages. We must even minutely experience God's broken heart. Therefore we shall experience being rejected by family, church, society, nation, and the whole world. We must overcome all these hardships and be grateful for sharing part of God's sorrow. Then we will be worthy to be called His sons and daughters.[21]

Second, this doctrine was elaborated to include Jesus as a "significant other." Thus on one occasion a minister publicly denounced Lester to his face as a neurotic in need of a psychiatrist. In the numerous later discussions of the incident, Lee explained that Jesus' brothers had also thought he was crazy. That is why Jesus asked: "Who are my brothers?" Lee would conclude: "We are following in the footsteps of Jesus." And Lester could reply: "Yes, it is a valuable experience to be able to feel what it was like in those times, to feel what Jesus went through." Chang was of course also a reference figure for necessary suffering. Thus DP's could at least in part write off their feelings of rejection.

A third strategy was less meek and long-suffering. More than simply believing that rejectors would get some vague punishment now and in the New Age, DP's kept a record of who rejected them and how it was done, so as to ensure later punishment. The detailed stories of specific rejections appearing in their news-

---

[21] *DP Newsletter* (December, 1960).

letter were, in fact, the documentary record of who was to be repaid. Once the DP's came to power, these files would be activated and used in ceremonies that, from Lee's descriptions, sounded much like the trials held immediately after more secular revolutions. Other bits of evidence were also saved, such as an uncashed check from a Baptist preacher who bought their book. This minister read the book, barred them from his church, and furnished the final slap in the face through noting on the check that it was in payment for "an occult book."

Fourth, people who rejected DP's not only began to use up their good credits in God's bank, but this grace accrued to DP's. The more rejection a DP received, the more grace he got. He should therefore not feel bad; he was better off because of it.

Finally, the rejector's shoe was often put on the DP's foot. In bringing the good news to an outsider, the DP was actually testing the outsider for his ability to recognize an emissary of the New Lord and the New Age. He failed the test by rejecting and was thereupon rejected by God.

These strategies may not have completely accommodated DP's to personal rejection, but they seemed to have at least helped to allay the pain.

*   *   *

This variety of perimeter experiences begins to suggest a part of the DP's power as a system for structuring a different kind of social reality. We now turn to the cult's internally generated experience for additional insight into the nature of this construction.

chapter 11

Faith and Cult Events

The DP's tendency to live together, of course, facilitated the circulation of supportive materials from the encompassing culture. Co-residence was in this sense an important arrangement in the maintenance of faith.

Perhaps more important, as an intensive interaction situation, the communal tendency itself created a range of supportive experience. The supportive nature of this association may be approached, first, through an examination of some types of internal cult events that might, on casual viewing, appear corrosive to faith. Later, I will discuss more obviously supportive events.

THE SUPPORTIVE SIGNIFICANCE OF NEGATIVE EXPERIENCE

MISS LEE'S MOTHERSHIP

As reported earlier, Lee presented herself to prospects as a permissive, gregarious, warm lady. With committed converts, however, she was often hard-driving, erratic, curt, and ruthless, particularly when confronted with internal opposition or the need for decision.[1] Such a leadership style would usually be most likely to produce disaffection and alienation among underlings. It may therefore be asked how, in fact, it was received and how "erroneous" (i.e., conventional) reactions were transformed into supportive terms. Before attempting to answer this question, some

---

[1] In addition, with high-status outsiders Lee projected herself as a giggling, shy, naïve, Oriental.

examples of this erraticism and authoritarianism should be reviewed.

First, Lee was almost compulsively concerned with the "proper" performance of everyday tasks. Thus she supervised Bertha and Minnie in minute detail during preparation of meals. The correct temperature, the amount of seasoning, the ingredients in salads, and the like were objects of hovering concern. Most of the time Lee seemed perturbed that the women had not accomplished some operation exactly as she would have done it. (This did not involve any ritual or mystic significance of food, but rather Lee's personal conception of recipes.) Dishwashing was likewise scrutinized for compliance to her own methods. In matters of personal hygiene, DP's received instruction on how to save water in brushing teeth, the maximum amount of water to use in the bathtub, and the maximum amount of time to remain in the tub. Although Lee could not drive, she sat next to the driver and issued a stream of stern orders regarding which lane to use, where to turn, and what to look out for.

Second, Lee controlled even the smallest of cult expenditures by maintaining a collective petty cash box to which only she had access. Converts even needed to ask her for daily streetcar fares, and in public service establishments she alone was allowed (or able) to pay.

Third, she tended to make decisions without regard for converts' desires, feelings, or capacities. Thus Elmer worked from 11:00 P.M. to 7:00 A.M. and arrived home bleary-eyed. But Lee frequently wanted him to perform some task or drive her someplace during the day. Elmer's frequent out-of-touch quality might well have derived from his lack of sleep. If he mentioned the necessity of sleep, he was scolded for being selfish.

Although 5:30 was the official dinner hour, Lee sometimes got hungry and ate at 5:00, with whatever converts were present. Those with the bad luck to arrive at the appointed hour and find the official meal completed ("official" being that which Lee did) were often unhappy about having missed the usual conviviality. (Lee was quite personable when dominating occasions such as this.)

Fourth, converts never seemed to work fast enough on projects around the Center. When Merwin and Elmer were patching and sanding the two upper flats of the DP house, Lee was perpetually complaining about their slowness.

Fifth, unlike "human relations" leadership, wherein underlings are privately sanctioned for misconduct,[2] Lee routinely shamed offenders before the group. Whether light (e.g., Elmer's continual shaming for talking out of turn) or weighty (e.g., sexual activity), Lee reduced violators to total repentance by such publicity. More serious offenses provoked threats of expulsion and a subsequent silent treatment from Lee. She called the latter "cutting off" and always uttered the phrase to the accompaniment of a swift, chopping, arm motion.[3]

Finally, although she was quite receptive to advice if she was unsure about something or had not made a decision, if she was sure, she would not tolerate dissent. Not surprisingly, overt dissent was rare. On one occasion the incompletely socialized Lester innocently disputed Lee's characterization of the Renaissance in the DP book. Lee thought this was insufferable impudence and launched into an angry discourse on the inordinate "persecution" and "resistance" presented by her followers.[4]

The most spectacular violation of Lee's decisions was Alice's refusal to give up her three children. At the time of the migration to Bay City, she had complied with Lee's wishes and left them with their grandparents. But nine months later she ran away from the DP's to be with them, and subsequently returned to Bay City

---

[2] Consider, for example, one of the eleven "rules of leadership" proposed by a leading theorist of the human relations school: "The leader will neither blame nor, in general, praise a member of his group before other members." George Homans, *The Human Group* (New York: Harcourt, Brace & World, Inc., 1950), p. 433.

[3] The emphasis here is on the more blatant methods of control. Lee also employed more subtle control tactics, such as praying to God for convert compliance. Thus she would plead: "Father, give X confidence; drive evil spirits away from him."

[4] She also appeared weary and discouraged over all the problems posed by her followers. Concern over maintenance of such strict compliance seemed, indeed, to require the expenditure of considerable energy.

with the children. Alice believed she could raise her offspring and be a DP too, but Lee thought it a waste of time (and money) in these last days. DP's said that Lee allowed Alice to be around only because she was Merwin's wife. She was a member "only on the surface" because she had violated Lee's will and had never relented or repented.

Elmer, Merwin, and Alfred, at least sometimes, felt that Lee was less than completely astute or rational in guiding the group and its relation to the encompassing culture. At times she appeared erratic and fickle to them. Thus an idea strongly vetoed at one time might later be adopted with no reason offered (e.g., to advertise or not, use the sound truck or not). They also wondered if Lee considered all the consequences of her decisions before making the group act upon them. Thus DP's were deeply in debt (incurred while renovating the house) when Lee ordered the 1962 dispersion. Many converts doubted that this was the most auspicious time to establish four new residences.

I have characterized Lee's leadership from a common-sense, sociological perspective and have thereby drawn attention to leadership attributes that are devalued by conventional culture (e.g., erratic and authoritarian conduct). Within conventional culture, such attributes are thought to provoke detachment among subordinates.

Although DP's betrayed some small moments of upset and reflection, Lee's leadership was by and large imbued with a radically different and positive character.[5] She elicited feelings of gratitude, love, and indebtedness, all of which contributed to the confirmation of faith.

Returning to the original question, then, how did authoritarian and erratic leadership generate positive attachment? This appears to have been accomplished by a rhetoric regarding Lee's identity and her unique relation to converts. As one of the earliest of

---

[5] Perhaps the largest slip from "correct" regard for Lee was expressed by Elmer during a long, late night conversation. Elmer was in despair at the time and thoughtfully said: "Sometimes I don't know if I am working with a genius or a paranoid." Given his special role as Lee's particular object of disparagement, this was small reservation indeed.

Chang's followers, she was far more advanced than local converts in her spiritual growth toward perfection. She stood, indeed, only slightly below Chang and God Himself in the spiritual hierarchy. Because of this and because she was responsible for their conversion, she was their "mother in faith," with the responsibility of raising her "spiritual children." Without her help they could not attain perfection, be worthy in the sight of God, or be temporal rulers. They had, then, to grow up under the mothership of Miss Lee.[6] This took the form of continual judging and testing by Lee. DP's, because of their low spiritual levels, could not always understand the reasons for Lee's actions. Her erratic, authoritarian appearance indicated only their lack of spiritual development. Moreover, doubting her judgment or resenting her treatment was clear evidence that the convert, because of his low spiritual development, had "made a base for Satan." It was understood that when Lee cut off a convert she was, in reality, scolding and driving away the evil spirit that had temporarily taken possession of him.

Lee was truly a hard task mistress, but after all, suffering was necessary for spiritual growth, was designed for their own good, and would lead to their greater glory in the New Kingdom. To be angry at or perplexed by Lee was the height of ingratitude, and such attitudes merely confirmed the need for growth. And in perceiving one's need for growth, one affirmed the DP system.

Such an arrangement suggests that erratic and authoritarian leadership may well be necessary for the maintenance of faith. If Lee were always understandable and amicable, converts could question her claim to special qualities and knowledge. Her inexplicable, ruthless conduct, however, showed that she acted on the basis of considerations that were inaccessible to lesser beings.

It might be said, in general, that the bizarre conduct of radical leaders does less to discredit them to followers than it does to provide additional evidence of their special powers.

---

[6]Thus one heard statements like Ludwig's: "I was born in Germany thirty-four years ago but raised in Bay City by Miss Lee half a year ago." When Minnie left Bay City for State U. City, Lee told her: "All teenagers have to leave home sometime. You are now ready."

PEER IRRITATIONS

The DP's appeared to get along among themselves about as well as one might expect any group with their variety of backgrounds and personal styles to do. As in any other group, some members were generally not well liked, and even positive attachments were punctuated by irritations and squabbles.

Bertha was the most intense "true believer" type among the DP's and was the most universally avoided, if not disliked. While the others could calmly converse about the Precepts, witnessing, and everyday topics, Bertha was continually the messenger of God. DP's felt that such a style, while acceptable in some types of proselytization, was inappropriate to everyday conversations. But Bertha gave the impression of regarding even her fellow converts as unregenerate outsiders. (She was, however, highly submissive to Lee.)

Furthermore, in everyday encounters, Bertha tended to represent her ideas as the point of view of God. Thus, on one occasion, two members were conversing about problems of witnessing. Bertha joined them and contributed the following:

You've got to have the spirit of God. You have to have God on your side. If you do, then you don't have to plan what you are going to do or what to say.

Merwin later commented:

Interesting mechanism that Bertha has. You can't win an argument with Bertha. Everytime God is always on her side, and what you are saying represents the forces of Satan.

Her evangelical fervor with prospects was also frowned upon. Peer DP's sometimes even felt it necessary to neutralize her membership through repeating Merwin's widely circulated comment: "You have to get past Bertha to enter the Kingdom of Heaven."

DP's also manifested the sorts of irritations and outbursts found in all groups. These were perhaps even stronger and more frequent here because of the pressure and rejection built into the DP role. In State U. City, for example, Lester was sometimes overtly irritated by Minnie's poor grammar and ignorance, and this cell had constant authority problems concerning household chores. And there were larger outbursts, such as that which occurred when Ludwig received, with elation, a letter and newspaper clippings from his mother, who had disowned him some months earlier. He joyfully displayed the material to Minnie, who replied by slapping it out of his hands with the comment: "That's a lot of junk."

The existence of peer irritations, which never became major conflicts, poses the question of how they were contained and prevented from growing into protracted and intense personal battles that could lead to defection or loss of faith. This was accomplished (and confirmation supplied) through the explicit expectation that they would have trouble getting along. Satan was there all the time causing trouble among peers. He was always after someone, flitting from one peer to another, attempting invasion. Minor irritations could be ignored as minor acts of His, but larger ones required a direct accusation of "making a base for Satan." Accusation usually caused Satan to leave (i.e., the accused peer apologized and altered his behavior). Minnie reported that she and Bertha could even sense one another's evil thoughts. Each would tend to deny the accusation, but upon reflection could discern some temporary league with Satan and confess it. According to Minnie: "It may seem cruel to an outsider, but it is the only way."

DP's also believed that, like Lee's tests, peer problems were God's tests and had to be endured. Indeed, every troublesome person was a cosmic test of one's ability to suffer. The latter was particularly applied to the plentiful irritations provided by Pierre and Leo.

The management of Lee's mothership and peer irritations suggest, then, the way in which presumably nonsupportive, disruptive experience was really confirmative and controlled both affect and conduct. A brief discussion of how this was applied in two additional areas will serve for amplification.

DOUBTS AND DEFECTION

Despite the flood of supportive experience, converts still had moments of doubt.

When doubt is defined as wrong or evil, doubters must deal with their lapses in secret. It would seem that repeated or prolonged unsocialized anxiety over such doubt would lead to complete falling from faith. In actuality, the necessity of maintaining secrecy diminishes group control over doubt. The problem can of course be managed through instructing believers beforehand that they should expect doubts, that everybody has them, and that they should not be overly concerned.

DP's employed this latter strategy and viewed doubt as simply one more way in which Satan attacked believers. Doubt was therefore not entirely one's own fault and was a matter of frank, unanxious discussion. Often Lee would recount episodes of her own and others' doubts in Korea, where believers would begin to falter over Mr. Chang's claims, but invariably regain faith upon coming into his presence.

Among DP's, Leo had the most persistent and overt problem with doubt. Almost daily he lamented that "everything in me tells me I should walk out of here." He received considerable sympathy and supportive treatment, although on days of intense doubt he was scolded, in an attempt to drive away the evil spirits that were molesting him.

Leo's doubts, however, were exceptional, and this kind of discussion was a minor theme in other converts' discussions. Converts sometimes related their most recent experience of doubt, particularly to newer converts, who might be having similar problems. But conversations quickly moved on to other topics. Thus, in one such episode, Ludwig humorously related to others an attack of doubt wherein voices whispered to him: "Who is this guy to say that he is the Lord of the Second Advent? How about other guys who said that and did nothing but make a little splash?" DP's of course understood and found it humorous; evil spirits had chosen to attack Ludwig in this way.

So far as one could determine, no total convert ever fell into a state of complete disbelief and defected from the DP. Up to the time when observation ended, DP's had yet to experience the threat posed by such a defection. However, there were at least four verbal converts who had fallen away, all of whom had been only partially accepted as members and were only partly committed to the DP's at the time of their exit. Thus it was never clear if they had lost all belief or if they had simply ceased participation. Even so, such exits would seem to be in need of management. So it was said that in the foreordained order of things a certain number of DP's would be taken away by Satan.

An account of one of Leo's numerous defections provides a concrete view of how this rhetoric operated. Leo spent Veterans' Day, 1962, unsuccessfully proselytizing in Bay City parks. Upon returning to the Center, he found that dinner had begun early. He announced that he was leaving and began to pack his clothes. Elmer went to dissuade him,[7] but Leo only kept repeating: "I can't do what I am supposed to do, so I am leaving."

Leo finished packing, came to the kitchen door, and thanked them for all their trouble. Everyone smiled weakly, and he walked out. There was a long moment of silence during which everyone engaged in studied eating. Then Lee began to define the situation. Leo had made a base for Satan that day by expecting great proselytization success. He felt low upon failing, and because of this he had "picked up a bad spirit and brought it home with him." Lee reflectively gazed into space as she slowly and without enthusiasm delivered this rhetoric. Again there was silence. Soon she recommenced, this time with considerably more enthusiasm. "There will be a certain number. Let us count those who have come and left. There will be a certain number." DP's nodded their understanding and agreement.

In this and other cases, the expectation of foreordained defection conveniently smoothed out present loss. A defection was merely a step in a prearranged cosmic process. As we are informed

---

[7] Lee had apparently ceased to care. Leo had packed to leave on the two previous days, and she had dissuaded him. This appeared to be the last straw.

in Timothy 4:1: "The Spirit says expressly that in after times some will desert from the faith."

POVERTY AND HUNGER

DP's required and practiced a life of extreme material simplicity and economic restriction. There were no personal expenditures beyond those necessary for subsistence and a proper face for the outside world. Conventional pursuits, possessions, and luxuries were frowned upon and forgone. Thus DP wardrobes were extremely limited and consisted in large measure of clothes they had owned before conversion. Worn clothes were replaced by shopping in charity and second-hand shops. They limited themselves to under a dollar and, following Lee, haggled with clerks to get the cheapest possible prices. The women had three or four different outfits, but the men had only two, one for work and one for dress. They wore the same garments day after day, month after month. As a result, DP's could accomplish changes of residence in the spirit of true deployable agents. Thus when Minnie moved to State U. City, she assembled her entire worldly possessions in two shopping bags.

The basic items of DP diet were rice and soybeans, which were purchased wholesale in hundred-pound bags. Although prepared in a variety of ways, these items were part of almost every meal (including breakfast). DP dinners were augmented by the cheaper meats and a vegetable or tossed salad. A variety of the more inexpensive fruits were kept on hand for other meals and evening snacks.

Furniture, as described earlier, was sparse and purchased from charity and second-hand stores.

This standard of living explains how DP's were able to assemble some rather luxurious group resources in spite of rather low earnings. Each convert lived on about a hundred dollars a month (of which sixty went for room and board), so that anything more went into the cult treasury. Thus in 1961-62 the group was able to secure an electric typewriter, a multilith press, a photocopier, a three-flat house, and a bus and still have money for advertising.

Poverty was not simply a matter of organizational necessity.

Like rejection, it was necessary for spiritual growth and was, in addition, a way of warding off Satan. Poverty, however, was not enough. It was further necessary for DP's to inflict biological deprivation upon themselves. This was accomplished through fasting, most typically by not eating for three days or by eating once a day for a week. Although the entire membership was never seen to fast simultaneously, at any given time one or more members were doing so.

The most frequent purpose for fasting was the winning of converts. Satan was always trying to win away prospects, but according to the indemnity precept one could ward off his attack through inflicting punishment upon oneself in advance. In this manner, the DP chose his own form of and time for paying. By thus carrying the prospect's burden of indemnity—and in advance —conversion was made easier, and one "outfoxed" the wily Satan.

Leaving aside the more obvious reasons for fasting, a possible faith-supporting function of it can also be suggested. The strongest faith may be produced where adherents experiment with the conditions of life itself, rather than continually existing above— no matter how slightly above—the limit of biological survival. Such experimentation may greatly heighten feelings of investment in the enterprise and the faith it represents.

MANIFESTLY SUPPORTIVE EXPERIENCE

Thus far, I have described experiences that might appear to be threats to faith. I have tried to show how they could, in fact, be managed by a reality construction that posits omnipresent, superempirical forces whose mortal struggle is continually manifest in the everyday world. The overall argument may be further elaborated by reference to some obviously supportive cult events.

SPIRITUAL EXPERIENCES

Although everyday life was filled with spirit-caused events, DP's maintained a more restricted category called "spiritual experiences," which was used to decode the purer or more forceful forms of spirit contact.

Spiritual experiences appeared to occur most frequently during sleep, or so DP's claimed. During sleep one's spirit body could leave the material body and travel in the spirit world. Thus Ludwig and others reported many pleasant journeys, such as the following:

I went into the spirit world to some temples, the beauty and colors of which were beyond description. To my great amazement I was treated there quite respectfully. This experience very much increased my confidence and in this way enabled me to overcome several attacks and temptations of Satan.

Of course Satan's spirits were as active here as elsewhere. Lester seemed particularly vexed by them. Tall, thin, blond men, in particular, kept beckoning him to homosexual acts, and on one occasion a nude male held him down, covered his mouth, and masturbated. Lester escaped and cried: "In the name of Our Lord, go away." The spirit departed.

Waking contacts were less frequent, but still represented a discernible flow of spirit activity. Thus, while consecrating the new house, Bertha and Santini saw pink angels dancing about the room. After the dispersion, DP's who visited Bertha or Minnie unannounced were likely to be told that just a moment before a spirit had announced their coming.

Evil spirits were also manifest in waking contacts. Ludwig and Minnie reported, for example, that the rooms they rented in the home of a practical nurse in State U. City were infested with low spirits. As a nurse, the landlady picked up all manner of low forces from sick people and carried them home. These spirits manifested themselves to Ludwig symbolically as mice, which crawled over his body and attempted to enter his bodily orifices. By fasting for three days, he was finally able to rid his quarters of them.

Complex verbal communications from spirits were quite rare. Lee, who might be expected to use continuing revelation to support her authority, was never observed to do so. (However, she did relate spirit communications from pre-DP and early DP times.) Minnie's encounter with the Apostle Paul was perhaps the most complex, yet was still quite simple.

Almost every minister I speak to always uses Paul's Epistle in trying to fight the Precepts, so I thought that I must study Paul's writing and know just what Paul said. I had spent almost the whole day in reading the Bible, so I was very tired and thought I would rest my eyes for a while. I had only laid down when someone appeared to me in spirit. He was saying in a crying, begging voice: "My Epistle must be rewritten." This was said over and over again. I said: "Who are you?" and he said: "I am the Apostle Paul." He seemed to be in such a state of suffering. Studying his writings and wanting to know about him made a condition for his spirit to come to me and let me know the truth from Paul himself.

Numerous tales of this sort were an important source of conversation among DP's. During dinner, after meetings, and so on, DP's told of the latest personal and second-hand tales of spiritual experiences. These stories were always well received and supported faith simply by having occurred and, frequently, by their specific confirmational content.[8]

KOREAN SUCCESS NEWS AND VISITORS

It was of course important that Bay City area DP's did not see themselves as the sole espousers of this world view. They were

---

[8] Some students of groups that claim revelations have pointed out the potentially disruptive consequences of allowing continued contact with the superempirical. To permit it is to foster the possibility that some member will get his own revelation and go out on his own. This is thought to be the reason behind the prohibition on spirit contact found in many religious groups.

Lee, in fact, reported that Chang discouraged spirit contact in the Korean group. If a member had such a contact, he was obliged to report it to Chang or his lieutenants, who then decided upon its validity.

Lee herself tried to make the best of both worlds. On numerous occasions she was heard to say that one had to be careful with spirits, for they could lead one astray. It was therefore best to tell them to go away if they came to you. On the other hand, she approved tales of spiritual experience, personally retold the latest contacts by members, and directed others to retell their experiences for the benefit of prospects who had not heard the latest events. In this way she retained the power to discredit any heterodox spirit communication, while permitting the practice and reaping the confirmation benefits it was felt to embody.

responsible for the salvation of America, but Korea was the chosen nation, the motherland, the real center of the movement. Thus the situation in Korea had an important bearing on how American-based DP's felt.

Their problem with conversion made Bay City DP's particularly attentive to the Korean experience and progress. Lee controlled ongoing news about the mother group by having sole linguistic access to its monthly newspaper and letters from Korean believers. Her reports from these sources contained only news of success. However, in June, 1961, United States DP's were in a deep, failure-produced crisis which prompted Lee to go beyond her typically scattered reports and set up what was called "The Korean Pattern." She wrote and reproduced a short history of the mother cult that detailed long failure and the beginning of success. It read, in part:

Our movement in Korea started as a group in 1954. It has been rejected as a heretic by existing churches, and accused by some people as being a communist movement. . . .

In the summer of 1957 this group sent out twelve teams of young people, mostly students, to spread the message of God's New Dispensation. These young people worked hard without harvest. . . .

[In] 1958 forty teams were sent to new [provinces]. These people also worked hard . . . and received little reaction from the local people. [In] 1959, . . . seventy teams of young people [went] to other new fields. Again there was little success. . . . Throughout these three years much opposition and all kinds of hardships were endured, yet there was little result.

[In] 1960 the group sent out 400 teams . . . to proclaim the Divine Precepts. Over 500 people applied for and undertook this project. This time the works met a different reaction in most places [i.e., met with greater success].

Last winter, 1960-61, the group sent out 700 teams to other new fields. Nine hundred . . . people . . . undertook this mission voluntarily.

Through the entire history of the Christian Church and its missionary movement, such a thing as our movement has been unheard of. This summer [1961] our group is planning to send out 2,100 teams, and this winter 7,000 teams.

Since last year, 1960, our group has been in an aggressive position, and no one is able to offer effective opposition.

Therefore, in the bleak summer of 1961, and in later months, DP's in America could remind themselves of the Korean pattern of long failure followed by growth and have faith that they would follow the same pattern.

Subsequent reports from Korea were not spectacular, but still encouraging. In September, 1962, Lee disclosed:

Nearly 6,000 men and women . . . went out on July 20th for another Forty-Day Enlightenment Movement, which is combined with evangelical work. . . . They have now come back to Seoul with many reports of victory in their work.

News of Korean success was positive but vague in 1963 but was overshadowed by a new source of excitement. The Japanese branch was now growing and reporting conversions among leaders of Buddhist millenarians. DP's thought there were some 2,000,000 of them and believed they would become DP's once their leaders converted. Lee reported in April, 1963:

After a forty-day training course in the Tokyo [DP] center, the leaders of the Buddhist group have been reforming within their own organization.

A Political College president, who has been following the Divine Precepts, offered a large building in Odahara Beach for the purpose of a training center, in which our group in Japan will open a Seminary. . . . As there are too many applications from the Buddhist [millenarians], they had to give a test for the selection of applicants.

Chang's wife provided DP's with a different kind of success in late 1962 when she gave birth to the required male heir of the New Kingdom. Chang's first child had been a female and the first perfect person born in the incipient New Age. But their son was cause for celebration and jubilant emoting, like that displayed by Ludwig in his letter addressed to "My Dear Little Prince":

It will probably be a few years before you can read this letter, but I want to send to you my loving thoughts from an overflowing heart.

Not only your parents, but all my brothers and sisters and myself had been waiting for you, and our hearts rejoiced when we heard of your birth. Now a great condition is fulfilled. You are yet but a sweet little bundle, but soon all the world will bow before you. Your father is the first man in history who could stand before God as a true man. He has given life not only to you, but to all those who follow him. At one time you will continue his great work.

We are working to build the kingdom over which you will eventually reign. . . .

With love and devotion.   Yours.[9]

The foregoing kind of news was brief and abstract. The world-wide scope of the cult came alive only through actually meeting some of its far-flung participants.

In 1961-62, Bay City DP's were treated to at least four visits by Korean members of the family. All were army officers passing through in connection with military duty. All of them spoke English and appeared to be personable, bright young men. Their appearance was cause for festive assembly. A wave of delight went through the cult, and use of kinship terms, such as "brother," "sister," and "family," greatly increased.

The most spectacular of these visits supported the feeling that DP political control of Korea was imminent. In November, 1962, the mass media reported the official United States visit of a Korean political figure known as the "Director." A feature story on Korea and the Director's visit appearing in a national news magazine said he was the mastermind behind the then current Korean military junta. He "provides the ideas, the drive, the plans. By his own immodest but unchallenged statement, [he] is the dominant figure of . . . [the] 'revolution.' " After talks with high level officials in Washington, the Director spent two days in Bay City before returning to Korea. He stayed in a luxurious hotel that flew the Korean flag over its main entrance in order to honor his presence.

---

[9] DP Newsletter (February, 1963).

The day of his arrival, Lee received a phone call from the Director's aide and interpreter, a Korean army colonel and DP. He told her that he had arranged an audience with the Director for Lee and her followers. Lee and five core converts appeared at the hotel the next afternoon, where they met another of the Director's aides, who had only recently converted to the DP. Before entering the Director's suite, the Koreans conversed excitedly in their native tongue, while American DP's stood around and giggled with joy. The audience with the Director himself consisted of Lee telling him of her work for the DP in America, after which each local DP gave a brief testimony to the DP's wonders and how it had changed their lives. The interpreter translated for the converts and for the Director, who continually smiled, nodded, and chain smoked. There were soft drinks, and toward the end of the hour the Director said that he was not a religious man but had great sympathy with DP's. He could not help them publicly in Korea, but he would secretly give them a hand whenever possible.

After the audience, DP's assembled in the interpreter's room, where pictures were taken and an air of family festivity reigned.

Dinner talk back in the DP Center focussed on the audience. Lee emphasized that such a meeting was unique and had occurred only because the Director had high regard for his two DP aides. Note was made of the recently converted Colonel being related by marriage to the junta head and thus having direct access to him. The Director's interpreter, Lee reported, was also his speech writer. When assigned to write a speech, he always got help from a top-ranking person in Chang's movement in order to give the speeches a DP slant. DP's had a strong suspicion that the two aides would eventually convert the Director.

Since Chang was to control the world by 1967, control of his home base would certainly come before that time. Although DP's in America were obscure and ignored, even the most skeptical had to agree that, for some months in 1962 at least, Korean control was not a fantasy. DP's had access to the people whose conversion could have given them power, if only in a short-lived coup. In any event, after their meeting with the Director, DP's possessed an important sense of being secretly near the center of power in Korea. Was this not testimony to the DP's truth?

KOREAN CHARISMA AND SUFFERING

More than being God's suffering people and, indeed, actively promoting their own discomfort, DP's had available a set of contemporary portraits of suffering so extraordinary that they could view their own travails as minor in contrast to them. No matter how uncomfortable American DP's might be, they could find some relief in and gain resolution from contemplating how well off they were in comparison to their Korean counterparts. Deprivation is relative, and in comparison to Chang and his followers American DP's had a rather plush life.

Thus there were frequently recounted tales of Chang's suffering in prison, especially in a North Korean prison camp, where he was made to carry bags of lime on his bare back and ate only half of his small rice ration "in order to build his will." He had of course imposed much suffering on himself over the years in order to "make a condition" and be able to discover the cause of man's troubles. Lee waxed most eloquent when recounting Chang's long suffering.

While all other people slept in comfortable beds, he knelt on a rock on a hill and cried out in prayers night after night to locate the mysterious problem. While all other people indulged in pleasure, he alone chose hunger to fight with the cosmic enemy. To liberate mankind he appealed to God by fasting day after day. When he realized the heartbreaking grief and sorrow of the Father in heaven, his heart was also broken, and he cried because of the whole situation brought about because of the failure of Adam and Eve. Since then he could not pray without tears which ran as a stream for mankind, for the whole creation, and for God. The tearful prayers were offered every day, month after month, year after year. He told the truth revealed to him, but no one would listen. He singly pioneered the way of life which no one had even thought of. Because of the truth, he was imprisoned a number of times by different regimes and severely tortured and suffered each time. It was a bloody battle, a tearful struggle, a lonely path, and a long suffering.[10]

---

[10] *Ibid.* (November, 1962).

Chang not only suffered, but possessed strange powers and perceptions that gave evidence of his special access to God. Thus during an air attack on the North Korean prison camp, he drew a circle around himself and announced that all who stood within it would be saved. He and two others who responded were said to be the sole survivors of the attack. These three escaped through the battle lines to South Korea by following a light that went before them at night and guided them unharmed through enemy positions and mine fields. Given such powers and aid, it was of course not surprising that he saw through to the true thoughts of all people and that nothing could be hidden from him.

Chang's charismatic gifts and unique spiritual sensitivity were reflected in his personal habits. In the days before the cult was large enough to provide him a car, Chang traveled on streetcars in Seoul. He was so sensitive to strangers' low vibrations that a group of believers went along to encircle him and block off low influence. He was also extraordinarily sensitive to the spiritual influences of even his own followers. Before the cult was large enough to provide him a private bathroom, Chang had to perform elaborate purification rituals in the communal lavatory before using it. Moreover, the entire DP premises in Seoul had to be scrubbed from top to bottom every morning in order to reduce spirit emanations and allow him to be more comfortable. While much of his conduct was explicable as spirit sensitivity, he sometimes performed acts that baffled even his followers. He would refuse to explain himself, saying his acts were between God and himself alone. Lee reported, for example, that no one quite understood why one day he raced out of Seoul in a jeep and drove at breakneck speed through the countryside for four straight days and nights.

Chang stood so far above all other people that DP's could easier idealize than emulate him. Their models were, rather, the "suffering saints," the ordinary rank-and-file Korean believers who set an example and provided inspiration. Lee made them out to be quite tenacious people.

In going out to the mission field, each person had to arrange for his own expense for food and room and arrange for a lecturing place.

The motto was to eat inferior food, no rice or meat, only barley and vegetables. The people, being undernourished, were very pale, but each person resolved to work for this cause even unto death. The workers ate the poorest food, gave the hardest labor in order to bring the highest message. I have been informed that a man and woman had fasted for forty days, and four persons fasted twenty-one days, drinking only water for the preparation of the forty days work. There were many who fasted three or four days during the work, some due to lack of food, some to overcome hindrances of the work. In this way they had paid their blood for their success.[11]

A letter from a Korean woman likewise reports extraordinary suffering.

My beloved family: My husband and I have been pioneering in different provinces, and to do this we had to send our four children into orphanages. My mission field is [in southeastern Korea]. I climb to a mount everyday and gather brush and wood to make two bundles of fuel to carry down to a village and sell. With the money I buy a few pounds of oats for my living. Supporting myself in this way I proclaim the truth day after day and month after month.[12]

Chang, indeed, gave special rewards to those who suffered most and had created within the Korean movement a publicly recognized stratum of extraordinary sufferers. A Korean believer reports the Master's ceremonial recognition of suffering on Children's Day, 1962.

The Leader gave special prizes to four persons . . . who have suffered most and for a long time and made a notable achievement in their works. Their prizes were nine copies of The Divine Precepts, including three English copies. They are the children whom the Father in Heaven is proud of. We all gave thanks for them and praised their works with many tears.[13]

"Brother and Sister Kim" of "Kyunpuk province," the suffering bearers of the word, were, then, heroic archetypes for DP's. They

---

[11] *Ibid.* (October, 1960).
[12] *Ibid.* (December, 1962).
[13] *Ibid.*

functioned as energizers and supporters of faith. Lester made much the same point about himself in response to the letter of the Korean worker quoted above.

I was very much inspired by [the] . . . testimony [of a rank-and-file-worker] in last month's *Newsletter*. How I wish that all our family could follow her example of steadfastness and devotion! We in America have such a comfortable and easy life in comparison to you in Korea. My heart and thoughts go out to you who are spreading the glorious news under such adverse conditions of bitter cold, poverty, and slander.[14]

SYMBOLS AND CEREMONIALS

DP's believed that all symbols and rituals were being fulfilled in these, the "final days." There was no longer a need for symbols because everything could express itself directly. Lee sometimes put it this way:

When Jesus came as the reality of temple, he naturally had to abolish the Mosaic law and the worship in the temple . . . in order to fulfill all those promises in reality.

Well, today, today we are living in the age of *reality*, fulfillment. Therefore, we don't bother with the symbolic rituals, because everything will be fulfilled in reality.[15]

In spite of rejecting trappings and frills and conceiving of themselves as no-nonsense realists, DP's were nonetheless evolving a variety of symbolic artifacts and rituals.

Such a contradiction between ideology and practice would appear to provide additional evidence for the proposition that all religious groups require devices that render faith concrete and promote the public expression of faith. Their existence, despite formal prohibition, suggests that such devices are a functional necessity.

---

[14] *Ibid.* (January, 1963).
[15] This sentiment was also expressed in their corporation by-laws: "We believe symbolic rituals such as communion service and baptism are unnecessary in the New Age when all symbols will be fulfilled."

The DP book itself was perhaps primary among DP symbols. Beyond its role as the "Completed Testament," attention should be called to the comfort provided by its mere existence as a *book*. In this slim volume, which was carried about and read from daily, a DP had the key to all existence. Consider the potency of the notion that all the enigmas and contradictions of man and the universe can be solved in the space of 200 pages.

DP scene rooms were conspicuously devoid of symbols, but the bedrooms were not. On an end table by Lee's desk, there stood a large, framed studio photograph of Chang, wearing a benign expression and dressed in Oriental robes. Next to this was a smaller, candid shot of him in Western dress, lounging before a window and smiling into the camera. The larger photo presented a dignified, fatherly figure, while the smaller one portrayed a "right guy." Another large, ornately framed photo stood on Lee's dresser. This showed Chang's wife with her back to the camera, an infant lying over her shoulder facing the viewer. This child was the daughter of the Master, the first perfect person born of the New Age. A framed drawing of a woman in flowing robes carrying a flaming torch stood on another small table. Properly instructed people could see that the flowing robes formed an outline of the Korean peninsula. They also knew that the drawing symbolized the motherland as carrier of the flaming truth.

DP's had made small copies of Chang's formal portrait and placed them in gold dime store frames. A new convert received his personal copy and kept it at his bedside. All DP's had this kindly likeness present to stare at them upon retiring and arising and to use as a vehicle of private prayer.

The ginko was the official tree of the New Age. Chang sent the group some seeds in 1962 and instructed their planting and growth as a symbol of the growth of the New Age in America. Lee carefully nurtured them in a hotbed box, where they sprouted but always seemed somewhat less than healthy. They were an object of occasional concerned inquiry by Lee's followers.

On a number of occasions Chang had been expected to visit America, and rooms in the Center had been prepared for him. When he did not appear, these rooms were not converted for other use, but set aside and maintained in an unpolluted state to be used by him if he should sometime make the trip. In Bay City, the two rooms were furnished with a variety of cheap new furniture, including a bedroom set and a vaguely Scandinavian chair. All the articles were draped in plastic covers. The floors were covered with the only full carpets in the house. Other DP's were content with a minimum of old, cheap furniture, but nothing less than their conception of the best would suffice for Chang. These rooms were entered only for cleaning and special ceremonies. They were becoming the sacred rooms of the Master, and their existence was kept secret from outsiders.

After the dispersion of July, 1962, Lee initiated a monthly newsletter, which contained, for the most part, a short article by herself and open letters to the family from converts in the missionary fields. Lee typed it on legal size, multilith masters, which Elmer ran off on the press. The average length was nine pages.

Lee stated explicitly that the newsletter was intended to "boost the morale of our workers." In some ways it seemed to be a more effective underpinning of faith than simply living together. The newsletter gave permanent expression to devotional vocalizing, resolutions to work, and admonitions to persevere. DP's frequently re-read their accumulated issues and seemed to gain new inspiration each time. The oral is ephemeral, but the written can become sacred and a source of ever renewed faith.[16]

Lee's lead article took up one or two single-spaced pages. As might be expected, her persistent and central theme was to work for the restoration. In a piece called "Heaven is the Kingdom of Use," she concluded:

This is the Time of God's Determination, His Final Judgment! Make yourself useful to the utmost degree for His Kingdom, so that the Lord will remember you. Do not be one of those to whom the Lord will say: "You wicked and slothful servant! . . . Cast the worthless servant into the outer darkness, there men will weep and gnash their teeth." (Matthew 25:26, 30)

---

[16] Compare the reasons for writing, the content, and the use of the early letters that survived to become part of the Christian Bible. Like the Christians, DP's saved their newsletters as sacred documents of the New Age.

Let us make everything we have useful to God, our health, time, wealth, education, talents, and experiences! Let them all be used for the highest purpose, for the Lord and His Kingdom. Your value in the kingdom will be determined by the degree of your Use. Jesus was the one whose value of Use to God was greater than others. The Lord of the Second Advent is the One whose value of Use to God is the greatest. Let us gratefully make ourselves useful to God, because all we possess are given by Him, for Him. We can ask God's favor according to our value of Use. Heaven is the Kingdom of Use.[17]

Being of use to the Kingdom naturally entails suffering.

It is absolutely impossible to become one with Him in Will and Heart without going through the same experiences as He did, even in a small degree. This is why our Master emphatically repeats over and over again and again that we should suffer as much as possible for His Will and His Kingdom.

The Kingdom of God cannot be expanded without the suffering of His children. The seeds of His Kingdom have been sown with tears, sweat, and blood throughout the Old Testament and New Testament Ages. Consequently they cannot be harvested without our tears, our sweat, and our blood.[18]

Suffering in order to be of use was not simply an obligation of personal salvation; DP's were "cosmic persons" who were responsible for the entire world.

We are the pioneers of the new world, whose restoration is solely dependent upon us. It is we who are laying the foundation of the New World. It is we who are going to be called forefathers of the Golden Age. The law of life we set, the pattern of worship we make will become the new law and the new pattern of life for the future world. The covenant Abraham made with God by circumcision became the law for his descendants, the pattern Jacob made became the pattern for his successors, Moses and Jesus, on different levels. Exactly what we do today will set an example for and affect our future generations.

There was no generation in the past whose task was related to the whole cosmos. We are cosmic persons who are responsible for the

---

[17] DP Newsletter (September, 1962).
[18] Ibid. (December, 1962).

restoration of the entire cosmos. This is why we have the highest privilege in all history.

This year we see that things are different from last year. People are more ready, spirits are more active. More and more we see the mighty forces of the heaven world working in and among people and nations.

The most favorable time in history to work for God has been given to us. Be aggressive in your approach! Hold high the torch of the Newly Revealed Truth of God, the Divine Precepts! The host of heaven be with you always.[19]

Open letters to the family comprised the bulk of most newsletters. These letters usually focused on an account of recent proselytizing efforts, often in a remarkably accurate and candid manner, although in a spirit framework. Spiritual experiences were also frequently related.[20]

Equally as important, the letters sometimes became highly demonstrative in expressing love for Lee and devotion to the DP. DP's were relatively reserved in face-to-face expression of love and devotion, but newsletters provided a mediated and therefore less embarrassing medium for expressions. Moreover, others could derive repeated comfort from these permanent expressions and, in turn, be stimulated to further emotional display. Under salutations such as "Our Dear Family" or "Dearest Mother Lee and Brothers and Sisters," the letters frequently opened with this kind of sentiment.

My thanks to our Leader and to you, Miss Lee, for bringing to this world the real light which not only has changed my own life, but will change the whole universe.[21]

Miss Lee, I . . . realize more and more each day how much I love you and owe you. The only way I can repay you even a little is by giving others what you have given me.[22]

Greetings to all, with all my love. What a privilege to be able

---

[19] *Ibid.* (May, 1963).

[20] Newsletter accounts of this variety are quoted in illustration of other points throughout the text.

[21] Ludwig (November, 1962).

[22] Bertha (August, 1962).

to belong to God's family! I am so very grateful to Miss Lee for showing us God's new plan and revelation. Had it not been for her I
would still be wandering in the darkness of this satanic world.[23]

I want to express my gratefulness and wholehearted thanks again to
our Leader and to my beloved teacher Miss Lee for setting me free
from the hands of Satan and bringing unto America this great truth.[24]

Unlike other converts, Lester addressed his letters to "Our Mighty
and Beloved Lord" (Chang).

May gratitude flow from my heart in an everlasting stream to you.
Thank you, Father, thank you, for your many efforts, for your accomplishments, for your devotion—to God, our Father, and mankind.
My lips pour forth praise, although my mind is still overcome in
awe at the immensity of God's imminent presence and working in
history through men.[25]

Lee was not alone in stressing the primacy of proselytization and
suffering. In their letters, converts rededicated themselves and
admonished others to do their utmost.

More and more it seems to be even a waste of time to sleep and eat.
I wish I could spend every minute of every day just teaching and
witnessing to the Precepts. So many people are hungry for the truth,
and we must reach everyone.[26]

God will only help us to accomplish our goal if we ourselves go to
the utmost effort. This is the question which I ask myself again and
again. Did I really go to the utmost effort? Or could I have done
more?[27]

Brothers and sisters, as I was praying this morning, I felt a great
urgency within myself to spread this Message! The responsibility of
presenting this Message to America is OURS! We cannot rely on
any efforts other than our own. We cannot sit back and wait for God
to work; WE must work, for we are His representatives on earth.
Let us keep our spiritual vibrations high by praying often, by reading

---

[23] Alice (April, 1963).

[24] Minnie (August, 1962).

[25] Lester (February, 1963).

[26] Bertha (October, 1962).

[27] Ludwig (January, 1963).

the Divine Precepts daily, by living the highest moral and spiritual life, by showing our separated brethren that we have found the Way, the Truth, and the Life! Every minute that we are not actively doing something to spread this Word is a minute given FREE to Satan. Let no one hinder us; let no one stop us. Let us be victorious! [28]

Also in the newsletter, Lee reported news from Korea and Japan, and she sometimes summarized liberal Christian and spiritualist views as confirmation of the DP. In the early months of 1963, she outlined the doctrines of the major world religions, on the theory that DP's should know the enemy.

Lee always put the best part, "the words of the Master," at the end of the newsletter. Typically, these words were but a single line, such as "Love God so much that you are not even aware of being hungry" or "The Lord will return to the people and the nation who love God most." Sometimes his words ran a page or more. These were translations of prayers he delivered at ceremonial occasions in Korea. The prayers recited DP theology, emphasized the merits of suffering, and called attention to time passing in the "schedule of restoration."

DP ceremonials were few, but growing in importance. In 1960-63, DP's observed two major ceremonies per year. The first, Parents' Day, or The Day of True Parents, celebrated Chang's marriage. It was observed on the first Sunday following the lunar March 1st (which is the last week of April or first week in May in the conventional calendar). The second, Children's Day, or The Day of Restored Children, observed the birth of Chang's first child by this marriage. It fell on October 1st of the lunar calendar (the last week of the Gregorian October).

These were not simply cult holidays; each was destined to become the equivalent of Christmas and Easter in the eternal "Cosmic Age" with its new "Cosmic Calendar." To be among those who celebrated these days was to be part of the tiny élite who first celebrated what *all* people would soon accept. These assemblies heightened the sense of being a true pioneer on the New Age frontier; for in a few years, early celebrants would be

---

[28] Lester (April, 1963).

publicly honored at mass celebrations of these days. Even in 1960-63, DP's looked forward to how they would reminisce in those glorious future days on these current "old days." The cult's insignificance, the smallness of its assemblies, only portended greater honor on Parents' and Children's Day in the fully restored world.

As might be predicted from a theory asserting the functional necessity of symbols and ceremonials, DP holy days were progressively elaborated over the three years, 1960-63. The days were merely simple evening gatherings in 1960, but by 1963 they had become all-weekend affairs held at the Bay City Center. The latter days were much in the spirit of the kinship gatherings that once prevailed in the rural sectors of America. DP women prepared a large Sunday afternoon meal, and everyone leisurely discussed problems and triumphs in a setting of relaxation, renewal, and festivity.

The daytime part of the celebrations were loosely structured in 1962, but became more ritualized in 1963 through the institution of an afternoon ceremonial in the Master's Sacred Rooms. Converts assembled, removed their shoes, and padded single-file into the Sacred Rooms, where they prayed, sang DP hymns, and received a report on the state of the corporation.[29]

The core ritual took place in the evening, which began with long prayers of thanksgiving, apocalyptic readings from the Christian Bible, and renditions of numerous Christian and DP hymns. DP hymns sung in Korean were emphasized. In the same manner that some other religions have sponsored liturgical languages, DP's honored their gods in "universal" but, to them, unintelligible speech. Lee had kindly provided transliteration for those who did not read Korean. Lee sometimes gave English translations of the hymns before singing; the favorite ones were entitled "Suffering" and "The Lord Has Come."

Praying, reading, and singing were introduction to the more

---

[29] Projecting a whimsical future, one can envision a minor secularized religion whose churches contain sacred rooms for the use of the Master upon his return from the spirit world. Or, perhaps, churches could be designed as bedrooms with an altar-bed around which the believers congregate for devotions.

festive middle period of the evening. Prior to the July, 1962, dispersion, Lee had tried to promote a party-like atmosphere through persuading participants to sing solos, duets, and the like. As with DP proselytization parties, this had been a faltering and embarrassing affair. After the dispersion, this entertainment was dropped in favor of convert reports from the mission fields, which were anecdotal talks emphasizing the ignorance of rejectors. In one such report, Ludwig drew gales of laughter with a description of how some outsiders respond.

There are those who say you are crazy and walk off. Those who agree with everything you say—"Sure, sure." You know you're never going to see them again.

Outsiders might feel themselves smugly superior and successfully deceptive, but DP's were on to them and knew they would get their just punishment in the New World. The strength of the laughter greeting each new anecdote suggested that this occasion provided an effective release of anxiety and promoted a strong in-group feeling of "we-happy-knowing-few."

The reports were frequently elaborated into personal histories of becoming a DP and testimony to the marvels of DP life. Interestingly enough, such accounts tended to dwell on the converts' own first contact with the DP and how, in their ignorance, they had not accepted the DP right away, and perhaps even rejected it. Such emphasis helped to define for others the tenuous nature of early acceptance and served to allay anxiety over initial rejections.

Also in the middle period, new converts made their debut, as it were, by declaring their faith before the assembled cult. However few there might be, even one new espouser strengthened faith.

The beginning and middle periods ran roughly two hours. By the end of the testimonial period, which was closed with more prayers, everyone was caught up in a festive spirit. The group then dispersed into small groups and conversed while feeding upon an elaborate assortment of cookies, cake, dried fruit, and punch.

It needs to be added that DP holidays were not simply celebrations that in themselves promoted veneration and faith. The passing of each holiday was also a milestone on the inexorable road to the New Age. Chang was married on the first "Day," and on each succeeding Parents' Day he matched up and married ever greater numbers of DP's in Korea. This yearly mating was part of Chang's schedule of restoration. It provided an internally generated event that marked progress toward the restored world. Regardless of progress, or lack thereof, in the encompassing culture, this accomplishment showed that things were really coming along.

However, DP's did not wholly lack external events that were related to the passing of a holiday and indicated progress in the schedule of restoration. Syngman Rhee's government was deposed after Parents' Day, 1960, *because* of Parents' Day, 1960. The Korean government was seized by a military junta shortly after Parents' Day, 1961, *because* of Parents' Day, 1961. The effect of Parents' Day, 1962, was less spectacular: the Korean government undertook currency reform. Parents' Day, 1963, caused the Korean government's return to civilian control. "It is no accidental coincidence," Chang said in Lee's translation, "that the Korean government has allowed political activities from this year, 1963."

CONCLUDING REMARKS

I have detailed some types of experience that supported faith in the DP as an accurate depiction of the real world. This enumeration is far from exhaustive, but is sufficiently detailed to suggest the plausibility of the initial argument: The DP world view was constructed so that every possible experience was evidence for its validity, at least in the short run. More generally, world views that operate on the premise of supernatural warring forces are not subject to negative evidence in the conventional meaning of that phrase.

It was no exaggeration, indeed, for DP's to tell prospects that "in the precepts the whole world opens up to you; you see everything differently" and "you see everything clearly." As we have seen, converts had an immediate and close sense of unseen forces operating upon their moment-to-moment lives. Missed (and caught) buses, automobile failure (and functioning), broken (and unbroken) dishes, poor (and good) health, missed (and kept) appointments, chance (and arranged) meetings, lost (and found) property—everything and anything, in short—belonged to a world of spirit causality and went forth by spirit action.

We might, in fact, entertain the possibility that such world views are superior to common sense in rendering reality explicable and meaningful. As Freud once suggested:

How we who have little belief envy those who are convinced of the existence of a Supreme Power. . . . How comprehensive, exhaustive, and final are the doctrines of the believers compared with the laboured, poor and patchy attempts at explanation which are the best we can produce.[30]

Users of common sense must struggle with the ambiguities and vicissitudes of meaning, purpose, evidence, and explanation. People like DP's live in a world of stable meaning, fixed and noble purpose, abundant and inexhaustable evidence, all of which are combined into a neat, cosmic explanation.

Unfortunately perhaps, even true believers are limited. This characteristic of their world view is successfully realized only in the short run—for days, weeks, and perhaps months. Paradox-

---

[30] Sigmund Freud, *Moses and Monotheism* (New York: Random House, Inc., 1955), p. 157. Although unemphasized in this analysis, it should be explicitly noted that the unambiguous understanding generated by this kind of world view promotes an "arrogant humility" and priggishness. These lowly, suffering servants of a Korean Christ wended their way through the day with a feeling of smug condescension. As Eric Hoffer has observed, "the vanity of the selfless, even of those who practice utmost humility, is boundless" [*The True Believer* (New York: New American Library of World Literature, Inc., 1958), p. 23]. "Humility is not renunciation of pride but the substitution of one pride for another" [*The Passionate State of Mind* (New York: Harper & Row, Publishers, 1954), p. 128].

ically, precisely those features that gave the DP's strength of faith proved to be their greatest long-run liabilities. This is the problem of empirical prediction (as distinguished from mere prophecy) and the mechanics of hope, to which we now turn.

chapter 12

Mechanics of Hope

Although the DP was thoroughly superempirical, it had the misfortune of being empirical in one important respect. It was deeply committed to the empirical prediction of making many thousands of converts in America. This was the cult's central goal and operating orientation. In disturbing contrast to this, very few people could be made interested in the DP and fewer still could be made verbal, much less total, converts. The most basic, enduring tension of DP life was this disparity between aim and actuality.

Rhetorical Mechanics

DP's of course had several types of rhetorics aimed at managing this tension and in some way reconciling the disparity. Perhaps the most popular was the previously mentioned "Korean pattern." It was said that Korean DP's spoke on street corners, in parks, and the like for three years before converts began to be made in any appreciable numbers. Americans might therefore make a similarly slow start. When people did start to take an interest, however, the rate of growth would be fantastic. Current failure was only part of the long calm before the storm. There could be a long period of failure because the time was not yet right. People were not quite ready, and DP's could therefore not expect success. "All mankind is ready, for it is the fullness of time," Lester once wrote, "but the *Kairos*, the exact time of announcement, has not yet arrived. . . ."

A second theme derived from the precept of restitution. Any

current nonconversion period was due to Satan's influence. Later on, God would counterbalance Satan by exercising more than normal "good weight" and pay back DP's with a large number of converts at one time. This was a seesaw imagery in which Satan kept people away for a while and God sent people for a while. An elaborated version held that lack of success was itself evidence of being close to success, or else Satan would not be working so hard to keep people away.

Third, conversion failure was sometimes explained by the proposition that God deliberately withheld or withdrew aid in order to see how well they could do on their own. According to Minnie: "God helps you for a while and things go along fine, and then He says: 'Well, I'll let My children go on their own for a while.'"

When individuals fell into despair over the distance between expectation and accomplishment, these rhetorics were trotted out in an attempt to define the situation and to build a sense of hope. Converts seemed, indeed, to carry on fairly close mutual monitoring in order to detect such moods. Minnie, for example, paid close attention to Lester and Ludwig when they came home at night. She sought to detect "low spirits" picked up in a day of failure, and upon finding them attempted to make her fellow converts more hopeful. While all of them experienced despair at times, some seemed more prone to it than others. Elmer packed to leave the residence several times because of despair over his inability to be a successful proselytizer. But these rhetorics generally did contribute to protecting DP's from inordinate concern over conversion failure and seemed to offer them hope.

ORGANIZATIONAL MECHANICS

However, something more than rhetoric appears to have been required to support a sense of imminent success. The DP's organizational history displays some rather curious features that seem best explained by reference to this problem of hope vs. despair. The adaptive maneuvers it manifests account, at least in part, for the DP's remarkable tenacity despite massive failure.

The four major cycles of hope and despair in the first three years of the cult may be examined for what they reveal about this problem.

Initial Hope Generated: Success After Preparation, April-August, 1960. DP's came into existence as a collectivity in April, 1960. Having conducted the Bible study group in Northwest Town for more than six months, Lee held the Parents' Day party in April, at which she first publicly venerated Chang's portrait and told Bertha, Minnie, Alice, Merwin, and Elmer that they were witness to the "crossing junction of good and evil." From that day, good was taking over the world, and things were going to happen as Satan fought a last-ditch battle to retain his supremacy.

The portrait veneration precipitated Mrs. Quinby's reporting Lee to the F.B.I. A local Quaker society also reported her at the same time. It happened that Lee was posing as a potential convert in this group in order to secure its sponsorship of Chang as a visitor to America. (Lee had said he was a "Christian religious leader.") Such sponsorship was rather routine for this group, and it had already begun taking the necessary steps to do so. They heard of Quinby's trip to the F.B.I., withdrew their support, and made their own report.

Lee and her still merely verbal converts learned of these events, both of which fulfilled the expectation (or hope) that the restoration had begun; Satan was becoming more active. (As numerous observers have noted, the worst enemies of a movement are often its best friends.) Merwin and Alice were impressed by this post-Parents' Day increase in opposition and invited Lee to live in their vacant cottage in Maple Hill. Lee moved and told no one in Northwest Town of her whereabouts.

The group now focused on preparing the DP book for publication. Merwin and Elmer sponsored the idea of renting an electric typewriter and typing multilith masters, which could then be inexpensively run off and bound by a printer. July and August were taken up with typing and proofreading stencils. There was also much discussion of how to promote the DP. Radio advertising was considered. They wavered between opening a local church or traveling around the country as preachers. At the same time, tension was mounting between Bertha and Minnie and their respective husbands.

April to August were the months for resolving hesitation and solidifying dedication. This period built an excited expectancy that once the book was finished, success would be imminent.

Despair and Migration. September-December, 1960. These glowing expectations were shattered by Minnie and Bertha's unexpected desertions of their families in September.

Lee had by now attempted to develop prospects in towns to the north and had generated particular interest among a quartet of lady seekers. In all, she had some twelve additional people "on the line." The Minnie and Bertha scandal caused all of them to fall away by November.

In Maple Hill, hostility toward Lee and the remaining DP's was running high. Bertha's husband threatened Merwin and Elmer with bodily harm should he ever catch them in the general store. He also tried to get Lee arrested as a homebreaker or thrown out of the country, but the local police and the F.B.I. said nothing could be done. However, the sheriff's patrol now cruised Maple Hill at night, throwing their spotlight on Lee's cottage. Both husbands also harassed the group, mainly by target shooting in the field across from Lee's house. Their gunfire was especially strong during Lee's study groups.

The group's plight was compounded by the recent arrival of one Yo Song Pak, also an early Korean convert. He was in the country as a student, studying at Baptist Seminary (a hundred miles north), but his aim, too, was the conversion of America. Both Koreans held nearly the same rank under Chang, and Pak began to vie for Lee's place as head of the American movement.

Minnie and Bertha wrote Lee that they were in Bay City, and Lee visited them toward the end of November. In view of the above problems, she decided to relocate the group there.

However, more important than all these problems, Lee's visitor's visa (she had dropped the student status) was going to run out at the end of December. The group was desperate, but saw no way to keep her in the country. She booked passage and instructed Merwin and Elmer in the conduct of cult affairs. Happily for the DP's, Lee was also trying to copyright the DP book and had consulted a lawyer about this only a few days before her scheduled departure. After she related her problem, the lawyer advised that copyright completion was sufficient grounds for visa extension. He obtained it for her. Such a dramatic, last-minute reprieve was of course the hand of God opening the way.

SECOND CYCLE

Hope Generated: Waiting for Chang and the First Assault, January-July, 1961. Now assembled in Bay City, DP's saw themselves as a saved remnant with a new world before them waiting to be conquered. Hope of imminent success was strong. As a matter of practical tactics, group migration, therefore, is a *first* major, and rather common strategy for regenerating hope.

We have seen that the first flurry of disembodied attempts at conversion was a failure. They were a bit more successful at the embodied level. Although DP's had killed their initial rapport with spiritualists, a number of other people were coming around regularly. Trouver began his association in April; Greta and Lucy came in May; Stein and Santini, Walter, Alfred, and a number of other people were regulars by June. DP's were hardly taking the city by storm, but they were not totally lacking in success.

However, all these events were overshadowed by the expectation of Chang's arrival in America. Lee had managed to obtain a visa for him, and he was expected to arrive in late May. In April, the group purchased a pickup truck and mounted camper unit, in which they planned to transport the Lord of the Second Advent around the country. This plan was disrupted by the Korean army's seizure of the government and subsequent prohibition on foreign travel for certain individuals. DP's expected the ban to be lifted momentarily; they waited hopefully into late summer, until they received word that Chang had decided not to come at all. DP failures in the spring and summer of 1961 must be understood against the background of this messianic expectation within a messianic expectation. Failures and reversals were neutralized by means of the notion that things would be different when Chang arrived. Although things were not happening now, they surely would when the Lord himself came on the scene. This points, then, to a *second* way in which hope can be maintained: by having the believers wait for the imminent, but unspecified arrival of a venerated person.

Compound Despair and Near Migration, August-September, 1961. By July, however, they had some new problems. Lee had managed to have her visa renewed in June by persuading Amhurst College's president to tell the immigration authorities that she was a teacher in his institution. She was not of course his employee, having lectured there only twice. Concerned over the legality of this, the president declined to support another extension. Trouver was now present and advised that incorporation as a nonprofit religious organization would provide a basis upon which to petition for permanent residence. If she were to become a legal minister with a congregation, deportation would be in violation of her communicants' religious liberty. The incorporation process and the uncertainty of Lee's residence in America lasted through the summer. (Her petition for permanent residence remained unanswered into late 1964, when it was finally granted.)

Trouver's romantic interest in Minnie became an issue in the late summer, as did the erotic high jinks of a resident male who carried on numerous affairs with non-DP women and, finally, with Bertha. Both men put the residents in a state of anxiety and concern over original sin. Moreover, Earl's bid to be proselytization leader extended into September.

The group's sense of imminent success was growing tenuous. In addition to grasping at the straw offered by Earl, they momentarily seized another possibility as a means of getting the group going again. As part of the first flurry, Merwin had placed an ad for the DP book in a national-circulation occult periodical.[1] The one response to the August insertion came from a Southern West Coast city reputed to be the mecca of perimeter religions. The order crystallized Lee's latest feeling that the group should move on to a new place. Lee, Elmer, and Bertha took the pickup truck on a long weekend to look over the city and meet the book's purchaser. Half a day was spent in reaching the buyer's residence, only to discover that he had not read the book and had little interest in doing so. They visited various occult groups, but found that such visits necessitated driving many miles and that public transportation was limited. Moreover, Elmer repeatedly got lost on freeway interchanges. Lee decided that they had best stay in the more compact Bay City.

In addition to their other difficulties, early one morning in the beginning of September, Alice arose quietly, packed her clothes, and stole away from the residence in order to join her children, who had been staying with her parents. Shortly after this, another resident lost hope and moved out.

The group's momentum was faltering: some new direction, project, or proximate purpose was desperately needed if hope was to be regenerated.

THIRD CYCLE

Hope Generated: Book Printing and House Hunting, October, 1961-February, 1962. As reported, Lee was unhappy with the language, syntax, and printing errors of the DP book. Yet it seems hardly coincidental that in the September period of despair Lee should assert the necessity for going ahead with revision and printing. It was also convenient that they should decide to do all the work themselves. An electric typewriter, photocopier, and multilith press were purchased in November. From then until February, everyone's time was filled with typing, proofreading, and printing.

---

[1] It read: "A COMPLETE NEW AGE REVELATION received by a Korean Master. 'The Divine Precepts,' $2.50—Merwin . . . , 420 Ash St., Bay City. . . . WY 8-5147."

DP's now defined their work as preparation, or "retooling." A revised book would make them better prepared for future proselytization. Merwin elaborated this in arguing that in the future they would need a large, permanent training headquarters. As in Korea, they were going to need facilities where missionaries could live for a few weeks while being trained. In addition, before a large facility was filled with converts, sections of it could be rented out, thus providing income and support for full-time missionizing. A thorough search for an appropriate dwelling was begun. In February, they purchased a three-flat (twenty-three room) building a few blocks from their original flat.[2]

Although this was a period of access de-emphasis, some prospects were present to provide a sense of progress. Greta, Alfred, and Santini passed the DP examination in October. Greta and Santini did not live in the Center, but they were at least "coming along." Trouver and others had not worked out, but Walter, a promising prospect had begun living with them in December. Pierre began residence in February, and perhaps something could be done with him. Also in February, four State U. students began coming around (Ludwig and three graduate students in sociology).

This interlude illustrates a *third* mechanism for keeping hope alive: the definition of the present as preparatory to a later time, when, helped by things done now, other things would *really* happen.

Hope Continued: The Second Assault, March-June, 1962. Moving to the new house in early March, DP's began to renovate the rundown, filth-caked tenement. Walls were cleaned, patched up, and painted. Floors were refinished, and the electrical system, fixtures, and plumbing were by and large replaced. They removed thirty years of accumulated grime and brought the building into a clean, tidy condition.

However, renovation did not greatly interfere with a new proselytization effort. When they first moved into the new house

---

[2] Actually Elmer and Merwin bought the house jointly by financing the purchase with G.I. loan benefits.

one sensed an air of expectancy, a feeling of being close to days of glorious conquest. A new handbill was printed, and Lee conducted her visits to local ministers during the last weeks of March. Converts stepped up covert presentations in religious gatherings. Bertha and Minnie began street preaching in downtown Bay City. At the beginning of April, Lee started the practice of convert rotation in leading DP meetings. She felt they needed more training in speaking in front of groups.[3]

DP's were now groping for new lines of action through which to implement their new hope. On May 4, Lee announced that she wanted every person to keep a record of how he spent each hour of the day, witnessing activity to be specified in detail. The reports were to be turned into her weekly. A week later, DP's traded in their pickup truck for a station wagon bus. Their mobility was thus greatly increased. At the same time, the DP sign was hung on the front of the house, but it was shortly removed at the request of the building inspector.

Other events were developing rapidly. Leo appeared at the DP's and was subsequently committed to a mental hospital. Pierre was ejected from the Center. In the following week, Brother Bob's storefront church was rented. It was after this series of tentative gestures that Lee settled on a new major strategy. In the first meeting at Brother Bob's on May 18, she promoted the Bible Week for Bay City, which would begin on June 12. Intervening meetings would be practice sessions in preparation for Bible Week. A few days later, she also decided to hold a series of parties in order to promote interest. DP's were now excited: these two lines of activity offered hope of imminent success.

The first two parties were ambiguously successful. Bible Week approached and, as reported, opened and closed in a single night. DP's agreed that the schedule of restoration was not sufficiently advanced to insure the success of a mass approach. Individual

---

[3] This "leading" amounted to the convert-leader stopping one person's reading and nodding for the next person to begin. Whenever discussion began, Lee took over. She found it difficult to sit by and watch her charges stumble through discussions with prospects. Thus she in fact continued to, lead the meetings.

embodied efforts were still necessary. The next week, core converts did not attend DP meetings as usual, but instead spent those evenings away from the Center attempting covert embodied presentations. Meetings were moved from the storefront church back to the Center.

Hope was turning to despair. They had barely begun a new assault, and it had stalled all too quickly.

Despair and Dispersion: July-August, 1962. On July 3, Lee assembled converts for a family meeting, at which time she laid it on the line. She was getting tired of working with people who did not work more swiftly. She threatened to leave and start work someplace else with a new group, because she was getting tired of "looking at the same old faces" and wanted to see new people. A choice was set: converts had to go out and start new works in neighboring towns, or else she was leaving. More than this, it was time that converts proved themselves by going out and working alone. They agreed and were dispersed by the middle of July.

There was little commotion during August, but the mission fields were providing new people. Bertha and Minnie's propensity to read politeness as concern was beginning to generate new hope of success as a round of new faces did, indeed, begin to appear in DP residences.

Geographical dispersion would appear, then, to be a *fourth* way in which a sense of hope can be produced. Moreover, it seems effective in producing a sense of largeness without any appreciable increase in membership. DP's felt that the group was expanding simply because they were spread over a larger area.

FOURTH CYCLE

Hope Generated: The State U. City Era and the Third Assault, September, 1962-April, 1963. The cult entered a new phase with Lester's conversion and the formation of the State U. City cell. Lester instigated an assault on State U. City seminaries, churches, and the university. These efforts produced only one convert, but the DP's were heartened by the opposition from ministers.

At the height of the assault and ministerial opposition— December, 1962, and January, 1963—there was even talk of moving the cult's headquarters from Bay City to State U. City. The latter was expected to be the center of DP expansion. The immediateness of expected success was perhaps typified in a comment by Ludwig during a discussion on tourists: "By this time next year [October, 1963], tourists will be coming to look at 706 Columbus Avenue [the Bay City Center]."

Nevertheless, by the end of January the State U. City assault had begun to stall. A count of the number of new persons signing the guest book shows a sharp downward trend in February and March:

Nov.	Dec.	Jan.	Feb.	Mar.
42	19	13	3	3

The State U. City faltering was somewhat abated by the discovery and attempted infiltration of middle-class, tongues-speaking groups. Attention was also diverted to an occult group composed of the wives of professors and other professionals at a nearby prestigious, private university. This group of some thirty women was led by a faculty wife who had received revelations asserting the leadership and dominance of women in an imminent New Age. Lee attended their meetings to promote the DP during February and March, but the DP's hopes of converting the entire group were dimmed when she was greeted with mere politeness.

By April, 1963, DP's could count eight new deployable agents in the Bay City area resulting from the dispersion. This was barely a dent in the several thousand needed to form America's contribution to God's saved remnant. The hope provided by the third assault was running out and turning to desperation.

Despair and Dispersion: May-June, 1963. Since the dispersion, DP's had begun to shuttle quite regularly around the Bay City area in order to meet with each other, ministers, occultists, and anyone else who displayed interest. (Lee was even something of a scheduled circuit rider between Bay City, State College Town, and State U. City.)

The developing tradition of much local travel provided inspiration for escape from an increasing sense of desperation. In April and May the cult was alive with the feeling that "we've got to get the word out to new places." Ludwig, troubled over Germany's insufficient representation in the foundation of the New Age, went back to Germany to missionize. Greta, who had finally converted totally, went with him. Lester now planned a missionary tour of the Southwest in the DP bus. Minnie, too, thought it was time she moved, and she traveled north to the state capital. A few weeks later, Bertha and a new female convert migrated to Sprawling City, several hundred miles down the Coast. Lee further sponsored this travel by announcing that time was too short to be wasted on public transportation. Additional cars were necessary. The cult purchased three used automobiles to be deployed as the need arose.

This dispersion to state cities was the functional equivalent of the dispersion to area cities in the previous year. It was a way in which a sense of imminent success was generated. DP's could not abide standing still. One way to stop this was to be literally on the move. A new sense of imminent success could be drawn from new places and new people. A feeling of greater size was drawn from the spreading of converts over an ever larger area. After the 1963 dispersion, DP's did indeed cover a large part of the West Coast, and because of Ludwig and Greta in Germany, they could with some slight justification claim branches "around the world."

Postscript

Although my observation and analysis of the DP ends with June, 1963, their saga, of course, continues. I had no contact with or knowledge of the cult in the subsequent year, but in June, 1964, after the foregoing report was completed, an independent observer made available some additional materials. The peculiar relevance of time to the DP lends interest to a brief postscript on developments through mid-1964.

Dispersion and Expansion

There were about thirty-five DP's in the United States and Germany following the 1963 dispersion. Located primarily on the West Coast, they were spread over eleven different towns and cities. June, 1964, presented a rather dramatic contrast. There were now *at least* 120 converts in some twenty-five places spread across America (and in Germany). The more important migrations and cell formations may be related to convey the extent and scope of this transformation.

In June, 1964, only four of the DP's in the Bay City area during the period of study were still there. Most had migrated to additional Western states and beyond. Minnie had converted two young, middle-class couples in the state capital and had moved on to an Ohio city in April, 1964. One of these couples had established a center in the state capital. The other couple returned to their native Germany to join Ludwig, Ludwig's sister Elsa, and Greta. Lester migrated to Texas in January, 1964, in order to exploit the assassination of President Kennedy two month's earlier. (He was soon joined by a missionary team of two new converts from Southern California, both of whom moved on to New York City in June, 1964.) In a southern West Coast city known for its fringe religions, Bertha had collected at least nine new, communally living believers. Merwin and Alice left the Pacific Coast in February, 1964, and set up shop in a Colorado city. Through visits to Merwin's home town in Kansas, they had converted Merwin's mother and three other people in and around Kansas City. After being with one other convert in a small West Coast city since August, 1963 (and making one additional convert), Alfred teamed up with a woman who had been with Bertha. They started a new work in an Arizona city in February, 1964. A State College Town convert who had been drafted into the army in the summer of 1963, had assembled three new young converts on an army base in Oklahoma. Another military convert who found the DP's through their phone book advertisement, was proselytizing aboard a large, well-known aircraft carrier and had made one convert among the crew.

Colonel Kim and Han, in the District of Columbia and Virginia, reported over fifteen believers in that area, including several members of the American military and a commercial airline pilot. Under the leadership of Yo Song Pak, Lee's rival missionary, there were now cells in three large cities in the Pacific Northwest. Through the frequent and wide-ranging missionary trips of Pak's lieutenant, small cells were reported in Idaho, Montana, Utah, and Illinois. (There was one cell in one large city of each of these states.)

In the Bay City area, two additional married couples were now the cult's backbone. One male was a junior executive for a well-known business form corporation. The other couple, a businessman and his wife, had become dominant in the conduct of cult affairs. [This latter couple were profusely "receiving" (hallucinating) types.] In the Bay City Center, a rotund former school teacher had given herself over to the DP, primarily in the role of cook and housemaid.

A graduate student in economics was leading the State U. City cell, which was composed of four new converts who were also university students. One of these, a graduate student in zoology, embarked on a university-sponsored zoological expedition to Madagascar in June, 1964. DP's commissioned him to convert South Africa.[1] Another State U. City convert, a German immigrant, returned to Germany with the German couple from the state capital. Still another moved to Ohio in June, 1964, to train with Minnie before starting a new work in Florida. Leo was still sporadically faithful and now resided in the State U. City headquarters.

It is important to note that this growth was not attained merely by the addition of people similar to those who were already DP's. There had been a significant upgrading in the level of social and verbal competence. Except for Lester, and perhaps a few others, previous to 1963 DP's did not convey a high level of interactional and intellectual competence. But now there was a significant proportion of espousers who had outgoing, warm, winning, competent interpersonal styles. Outsiders could no longer so easily dismiss DP's as sickly incompetents huddling together in an obscure religion. The cult was acquiring converts who could give it a respectable front.[2]

The most important of the new converts was a British citizen in his fifties, formerly heir to the rajah's throne in a small southeastern Asian kingdom, which had been taken over by the British in the late forties. In later years, the heir had occupied himself (and his trust fund from the British) with religious and occult matters, becoming leader of an English metaphysical group. Bertha proselytized him in February, 1964, while he was visiting the southern West Coast branch of his group. He was impressed by Bertha's tale and flew to Bay City to talk with Lee. Even further impressed, he then flew to Korea to meet the Master. Accompanied by Lee, the heir stayed in Korea several weeks, made a

---

[1] He was, however, a problematic disciple, periodically a resident of the university psychiatric ward for, among other things, wandering around nude in public.

[2] This is only to say that many new converts did not wear their physical and mental sores so openly. They all seemed to be troubled people as pre-DP's. The very respectable and competent new recruits were simply better bandaged and made up for public display.

number of radio and television appearances, and returned to Bay City in April. DP's who met him at the airport rejoiced in his disembarking exclamation: "It's true! It's all gloriously true!" In a long speech to some thirty DP's that evening, the heir witnessed:

Since I've been in Korea, I've never had any doubt at all. I've met several great religious leaders—but when one meets Soon Sun Chang —he's a gloriously great man. You can see the colossal powers of leadership he has. I have no doubt at all that He is the Messiah. We are at this moment of time . . . seeing the fulfillment of all Bible prophecy, and we are to see the world come under Love and Truth.
I know the Second Coming is in our leader, Soon Sun Chang.

The rajah visited DP's in Southern California, Colorado, Oklahoma, Texas, Kansas, Ohio, and the District of Columbia on his way back to England. His unusual background enabled him to appear on radio shows and witness for the DP in Colorado and Kansas.

PROSELYTIZATION

DP's strategies of access appear to have persisted with but small changes in how much they would disclose on first contact.

In the Bay City area there were two primary flurries of disembodied access in 1963-64. The first was prompted by President Kennedy's assassination. About a week after the event, readers of the Bay City *Times* and the *University Daily* were treated to display ads measuring two by three and five by six column inches. One of the largest read:

ATTENTION

Christ has returned and is now on earth to draw man's heart to him. God is now removing the idols of power and money. Within a week America will undergo a great crisis.[3] For more information,

---

[3] Through unknown processes, DP's perceived Kennedy's assassination as the beginning of the overt end of the current order. It was thought that from

come in [the] evening at 7:30 to any of the following addresses: [addresses of the Bay City, State U. City, and the new "Slum City" cells].

These and some other, smaller ads brought small success and were stopped toward the end of December, 1963. In April, 1964, after the conversion of the rajah heir, DP's again turned to the *Times* and the paper of a large state college with a series of personals that were quite sophisticated. Two of them read:

IF YOUR CHURCH can and has answered ALL your questions about the "Mysteries" contained in the Bible, has given you proof of the continuation of life after "Death," you have no need to phone

WY 8-5147.

*   *   *

LOST

One family of man; color: white, black, red, yellow, brown; missing the past 6000 years [and] last seen wandering in the dark; is in the habit of fighting and displays tendencies toward self-destruction. WY 8-5147.

FOUND

A way to lead this family to unity. WY 8-5147.

The emphasis on relatively covert presentations in religious gatherings persisted and was taken up by new converts. It seems, in fact, to have become a highly institutionalized (standard operating) procedure. Thus upon arriving in an Ohio city in April, 1964, Minnie wrote back to the Bay City headquarters:

---

that dark day, secular powers would begin to disintegrate. Among these imminent crises, it was expected that at any moment—"within a week" said this December 6th advertisement—the American economy would collapse. Inflation would make the dollar worthless. Throughout December, DP's milled about in tense expectation of calamity. They prepared for the worst by hoarding and filling a basement room with flour, rice, soybeans, and the like, and by buying work clothes in the expectation that it would soon be possible to get only the lowest of menial jobs. Sometime in January it was finally acknowledged that the economy had survived. The failure of the prophecy was interpreted as a test of their faith and a way to teach them that they should not be concerned with money. They should instead convert their money into material goods. It seems likely that the dispersion of January and February was in response to the failure of the December prophecy.

I bought a paper yesterday—three pages of nothing but churches, so you can see what a job I have ahead of me. This is a big, big city.[4]

In the next newsletter Minnie reported:

Dearest Family: I have just returned from a church. I went there for the first time Thursday night. They didn't even know me, but I was asked to talk. I talked for about fifteen minutes. They asked me to speak in the minister's place this morning, but I refused. I went tonight and they asked me to speak again, so I am telling them the Precepts, little by little. I have been asked to speak in the Jewish temple sometime and also to lead a prayer meeting next Saturday at a home here in [the city]. I do not know how long I will be able to hold it from them that the Lord is on earth. I thought if they could get to know me first, they would trust me much more and listen.[5]

In Arizona, another convert had found covert presentations in religious places to be a way in which one could get into a somewhat different kind of organization:

This week I went to the State Mental Hospital . . . with a group from the Presbyterian young adult organization. They sponsor a social night once a month for the patients. We were forbidden to talk religion or politics with the patients, but the subject just couldn't be avoided. They warned me twice, but it seemed that [the patients] just came to me with questions and ideas and I had to speak. Many of them have had deep spiritual experiences, have seen the spirit world, and have brilliant minds. They all seemed to be crying out for love and freedom. I also talked to one of the doctors and he seemed more mixed up than the patients. I hope to go again if they let me. What a day it will be when all the prisons and mental hospitals will be opened![6]

And Lester, the master of the covert stance, was of course plying his trade in Texas:

On . . . Sunday, I went to a nondenominational, fundamental, full-gospel church, and the Spirit was really present. During the Bible

---

[4] Newsletter (May, 1964).

[5] Ibid. (June, 1964).

[6] Ibid.

study, a number of people spoke in tongues . . . and prophesied, and the Spirit fell upon me, and filled with boldness, I stood up and spoke of the coming judgment and return of the Lord. How much I desired to tell them the Lord was already on earth, but they believe he will come physically in real honest-to-goodness clouds—so wisdom was required. I have found from past experience that people will more readily listen to what one has to say if they are assured beforehand of the speaker's love, sincerity, and integrity.[7]

The covert motif persisted, but DP's also appeared to have become more willing (perhaps in response to Kennedy's assassination) to give the conclusion in early contacts with outsiders (as seen, also, in the "Christ has returned" advertisement). Thus the peripatetic Lester reported that during preaching with Bertha in a famous soapbox speaker park in Southern California, "people . . . listen, especially when we hit them between the eyes with the statement: 'Christ is on earth!'" And Alfred reported from another Southern California city: "Harry and I have been very positive—'Christ is here!'"

Also under the stimulus of Kennedy's assassination, in late 1963 and early 1964, the DP's in Bay City began soapbox preaching in the local square known for that activity. Lester reported:

Every Sunday [six to twelve of us] . . . drive down to . . . the main street and walk about ten blocks, carrying signs: . . . "New Revelation," "Christ has returned and is now on earth!" We pass out cards to people on the street, inviting them to come to our meetings. At the square, we sing American and Korean songs, and then one of us will stand where he can be noticed and present the Divine Precepts, shouting in a loud voice. The first time we did this, it started to rain, and when we began preaching the Precepts, the rain really poured![8]

Much larger changes had overtaken DP promotion vehicles. The recorded briefing session was entirely dropped by the fall of 1963. Great emphasis was placed instead upon lecturing an introduction to prospects. The process of working up an effective set of lectures had led to a simplification of the world view's

---

[7] *Ibid.*
[8] *Ibid.* (February, 1964).

presentation. It was now something of a slogan to say that there were *only three* central precepts.[9] Other parts of the DP were simply deductions from, or elaborations of, these few basic principles. In moving from a relatively complex formulation to a more straightforward and readily understood version, DP's were following the classic process of generating a popular form of an erudite, abstruse, abstract body of doctrine. It will probably not be long before they have worked up a doctrine with a "popular character;" that is, a guise in which the "ideology takes the form of emotional symbols, shibboleths, stereotypes, smooth and graphic phrases, and folk arguments . . ." which is presented ". . . in a form that makes for [the doctrine's] ready comprehension and consumption." [10]

The DP's were now frequently meeting for lengthy sessions in which each lectured the others and received a critique of his performance during a tape-recorded playback. It was reported that even Elmer was becoming adept at public speaking as a result of almost a year of participation in such sessions.

Serial, oral reading from the DP book was also a thing of the past. Prospects who got beyond the introductory lectures received, instead, individual or small group tutoring and spoken talks on the DP. One now read the DP book on one's own and discussed chapters when meeting with DP's.

The planned fourth version of the DP book was published in the summer of 1963. Produced by a professional printer, the volume no longer had a homemade quality. It had the appearance of a volume issued by a good university press. The content was essentially the same except that future tense statements were now in the present progressive (i.e., "will" and "shall" were now "is being"). In the spring of 1964 Lee decided to revise it yet again. The projected fifth version was even more "scholarly" through an

---

[9] These were the first through third of the six precepts described in Chap. 2. In addition, a number of disciples around the country were reporting a variety of DP synopses that emphasized only a few key chapters in the DP book. The German cell had even printed its own summary version.

[10] H. Blumer, "Collective Behavior," in A. M. Lee, ed., *Principles of Sociology* (New York: Barnes & Noble, Inc., 1951), p. 210.

increase in allusions to materials in physics, biology, philosophy, and religion. It would also contain information on the character of life in the New Age that Miss Lee was getting from Master Chang during her visit in Korea.

Unfortunately, one can only wonder about the causal connection between all these proselytization changes and the DP's rather dramatic growth in the space of a year.

FAITH AND HOPE

Needless to say, DP's gained increased faith and high hope from a tripled membership and wide geographical spacing. The conversion of the wealthy Englishman was also a major supporting event. Letters from Korea in the spring of 1964 reported great growth and spoke of 700 to 1,000 people attending nightly DP revival meetings in various Korean provinces. It was said that the Korean government had finally recognized the DP as an official religion and that the Christian churches were no longer bitterly opposing Chang's movement. The mass media were of course supplying more than adequate indication of the end of the world. Among the array of crises in 1963 and 1964, the Kennedy assassination was, needless to say, paramount.

Relative to the functional necessity of symbols and ceremonials, the 1964 follow-up found these items to have been progressively elaborated. Instead of two cosmic holidays, there were now four. "World Day," celebrating the restoration of the nonhuman (physical) order, was observed in June, and Chang's and his wife's simultaneous birthdays were now an occasion of assembly and rejoicing.

The celebrations themselves were also more elaborate. Chang's room in each DP center now contained a candle-flanked altar on which stood a picture of him and his wife. Believers lined up in the Sacred Room, men on the right and women on the left. After much praying and hymn singing, each believer ate a small piece of food that had come from the leader's table in Korea. In units of three, they came before the altar and bowed down on their knees with their foreheads touching the floor, an explicit posture of submission to the Master. Special priestly garb was added to this observance on Parents' Day in Bay City. Lee was still in Korea, so Elmer, as the earliest attendant convert, led the ceremonies dressed in a Korean costume.

There was also a remarkable increase in the number of little daily rituals. Converts slept with their DP books open by the bed in order to keep evil spirits away. (Leo even felt it advisable to sleep with one's DP book over one's heart.) Some slept with their bedroom lights on or with salt in the room to keep spirits away. Dust was assiduously kept from under one's bed because of the attraction it held for evil spirits.

DP living places had always been dedicated with prayers and singing, but dedications were more elaborate in 1964. As Minnie wrote:

When we [fifteen DP's] arrived at our new headquarters [in the state capital], we got out of the bus and marched three by three around the house three times to claim it as the Kingdom of Heaven. Then we marched inside and sang many more songs and prayed several prayers. We had a bag of salt, and each person took a handful and put it in every corner of the house. This was to drive out any evil spirit that might try to hide in the corners.[11]

Now that converts were spread over the globe, the *Newsletter* assumed even more importance as a source of inspiration. (Personal letters—in addition to those written for the *Newsletter*— also circulated in profusion, along with tape-recorded letters.) Convert references to their love for the *Newsletter* became very frequent.

I don't have to tell you the experience of great uplifting and the urge to accomplish more and more that the newsletters bring.

We thrive on those wonderful newsletters which inspire us with the love and devotion of our Family.

A soldier disciple in Oklahoma seems even to have gone into some kind of ecstasy upon receiving his latest *Newsletter*.

---

[11] *Newsletter* (April, 1964).

There I sat eating lunch when the mail clerk dropped the latest news-letter off at my table. . . . My face was flushed and my heart panting as I read through the first page and on to the second. . . . I . . . had lost my appetite, and . . . I had to get away so that I could express my feelings outwardly alone. I felt like I was going to burst any second! I hurried out-of-doors. . . . I thought for sure I was in spirit only, for I couldn't feel the ground under my feet; somehow I seemed to float.

With the message given by [a new and "mediumistic" DP], I had been engulfed into a new reality of how much more wonderful, joyful, and great life shall be in the New World with our Master; truly a Kingdom of Heaven on Earth.

I was in complete peace and joy for the space of an hour as I read the letter to the end.[12]

Given joyful responses such as this (and an increased number of letters among an increased number of DP's), it is perhaps not surprising that beginning in March, 1964, the *Newsletter* began to be issued twice instead of once a month.

Finally, but certainly far from least, there is the crucial matter of the DP prediction for 1967. Through an unknown process the prediction for a great upheaval in 1967 had become both some-what more specific and somewhat attenuated. During my obser-vation in 1962-63, DP's expected to rule the world, or a significant part of it, by 1967. In June, 1964, the insider understanding was that the international foundation of perfected couples would be laid *in America* by or before 1967. This colony would then live in perfection some place in the United States. Chang himself would journey to America to do the matching and the blessing.[18]

It was important that this foundation be completed by 1967, because at that time the "Spirit of Truth" was going to appear in the sky and be visible to everyone in the world simultaneously. Upon his appearance hordes of low-level spirits would descend to earth and become visible as "black blobs" and "hairy things"

---

[12] *Ibid.* (May, 1964).

[18] In the spring and summer of 1964, Chang was again expected to arrive in America imminently. This was the fourth spring and summer in which he was expected to arrive imminently!

(among other forms). They would interfere with people's lives and play a part in everyone on earth having a spiritual experience. There had to be a foundation of perfected couples because the world's population would then turn to the DP to ask what all this meant. With their foundation, the DP's would be able to set an example and show the way to perfection—and to avoidance of unpleasant contact with "black blob" spirits. Mass conversions would begin to occur at that point. This, however, would only be the beginning of restoring the world to perfection. The actual work of making the entire world perfect would take until about the year 2,000.

Curiously, this vision of the future has an uncertainty clause: the Spirit of Truth would appear and the spirits would attack in 1967 no matter what, but it was possible for the DP's to fail to lay the international—American—foundation on time. They might lack the requisite number of converts. In that event, Chang could postpone this foundation laying for seven years. Mankind would simply have to suffer with spirits and perplexity in the interim.

It might be said, then, that while the DP's had backed away from prophesying total transformation in 1967, they still had a prediction that could be rather clearly disconfirmed (that is, if Chang did not get a new revelation postponing the millennium even further).

In view of the way in which the DP's future is dependent upon the passage of time and is still problematic, it may be that the most interesting part of their story has yet to unfold.

* * *

As of June, 1964, then, the DP was still quite small, but was experiencing healthy growth. The disciples' propensity to keep moving is likely to cause continual growth. It will not be long before they effectively blanket the country with a thin, but active layer of proselytizing true believers.

Appendix
How the Data Were Collected

Observation in the Cult. In one significant sense, my involvement with the DP's began by chance. While observing a flying saucer convention in State U. City one Sunday afternoon in early February, 1962, I was approached by a young woman who claimed to possess a "wonderful message from Korea." In some two hours of conversation with her (Bertha) and her friend (Alfred) that afternoon, I extracted little more than the millenarian thrust of their beliefs. They insisted upon my attending their tape-recorded lecture in Bay City so that I might obtain further information.

In response to their inquiries, I described myself as a graduate sociology student interested in new religious movements. I commented that their group sounded very interesting and that I might like to study it in a year or so. Being the hustler she was, Bertha suggested I study their group now. She said that Miss Lee had been a professor and liked people to study. I took this as a mere gambit to get me interested so as to secure my conversion.

Bertha insisted that hundreds of people were attending their lectures "at all hours of the day and night." The impression I received was that of some quiet but large movement in the underground of Bay City. Although in fact I suspected this group to be very small and not really worth investigating, I was nonetheless intrigued and promised to visit them that evening.

I contacted my colleague Rodney Stark, and we went off to hear the new words of salvation. At the flat, Bertha introduced us to Miss Lee, and we were quickly taken to their "scene room," where we sat alone with a tape recorder. Bertha's taped voice droned on for two and a half hours as we alternately fought stupefying boredom and rollicking laughter. (The latter was to be avoided as Lee and Bertha could be heard moving about in the hall and nearby kitchen.) An eternity later, the tape finally ended. Lee came in to find out our reaction. Although exhausted and bored, we managed some polite and sympathetic answers ("It was very interesting") as well as a few questions. Lee issued warm invitations to their study groups, and we promised to come, although actually we wrote the group off as too small and too dull.

A week later I read an occult magazine advertisement that announced: "I am God's Messenger." The messenger was in Bay City, so Stark and I paid him a visit. The evening was dark and cold and we had turned up the collars of our trench coats, which apparently gave us police-type appearances. When we told God's Messenger that we had seen his ad and had come to meet him, he stammered that he was unable to meet with us as he was leaving the country the next day, and he slammed the door. Thus foiled, Stark recalled the meeting with the other Divine emissaries and suggested that lest the evening be a total disappointment we revisit Miss Lee and Bertha.

We appeared at the DP's and received an impression drastically different from that of the first visit. The revised DP book was introduced that night, and we were impressed to learn that the group had done most of the work in producing it. We also noted that they lived communally and learned that they had been "spreading the message" in Bay City for more than a year. For the first time we felt that the DP was not just so much peculiar rhetoric, but a living, radical faith.

Our passive interest was transformed into fascination. Unlike the ideological permissiveness of the occult milieu, the DP was a sharply defined, intense microcosm markedly out of step with its environment. After this meeting, we believed that the group had to be studied. The project was broached to another friend, Fred Templeton, and the three of us decided to engage in an extracurricular spring project.

Relays of meeting attendance and sociable conversations with DP's were set up. We assumed the standard seeker's posture, namely, interested and sympathetic but undecided. Outlines of the converts' biographies, a vague group history, and some notion of proselytization procedures were pieced together within four weeks. We noticed, however, that the amount of new information declined with each successive encounter. In first meetings, we could legitimately inquire into backgrounds (in exchange for personal information about us) and ask about past and present group activities. This is permitted by the norms of the acquaintance process, which unfortunately prohibit successive occasions for such concern.

Perhaps more important, the seeker posture was leading to considerable conversion pressure. DP's kept inquiring, "What do you think of the Precepts?" Continued expressions of sympathy and interest became more difficult to align with the profession of being undecided. Each of us was receiving suggestions to move into the Center and study the Precepts with Miss Lee. We were finding that this was no casual Sunday afternoon with the permissive flying saucer people. The DP's were out for full commitment and had marked us as prime targets. They said that one should take his time in deciding, but (it seemed to us, at that time anyway) that one should not take too long. Further data-collection progress threatened to be slow and ever more difficult.

We considered other role strategies. The possibility of feigning conversion was discarded as too demanding psychically, morally, and economically. Open observation as sociological students was the only other major alternative. This was problematic, however, for unlike myself, Stark and Templeton had been disavowing sociological interest in the DP and espousing innocuous, non-religious areas of sociology as their professional concerns. That is, they claimed their interest in the DP to be purely personal. To become open observers would be to admit deception. From my first encounter with Bertha, however, I had been relatively straightforward and continued to say that, while I was personally interested, I was also professionally interested.

During this period of observation, I had become interested in a long-term study of the group, rather than simply in a lark. In view of the above problems, we decided that I should attempt to secure acceptance as a sociological observer. If Lee said no, that would be the end of the project, but assent would lead to a close study of an obscure but grandly cosmic group of cultists. In meetings with the relevant members of the State U. faculty, I received informal approval of the topic as a Ph.D. thesis, after which (March 21, 1962) I met with Lee.

Lee already knew me as a "sociologist interested in social and religious movements." We had discussed other movements on several occasions, and at her request I had even loaned her monographs on several of them. Thus it was not difficult to say that I had become interested in studying her group. I was surprised (then, but not later) to find her not only receptive, but enthusiastic about the project. In fact she cast me in the role of chronicler of the beginning of the New Age in America. Although she kept brief notes in a diary, she felt the need of a more detailed account of what happened in the early last days. People in the New Age would want to know what things had been like in these times.

After giving her assent, Lee demonstrated her sincerity by spending the next two hours in a detailed account of DP activities in Northwest Town and Bay City. I later discovered some major omissions and revealing distortions (aside from theological imputations of meaning), but her story was nevertheless amazingly candid. It was from her that I first learned of the sensitive and secret matters of Bertha's and Minnie's marital difficulties and desertions of their husbands and children.

This, then, is how the DP study began. Stark and Templeton decreased their cult visits and by the end of April had stopped going altogether. In May, DP's occasionally inquired of their whereabouts but by then they had more pressing concerns (see Chap. 12).

Teaching duties, course requirements, and language- and Ph.D.-qualifying examinations limited my observation to about fifteen hours a week from February through October, 1962. During that period, I attended DP study groups, ate with converts in the Center, helped in renovating and maintaining their house, acted as messenger and car driver between cities after the cult dispersed, and, at Lee's request, functioned as copy editor for her prose.

DP's used the phrase "studying the Precepts" to denote non-converts around the cult. I had accepted their invitation to move in as soon as I was free of other obligations, so my announced desire to study the Precepts reduced the problems of assigning me an identity. DP's assumed that most people knew little about the occult and that they had to be taught the "true nature" of reality. DP's were happy to spend time with interested persons. It was therefore relatively simple to present myself as one who knew little about the "real world" and to promote an impression of the naïve young man who was anxious to learn. In interaction with DP's, I was almost always a student being taught by an experienced and learned mentor.

The DP's desire to explain the world to me (and secure my conversion) thus fit perfectly and very conveniently with my desire to secure information on biographies, group activities, and beliefs. Because events were "spiritualized" and, I suppose, because they trusted me, they even revealed discrediting episodes. Thus my initial information on Maple Hill and a variety of personal conflicts came from members themselves.

Interestingly enough, my group interest was similar to theirs. From the beginning, I said that one of my main concerns was how one went about gaining converts and building a movement. This was of course central to their concerns, and thus I could make repeated inquiry into past and present proselytization activity.

By July, 1962, my understanding and appreciation of the subjective meaning of being a DP was greatly increased by the good, though guilt-tinged fortune to have developed relatively close friendships with Merwin, Elmer, Alfred, Ludwig, and Minnie. It was in a number of reflective late evening conversations that I came to a closer understanding of what it meant to be a "true believer." Although DP's rarely displayed "role distance" or "came out of role" at these moments, one could nonetheless glimpse them as wondering about the meaning of the part they played.

From November, 1962, through January, 1963, I lived in the Bay City Center four days a week. During most of this period, I functioned as copy editor of the fourth version of the DP book.

I had been aware of Lee's "mothership" style and the DP's reality construction, but came to have an intimate sense of these and other matters only through this subjection to their social round.

Through all these months, there *appeared* to be a shared understanding of my interest in the DP: I was personally sympathetic to, and accepting of, them and desired to understand their endeavors, but I was not likely to be a convert. There were understandable and kidding suggestions that I should "witness" and convert, but the ostensible reason for my presence was to study the movement.

Then, in January, 1963, Lee told me that she was tired of playing the "studying the movement" game. She made it clear that she was very concerned that, after all these months and all that the members had told me, I had not become a convert. I responded that my interest was necessarily professional. Lee expressed regret: "If I had known from the beginning that you only looked at our Precepts as a scientist—why should I have bothered?"

It seems, in fact, that for eleven months I had unwittingly and systematically misled the DP's with the *standard participant observer's* open, permissive, sympathetic stance. While I was trying to appear noncommittal, although very interested, the DP's were reading this as existential concern. Lee now decided I was unlikely to convert, and so there was no longer any justification for my presence.

Once that decision was reached, I was defined as a positive threat to the group. As a nonbelieving repository of sensitive material, I might write a negative report that would retard conversion progress and hold up the entire course of universal restoration. Indeed, according to Lee, to present only the "sociological part" would be to grossly distort the movement: "You only see the very tip of the Divine Precepts, the sociological part. There is a vast underlying part that you can't see. Without the spirit world this is nonsense."

Lee undertook to control my report on the DP by demanding complete censorship. This was of course impossible. I reaffirmed

my March, 1962, offer of prepublication review and commentary
rights and withdrew from the cult. But fortunately I continued
to acquire information on the group through June, 1963. At about
the time of my exit from the group, DP's witnessed (independ-
ently) to two young sociology undergraduates who on their own
had become fascinated by the DP as an object of study. They
learned of my work and offered their services as observers. One
of them decided to feign conversion, was accepted as a convert,
and became an insider to the State U. City cell.

Interviews with Local Outsiders. Some of my interests required materials on group history, witnessing activities, and biographies. At the time of leaving the cult, my data consisted largely
of convert reports. I assumed that this material was biased and
undertook to interview relevant persons in order to assemble independent accounts. Plural accounts, assessed for internal consistency and multiple report agreement, were assumed to yield as
truthful a depiction of concrete events as possible.

In order more accurately to describe proselytization procedures,
I interviewed a variety of ministers, church laymen, occultists,
co-workers, former employers, and neighbors who had experienced
the DP's. I was uncertain of the willingness of many of these
people to inform on or gossip about others and approached the
interviews with some trepidation. But I was continually surprised
to find that everyone was at least interested in relating his experience, and most seemed enthusiastic. With many it was almost
as if they were happy that someone was "getting the goods on
those people." (This was of course mixed with proper psychiatric
concern or allegations of anti-Christ.) Encounters with DP's were
not seen as meriting the rules of confidence and privacy that are
generally extended to others. I even felt a certain chagrin at the
promptness with which religionists in particular related discrediting
material to a total stranger claiming to be a graduate student in
sociology studying the DP's.

To round out and evaluate the activities of 1961, most of the
former boarders and some other nonconvert associates were inter-

viewed for their recollections of DP activities. Where the DP's and the outsider were in conflict, I made a special effort to get the latter's version.

In all, seventy interviews were conducted in the Bay City area.

Interviews in Northwest State.   The interviews provided independent material on local group history and activities and the biographies of local converts. I still lacked independent accounts of Northwest Town activities in 1959-60 and biographies of converts from there. I spent two weeks in Northwest Town in May, 1963, interviewing clergy, landladies, formerly interested but unconverted prospects, neighbors, teachers, and the two deserted husbands, a total of thirty interviews.

These people, too, were highly cooperative. DP's had portrayed Minnie's and Bertha's deserted husbands as ogres of a sort, so I expected a difficult time with them. In fact they gave me long and enthusiastic (although appropriately biased) accounts of the entire affair.

*   *   *

The observation and interview material came to over nine hundred pages of single-spaced typed notes. Several hours of tape recording also accumulated, in addition to a variety of documents. The analysis was constructed from these materials.